T0178712

Metaheuristics for Maritime Operations

Optimization Heuristics Set

coordinated by
Nicolas Monmarché and Patrick Siarry

Volume 1

Metaheuristics for Maritime Operations

S. Mahdi Homayouni
Dalila B.M.M. Fontes

WILEY

First published 2018 in Great Britain and the United States by ISTE Ltd and John Wiley & Sons, Inc.

ISTE Ltd
27-37 St George's Road
London SW19 4EU
UK

www.iste.co.uk

John Wiley & Sons, Inc.
111 River Street
Hoboken, NJ 07030
USA

www.wiley.com

Library of Congress Control Number: 2018932787

British Library Cataloguing-in-Publication Data
A CIP record for this book is available from the British Library
ISBN 978-1-78630-280-9

Contents

Introduction

If this book is delivered to you as a hard copy, you may read it on a paper made from Canadian woods manufactured in USA paper mills, while you drink a fine Brazilian coffee beside a delicious British biscuit. If you read the book as a soft copy, most likely you use an electronic device whose monitor was manufactured in South Korea, its processor was fabricated in China and its hard drive was made in Thailand. Globalization is the process of worldwide interchange of products, money, ideas and culture. In fact, globalization started hundreds of years ago, when merchants started to trade commodities all around the known world from China to Persia, and from India to Rome. Ships from Europe sailed round the southern tip of Africa to reach India, China and Persian coasts. However, in the late 19th Century, large-scale international connections among the economies all around the world were expanded very quickly, most likely due to advances in transportation. Maritime transportation, new worldwide maritime routes (after digging the Suez and Panama Canals), and larger ships are among the most important reasons for this boom in globalization.

Maritime transportation requires large capital investments in ships, seaports and post-port transportation. A small percentage reduction in the expenses of a shipping operator or a seaport authority leads to millions of dollars savings that can be invested in further expansion. Expansion of maritime transportation capacity and world trade development depend on and support each other. Therefore, many planning and scheduling problems need to be addressed in order to use maritime transportation in a more efficient and more cost-effective manner. The recent growth of ships' size has led to drastic reductions in maritime transportation costs. Nowadays, the largest containerships can carry up to 21,000 TEUs. For such a ship, 9,000 handling moves are expected for a 24-hour cycle time, or 375 handling moves per hour. This is more than twice the current productivity in the major container terminals in the world. Such a doubling of productivity will require dramatic innovation in the handling systems and operational methods.

New technologies in the seaports allow the operators to pursue loading and unloading tasks for the ships, simultaneously. Furthermore, the new handling equipment in seaports is capable of handling two or more containers at the same time. However, further technology and equipment innovation is not expected to provide a much higher productivity for the seaports. Thus, innovative planning and scheduling methods are critical for the successful performance of seaports. To add to this, higher environmental concerns by governments and societies all around the world, as well as increasing fuel prices, pressure the ship owners and operators into quicker turnarounds, and more efficient travel. Evidently, all parties involved in maritime transportation are forced (and enthusiastic) to optimize the operations that deal with maritime transportation.

This book is dedicated to the major optimization problems related to maritime operations both at sea and in ports. However, problems regarding the transportation from the ports to the final customer are beyond the scope of this book. Most of them are known to be NP-hard problems, and thus a considerable part of the studies addressing them focus on developing (meta)heuristic algorithms.

Many of the problems and issues presented in this book have been researched in two directions, namely the management side and the optimization side. Although we defined the problems from the management point of view, the main concern of the book is the optimization side of the problems, rather than the managerial one. Moreover, for most of these problems, several versions of the problem and problem definitions have been reported in the literature; however, for each problem here, a simple and widely accepted version of a mathematical model is reviewed. We describe a general version of the problem and then review some of the solution methods proposed in more detail. Regarding the notation, for consistency we use the same throughout the book, thus ignoring authors' notations when reviewing specific works. In addition, and still having in mind the book's consistency, in some cases, the mathematical model is presented in a slightly different way, though equivalent to the one originally proposed. A final note goes to the pseudocodes given throughout the book; they were taken from the work being reviewed and their presentation adapted for consistency or written whenever not provided by the authors.

Although we list some of the related literature for each problem, a literature review is not the prime objective of this book. We only searched for studies that are directly related to the optimization problems in any maritime transportation; among them, only studies that propose metaheuristics have been considered. Owing to space limitations, we selected some comprehensive works published in English and in refereed journals or edited volumes, using criteria such as a full description of the proposed algorithm, algorithm simplicity and data availability. Since the metaheuristic approach, the design process and structure are top of our concerns, approaches using commercial software packages or other optimization predefined tool boxes are not considered here. Regarding some of the specific maritime operation problems discussed in Chapters 3–5, due to space limitations, we will review one work with state-of-the-art results, in detail.

The target audience of this book are expert practitioners and researchers who seek a basic, but integrated overview of maritime operations and transportation, and the related optimization problems.

The book consists of five chapters; two of a more introductory nature and three on the main specific optimization problems that arise in maritime operations. Chapter 1 provides the motivation for addressing maritime operation problems, as well as a short overview of the main problems. Chapter 2 introduces the basic principles of metaheuristics and provides a brief explanation of the most commonly used ones. Chapter 3 is dedicated to the optimization problems related to ships and it includes network design problems both for liner and for tramp ships and speed optimization in green ship routing problems. Chapter 4 is on seaside operations in seaports, in which we review berthing time allocation, berthing space allocation, crane assignment and integrated berth allocation. Finally, in Chapter 5, the works related to the operations in the storage yard are reviewed. It includes but is not limited to storage space allocation and crane scheduling problems. As a pioneering way of innovation and improvement in the port throughput, we dedicated a large portion of Chapter 5 to integrated planning and scheduling problems.

A Review of Maritime Operations

Maritime transportation is the least costly mode of transportation and, as such, it plays a major role in the world trade expansions. This chapter provides an overview of the importance of maritime transportation in current global economic conditions (section 1.1) and introduces various types of loads and ships in maritime transportation (section 1.2). Containerization, a revolutionary concept in maritime transportation, is reviewed in section 1.3, followed by a brief introduction to handling equipment in seaports in section 1.4. A short overview of the main optimization problems faced in maritime operations is presented in section 1.5 and the chapter is concluded in section 1.6.

1.1. Maritime transportation

Nowadays, supply chain networks are increasingly complex, and the logistics associated with them present more challenges than ever, mainly due to the fast trend of globalization. The ever-increasing importance of sustainable development strongly depends on the development of transportation infrastructures. Although there is no explicit hint to transportation in the United Nations' sustainable development goals [UNI 18], it is considered as the most critical factor to reach its goals and targets.

As an essential tool, maritime transportation lies at the heart of globalization and the international trade boom. This mode of transportation revolutionized industries by enabling almost any company, regardless of its size and location, to export its products all around the world. Maritime transportation, mainly ocean and deep sea, is considered as the corridor of global international trade. Conceptually, any goods, other than time- or content-sensitive ones, can be moved by sea. Although maritime transportation is one of the slowest modes of transportation, due to its higher transported volumes and lower operational costs, it is a widely used intercontinental transportation mode for all types of loads, from heavy loads such as ores, grains, coal and coke, to liquid loads such as crude oil and liquefied natural gas, and to final products such as cars, digital instruments and household appliances. If the delivery time is not an important matter, larger, odd-shaped products including engines and propellers may be moved via this mode, as well. Many types of cargo can only be transported by sea since, due to either their size or shape, there is no other physically or economically viable option.

According to Yuan [YUA 16], almost 85% of total international trade is transported by sea. More specifically, for the EU member states, 75% of their imports and exports depend on maritime transport [EUR 15]. It is the leading mode of long-distance transportation in the world, with a transported volume of over 10.6 billion tons in early 2017, almost twice that of 1995. Although this increase represents an annual average growth of almost 3.5% in the past 22 years, a similar and steady annual growth is expected in the near future, approximately 3.2% during 2017 to 2022 to reach 12.5 billion tons of transportation by 2022 [UNC 17].

The fast increase in the worldwide fleet size and fleet capacity, consisting now of more than 93,000 commercial ships with a total tonnage of 1.86 billion deadweight tons (DWT), has been a key factor in globalization and lies at the center of global support supply chains. Massive transportation capacity, as well as low carrying costs, has led most countries to increase the throughput of their maritime transportation, especially developing countries, which by 2016 accounted for around 59 percent of loaded (i.e. exports) and 64 percent of unloaded (i.e. imports) total volumes of international maritime trade [UNC 17].

Although maritime transportation has almost the longest transit time and needs the highest level of capital investments, it is known as the least expensive and safest mode of long-distance transportation. Additionally, while the size and weight are an important issue for air transportation, this is not the case for maritime transportation. Although ships usually need to travel a longer distance compared with other modes of transportation, maritime transportation is still the mode with the least CO_2 emissions.

Nevertheless, the maritime industry itself is seriously affected by the impacts of climate change, such as rising sea levels and more extreme weather [VIL 15].

To compare different modes of transportation, we selected a very common route between Shanghai in China (busiest container terminal in the world), and Rotterdam in the Netherlands (busiest container terminal in Europe). To have a fair comparison, we estimated that one twenty-foot equivalent unit (TEU) container, a common unit to count carrying capacity by train, trucks and ships, is able to carry 20 tons of load, on average. Table 1.1 shows an estimation of the average transportation costs for one TEU by a ship or a train and 20 tons of load by plane or trucks. The data presented in this table have been gathered through surveying duration, distance and cost from [SEA 18, CAR 18, UNC 17], and emission rates from [HIL 18]. The emission rate is counted by grams of CO_2 per ton-kilometer (g/tkm). Although maritime transportation is the longest mode of transportation, it is the cheapest and greenest mode of transportation, as well. It is noteworthy that air cargo produces almost 100 times more CO_2 than maritime transportation.

Mode of transportation	Duration	Distance	Emission rate (CO_2)	Emission for a 20-ton load	Cost
Air	1–10 days	9,000 Km	1278 g/tkm	230 tons	50,000 $ for 20 tons
Road	10–15 days	11,000 Km	59.8 g/tkm	13.1 tons	8,300 $ for 20 tons
Rail	18–25 days	11,000 Km	22.6 g/tkm	4.9 tons	3,000 $ per TEU
Sea	32–43 days	19,000 Km	5.6 g/tkm	2.2 tons	700 $ per TEU

Table 1.1. *Comparison between the four main modes of transportation in a route between Shanghai and Rotterdam*

1.2. Types of ships and cargo

Bulk cargo is mainly divided into four categories, dry bulk cargo (e.g. grains, sand, coal, ores, etc.), liquid cargo (e.g. crude oil, LNG, liquid fuels, chemicals, vegetable oil, etc.), other main bulk commodities or break bulk (e.g. goods in sacks, cartons, crates, wood, paper, steel, autos), and containers. These four main cargo categories have a certain portion of the maritime transportation market, depicted in Figure 1.1, based on the data from [UNC 17] for the year 2016.

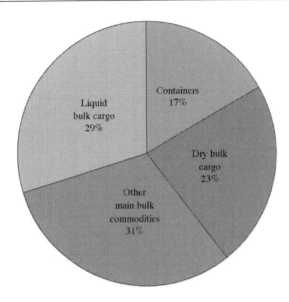

Figure 1.1. *Market share of cargos transported by sea in 2016*

There are currently three main routes in the world for maritime container transportations, namely from Asia to Europe, from Asia to North America and from Europe to North America [GEL 13]. Main routes for oil and gas include the Persian Gulf to Asia, Europe and North America. For the dry bulk cargo (mainly iron ore and coal), the main routes are from Latin America to Europe and to the Far East, and from Australia to the Far East. Other commodities are transported all over the world, but mainly from the Far East to Europe and to North America. Cargo flows are set to expand across all segments, with containerized and dry bulk cargo trades recording the fastest growth.

Beside leisure, educational and passenger ships, most of the larger ships are used for merchant purposes. The smallest portion of the world fleet belongs to the Ferries and passenger ships with less than 0.3% of the total tonnage.

Huge tanker ships transport fluids such as crude oil, petroleum products, liquefied petroleum gas (LPG), liquefied natural gas (LNG) and chemicals, also vegetable oils, wine and other foods. Currently, tankers have more than 500 million tones of DWT accounting for 28.7% of the world commercial fleet deadweight [UNC 17]. However, the largest portion of the commercial fleet is dedicated to the dry bulk cargo ship with almost 800 million tones of DWT, which represents 42.8% of the world fleet deadweight. Break-bulk cargo ships represent just under 4% of the world fleet deadweight. A special version of the break bulk cargo ships, known as roll-on/roll-off (RORO), are used to carry wheeled cargo such as automobiles, trailers or railway carriages. RORO ships have built-in ramps that allow the cargo to be efficiently "rolled on" and "rolled off" from the ship when in port. Perishable goods such as fruits, meat, fish, vegetables and dairy products, which need temperature-controlled transportation, are transported in refrigerated ships (reefers).

The most preferred mode of transportation for containers is the containerships, which, with 245 million tons of DWT, account for 13.2% of the world fleet DWT. They are, typically, operated on fixed maritime routes that include various container terminals worldwide. For the deep-sea containerships with a general capacity of several thousand TEUs, the deck is subdivided into several holds, each of which can carry between 200 to 400 containers. Containers may be stacked on the deck or below deck. Deep sea containerships are mainly used for interlinking Europe, North America, South America, the Far East and the Middle East. For the shorter distances between the countries or intra-continent, short-sea containerships with a capacity of several hundred TEUs are in service. Feeders and Barges are two other types of ships for carrying containers. The former carries up to several hundred TEUs to/from deep-sea ships, and the latter is a small size ship with a capacity of dozens of TEUs that serve the hinterland of a seaport via rivers and channels.

1.3. Containerization

A shipping container is a box designed to enable goods to be delivered from door to door without its contents being physically handled [CHE 05]. In the last 60 years, containerization has revolutionized maritime transportation by making it much more cost-effective. A major part of today's maritime transportation is performed using containers. Although the first ship built to carry containers dates back to 1926 (four containers were used to carry passenger luggage in a regular luxury connection between London and Paris), regular sea container service between the US East Coast and points in the Caribbean, Central and South America started in 1961. The standard dimensions of containers are 8 feet wide, 8.6 feet high and either 20 or 40 feet long. However, other lengths can still be found, namely eight, ten and thirty feet. A 20-feet-long empty container weighs approximately 2.2 tons and it can be loaded with up to 22.7 tons [KEN 13].

Standardization of these metal boxes allowed for easier loading and unloading processes, the design of standard handling equipment, protection against weather and theft, and scheduling and controlling in seaports. The aforementioned advantages resulted in a larger physical flow of cargo and an increased acceptability of the containers, which led to higher profitability. It is important to note that ships are productive only when sailing. Currently, on average the general cargo ships spend 50–70% of their time in ports to be loaded and/ or unloaded; while containerships spend only 15–30%, making them more profitable [CHR 13].

Container terminals (CTs) are an area in the seaports, where containerships dock on a berth to be loaded or unloaded [VAC 07]. The goal of the CT is to move the containers as quickly as possible and at the lowest possible cost. Therefore, it is essential for a CT to be able to efficiently and rapidly receive, store and dispatch containers. The ever-increasing demand for containerized transportation has compelled ports to improve their facilities. This is one way of developing economies to benefit from greater connectivity to world markets, improve trade and lower their transport costs. These countries have many plans to construct new CTs or to increase the capacity of existing ones. The economy of developing countries is highly dependent on the extension of their loading/unloading capacity of containers, concurrent to their cargo fleet; however, future improvements and investments in facilities and operating knowledge highly depend on global economic conditions. The growth rate in developing countries varies over the years due to strong fluctuations in trade and a need to improve reports and a lack of data.

The world fleet continues to expand; by mid-2017, there were 11,150 containerships with a total capacity of 22.3 million TEUs. Germany holds a predominant first place followed by China, Greece, Denmark and Hong Kong, which together hold 52.1 percent of the market share. Overcapacity and poor market conditions are the two most important challenges for both the container terminal operators and the containership owners. However, the latest reliable statistics for 2016 published by [UNC 17] indicate that 699.7 million TEUs have been moved through container ports all over the world. This is more than three times the 231.7 million TEUs moved during 2000. It seems that container transportation has achieved its potential market share, since most of the suitable cargos are already containerized; thus, the future growth of containerization will mainly be due to global trade growth. Figure 1.2 shows the top twenty CTs in the world, which collectively accounted for 45.2 percent of the world container terminal traffic in 2016. The ports are sorted based on their throughput in 2016, according to data gathered from [UNC 17].

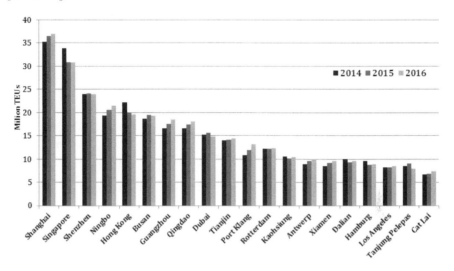

Figure 1.2. *Annual throughput (million TEUs) of top twenty CTs in the world ranked as of 2016*

Huge maritime ships transfer containers between the continents. The size of these ships has increased enormously, e.g. the nominal capacity of the largest containership in service is 19,224 TEUs [UNC 17], and the next generation of containerships are conceptually designed for 22,800 to 24,000 TEUs [LIN 17a]. These much larger containerships demand a quicker turnaround of ships and thus, CTs have to resort to new techniques and technologies to coordinate all types of handling equipment, leading to more efficient container terminals. Therefore, it forces changes such as the replacement of manually operated cranes by automated cranes and manually driven carts by automated guided vehicles (AGVs), among others.

Automation of handling equipment in CTs is a response to the ever-increasing container traffic. Automated container terminals are fully automated terminals, which integrate automated storage yard, AGVs and quay cranes. This is a general solution for the increasing demand for CT throughput. Researchers have introduced automated container terminals to reduce operational costs, especially labor costs, and to increase the throughput of the CTs. Although initial investment for automated container terminals is definitely higher than this for traditional CTs, the operational costs of automated container terminals are less than those of traditional CTs. Thus, being able to pay for the investment in a shorter period of time.

Euromax CT in Rotterdam, Netherlands, Altenwerder CT in Hamburg, Germany, New Qianwan CT in Qingdao, China, Victoria international CT in Melbourne, Australia, the Pasir Panjang terminal in Singapore and the Kawasaki Port in Japan are examples of container terminals that are partially automated with plans for full automation in the short term.

1.4. Handling equipment in seaports

A seaport can be defined as a facility situated at the edge of an ocean or sea for receiving ships and transferring cargo to and from them. A seaport is further categorized as a "cruise port" or a "cargo port". Sea cargo ports serve containerships (see Figure 1.3 for a top view of the CTs), tankers, dry bulk carriers and other general cargo. The port of Shanghai in China is the largest and busiest port in the world regarding cargo tonnage, followed by the ports of Singapore and Hong Kong; while the busiest in Europe is the Port of Rotterdam, Netherlands.

Seaports primarily serve as an interface between different modes of transportation, e.g. domestic rail, truck transportation or deep sea maritime transport. In seaports, a ship moors at a berth and waits to be loaded or unloaded. It is common practice to dedicate a part of the seaports (known as a terminal) to a specific type of load (i.e. for dry and liquid bulks, or for containers). Although various types of loads need different types of equipment in a seaport, generally similar activities are performed to load/unload a ship. The exporting loads are received from the hinterland through the terminal gate. After the initial legal inspections, they are transferred to the storage yard waiting for the expected arrival time of a ship. After its arrival, the load is retrieved from the storage yards being transferred to a crane or loader to be loaded into the ship. The importing loads (unloading from a ship) go through the same process but in a reverse mode;

that is, the load needs to be transferred to the storage area, from where it will be delivered to the final customer or to another mode of transportation (e.g. trains, smaller ships, or trucks). Commonly, the unloading process of a ship precedes its loading process.

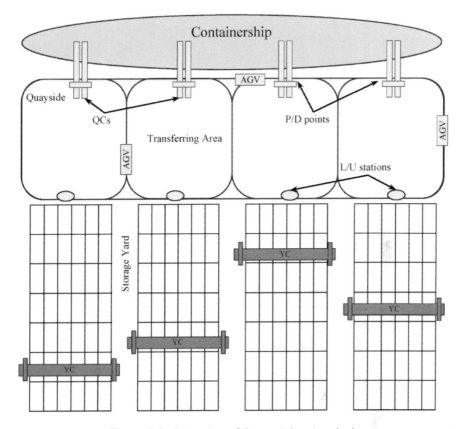

Figure 1.3. *A top view of the container terminal*

The third type of load is the transshipment one (quite common with containers), in which containers are unloaded from a ship, stored temporarily in the yard and then loaded to another ship. More specifically, some of the large container terminals in the world are known as hubs for transshipment containers. For example, 80% of the handled containers in Pasir Panjang terminal in Singapore, the largest hub in the world, are transshipment, while 70–80% of the containers are either imported from or exported to the largest European port in Rotterdam, Netherlands [KEN 13].

A seaport can theoretically be divided into five main areas: berth, quay, transferring area, storage yard and terminal gate. Usually, the berth and quay areas are known as the seaside, and the transferring area, the storage yard and the terminal gate are known as yard side. In this book, we concentrate on the optimization problems related to the ships, seaside and yard side operations except the ones associated with delivering loads to other modes of transportation or final customers. The next sections introduce some special handling equipment used in seaports.

1.4.1. *Quay cranes*

The aforementioned four types of loads need specific types of cranes to be loaded and/or unloaded to and/or from the ships. Liquid bulk cargo is usually pumped through the pipelines from and/or to the storage tanks, and then distributed to the other modes of transportation. Dangerous materials are commonly handled at special berths constructed for such a purpose, usually not too far from the main berth area of the seaport.

Dry bulk cargos are divided into two main categories, namely: major bulks and minor bulks; the former representing about two-thirds of the dry bulk trade. Major bulk deals include ore, coal and grains; while minor bulks include several goods such as steel, forest and agricultural products, fertilizers, and cement, among others. The handling equipment needed differs depending on the good being handled and may include loading shovels, bulldozers, clamshell grabs, hoppers, suction pipes, and conveyor belts. Common to all of them is the fact that their loading and/or unloading are highly mechanized, requiring very few people to be involved.

Break-bulk cargo refers to goods that must be handled individually, which is usually done by a floating crane either installed on the ship itself, or in the quayside. Goods are fitted in containers, boxes or bags, which are then placed in pallets. The pallets and/or containers are fitted with lifting slings and then lifted, usually in groups, to be loaded to or unloaded from the ship. Most of the preparation for lifting is done by manual labor, which is the main reason for the large costs associated with handling this type of cargo.

Container cargo refers to the transport of containers, regardless of their contents, usually truck-size intermodal containers. Since containers are large and heavy, specialized material handling equipment is required for transporting them within the terminal. Most of the types of handling equipment are able to carry only one container at the time, and there are limitations to how far they can carry a container. Containerships dock on a berth and containers are loaded and unloaded using huge cranes, typically rail-mounted, quay cranes (QC) or container cranes. The QCs are equipped with trolleys that can move along the crane arm to transport the container from the ship to the quay area and vice versa. In unloading tasks, the spreader of a QC clutches a container on the ship, lifts it vertically to a safe height, moves it horizontally over the dock and places it either on a vehicle or on the ground (i.e. buffer area).

Typically, in container terminals two to six QCs work on a ship at a time, depending on the size of the containership, the number of containers to be unloaded and loaded, and the expected departure time of the containership. Conventional QCs can handle about 30-50 moves per hour [BAR 13]. However, the larger containerships force the CT authorities to expand the capability of the QCs. According to Chao and Lin [CHA 11] in the beginning of 2009, more than 18% of total capacity of worldwide containerships belonged to ships larger than 7500 TEUs. Since the first application of QCs in 1959 in Alameda CT – USA, the size of QCs has been doubled [BAR 13]. Nowadays, a Post-Panamax QC serves a ship with up to 65 meters in width (a row with 21–23 containers) and can lift a container 42 meters above its rail.

Selecting and using such expensive equipment is a multi-criteria decision-making process. Space restrictions and economic and historical factors are the key issues for port authorities when selecting the handling equipment for the CTs. One way to increase the throughput of the CTs is to replace the older equipment with a more efficient alternative. Dual-trolley QCs can work independently in two or more containers. In addition, modern spreaders make it possible to more two to four 20-feet-long containers simultaneously (twin-lift mode). An alternative way is to improve the scheduling methods for the QCs.

1.4.2. Vehicles

Loads are transferred to the yard for temporary storage. For the liquid bulk cargos, it is common to use pipelines, while for the dry and break-bulk cargo, yard trucks (YTs) are the most typical mode of transportation.

However, for the container, a wide variety of vehicles have been used since the beginning of containerization. Initially and for a period of time, only conventional YTs and rail-based handling equipment were used; mainly due to their comparatively low investment cost and large capacity. However, they need human drivers which lead to increasing operational costs [CAR 14a].

More recently, the choice has been automated guided vehicles (AGVs), which are completely automated; they are controlled by a central computer which decides on the dispatching and movement of each vehicle. However, AGVs are not able to lift the containers by themselves. Thus, they need a crane to receive and/or deliver the containers. AGVs have been widely implemented in modern automated container terminals, e.g. Euromax CT in Rotterdam, Netherlands and Pasir Panjang terminal in Singapore. AGVs usually follow a fixed path guided by markers, wires, lasers or computer vision; however, more intelligent and flexible AGVs have been introduced that travel freely in the transferring area, and avoid collisions and congestion. Today, AGVs can transport up to one FEU (single-load) or two TEUs (multi-load), in a trip.

Transport vehicles are classified as passive or active. Passive vehicles (e.g. yard trucks and AGVs) are not able to lift containers from the ground autonomously and thus, need to interact with other equipment, which requires a higher degree of coordination between the various equipment types. On the other hand, active vehicles (e.g. straddle carriers (SCs) and automated lifting vehicles (ALVs)) are not dependent on other equipment to lift a container. This means that they can lift and transport the containers between the ship and buffer area; although the size and availability of buffer areas is an important issue for the practical use of active vehicles.

Straddle carriers are able to stack containers on top of each other (usually up to 3 or 4 containers). Although this is a positive point for the SCs it causes a lower transportation speed of the SCs, because they are intra-mode transportation equipment. Moreover, if the CT operator decides to use SCs as a stacking crane, a special storage yard layout (in which only one container can be stored in a row) is needed, since SCs need clearance on both sides of containers in order to handle them. However, SCs are among the most adopted transportation/stacking equipment for small- and medium-sized container terminals. Note that typical SCs are manned. ALVs have been designed based on the concepts of SCs to lift/deliver the containers from/to the ground and to move them automatically and more quickly, similarly to an AGV. Obviously, ALVs have an independent work cycle from that of the QCs or the storage yard cranes and do not have to wait for a transport vehicle.

Initial simulation studies to compare AGVs and ALVs have shown that on average, the number of required AGVs in a CT is 50% more than that for the ALVs, in order to achieve the same performance [VIS 04, YAN 04]. Thus, ALVs are superior to AGVs in terms of productivity, as they reduce the waiting time in the buffer areas at the quay cranes. The AGVs fail to meet demands of tandem double-trolley QCs, where a pair of containers is ready to be unloaded in very short intervals; however, the ALVs are capable of serving such types of QCs [BAE 11]. However, Homayouni *et al.* [HOM 14] stated that by using more effective scheduling techniques (i.e. integrated scheduling), the required number of AGVs for a specific set of loading/unloading tasks can be decreased by half.

1.4.3. *Storage equipment*

The temporary destination of the loads in seaports is the storage yards. Stacking in a very large yard is the most common method of storage. A typical storage yard in CTs consists of multiple rectangular blocks, each of which consisting of several rows of containers stacked in tiers with up to six containers (see Figure 1.4). For a full description of the yard layout in CTs refer to [CAR 14b].

Yard cranes (YCs) are the most common yard handling system in CTs all around the world. YCs are non-automated rubber-tired gantry cranes, which have the flexibility to travel freely within the blocks. YCs can rotate their tires by 90° to move between the blocks as well, although this is a slow process (takes approximately 15 minutes [CAR 14b]). The second most used handling system in CTs is a straddle carrier, which is basic manual equipment to move the containers in the storage yard and stack them; however, it can only stack up to four containers. The containers self-lifting capability and the ability to move around the CT are the two most important characteristics of SCs. Thus, they are used in CTs both for transferring containers between the quayside and the storage yard, and for storing containers in the yard. However, a special layout for the storage yard is required to implement the SCs, since they can only move on the top of one row of the container. Automated yard cranes (AYCs) are also commonly used, however, since they are rail mounted gantry cranes, their movement is limited to the rails. AYCs can be operated without human intervention; although for safety reasons, when interaction with non-automated vehicles occurs, it is preferable to operate them manually. YCs and AYCs can move on the top of six rows of containers.

A simulation model was developed by Vis [VIS 06] to compare the performance of manned SCs and AYCs, in terms of average total travel (including both loaded and empty travels), hoisting and reshuffling times. They concluded that since there is no restriction of width (based on number of containers) for manned SCs versus AYCs, if the number of rows for each crane is between six and eight, then the AYCs outperform the SCs. However, for a block with nine rows or more SCs perform better than AYCs. In fact, SCs are the most suitable equipment for small-, with one berth segment [CHU 05], to medium-sized CTs [CAR 14b]. Nevertheless, for larger terminals, the land utilization and controlling issues may affect the performance of SCs; and they are outperformed by YCs and AYCs.

The main advantages of introducing new equipment in storage yards are the automation of equipment and its ability to use the land more efficiently. According to Stahlbock and Voß [STA 08], simple chassis-based lift trucks can store up to 250 TEUs/Hectare. The SCs can stack up to 750 TEUs/Hectare, while the higher number of stacked containers increases the land usage up to 1000 TEU/Hectare for YCs, and 1100 TEUs/Hectare for AYCs.

Once an exporting container of a specific ship is stored in a block, to decrease digging activities of cranes, the whole column (or columns in a row) of the location is reserved for containers of the same ship. The same happens when a portion of a block is dedicated to a shipment. Therefore, if the arrival of the whole shipment lasts for one or two weeks, the arriving containers are stored in the assigned portion of the storage block. In some other CTs, exporting containers of the same containership are often distributed among blocks to smooth the yard–block work balance, which leads to an additional vehicle traveling time. The reshuffling of the containers is another unproductive process in CTs; however, it is required when the desired container has been stacked below some other container(s). These are the main reasons for conventional yards to have storage land utilization indices much lower than the nominal capacity, regardless of the type of equipment used.

Increasing storage yard size is difficult, since, on the one hand, many container terminals have nowhere to expand and, on the other hand, land costs are sometimes prohibitive. In addition, reshuffling operations required in stacking storage yards are too time-consuming. Thus, to increase storage capacity researchers have recently been considering the principles of automated storage and retrieval systems to be implemented in CTs. For example, the split-platform automated storage/retrieval systems (SP-AS/RS) [CHE 03, HU 05], in which not only the land utilization is higher than the conventional storage yard, but also, storage and retrieval operations of various containers are not dependent on any other container in the storage area, which results in quicker access to containers and no reshuffling.

The storage system in the SP-AS/RS comprises several storage racks, each of which consists of two bays. Each of the bays has a certain number of rows accessible using the vertical platform (VP). Storage cells in each row are served using horizontal platforms (HPs). Load/unload (L/U) stations are places for the containers to be picked up/delivered to the vehicles. Expected travel time models for the SP-AS/RS have been developed by Vasili *et al.* [VAS 06], Hu *et al.* [HU 08] and Vasili *et al.* [VAS 08], and its physical and economic feasibility has been proved theoretically [HU 05]. More details of such a system and how to schedule storage and/or retrieval operations are provided in section 5.5.

1.5. Optimization of maritime operations

Optimization problems in maritime operations like any other major decision-making area are divided into three main levels, namely long-term or strategic, mid-term or tactical and short-term or operational. Decisions like cooperation between seaports, investment in new seaports or expansion of the current ones, seaport equipment type and degree of automation, ship fleet mix and size are among the strategic problems; while, decisions such as ship routing, storage yard layout and mid-term ship scheduling are usually categorized as tactical decisions. Real-time ship scheduling, speed optimization, berth allocation, crane scheduling and yard vehicle scheduling are among the day-to-day or operational decision problems. A schematic view of these decision levels is depicted in Figure 1.4. Note that each decision level imposes a set of constraints to the lower level of decision-making, while lower level decisions affect the level of accomplishment of the goals set by upper decision levels.

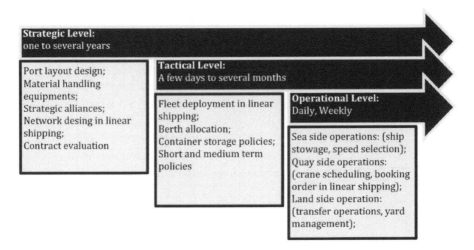

Figure 1.4. *Three levels of planning decision in seaports*

Owing to cumulative competition among geographically close seaports, the expected capacity of seaports has increased considerably, and forced the seaport authorities to improve the performance and productivity of the terminals. The efficiency of storage yards and handling equipment are key factors for more productive and efficient seaports. Massive containerships need to be unloaded/loaded in a shorter amount of time to reduce the inactive ships' time and this decreases maritime transportation costs. In most of the cases, both equipment and decision-making improvements are essential to decrease waiting times in seaports.

Although decisions made in strategic and tactical levels have a great impact on the performance of the seaports, the daily operations are the most challenging and time-consuming problems for the seaport authorities. Especially for container terminals, since, due to the degree of automation required, a very large number of complex problems needs to be dealt with. Figure 1.5 illustrates the main operational problems in maritime operations. The upper level decisions constrain lower level problem solutions dedicated by the available resources.

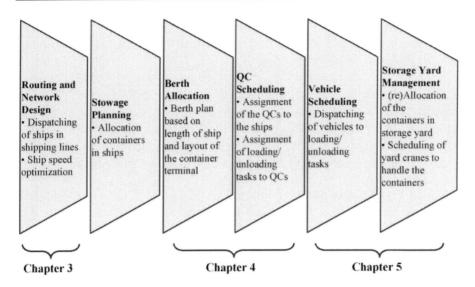

Figure 1.5. *Major operational problems in CTs*

Commonly, ships travel between multiple seaports around the world either based on a predetermined fixed or cyclic route (in liner shipping) or based on a route of demanded seaports (in tramp shipping). Designing the cyclic routes for liner shipping requires that one determines which ports the ships should visit, and in which order it should be done. Such decisions are, obviously, constrained by fleet size and ship type. Speed optimization of the ship along the route is another important issue. Traditionally, quick and shorter routes are the target of routing and network design problems [MEN 14]. However, energy-efficient routes and speed optimization problems have recently gained much more attention in the literature [PSA 13, PSA 14]. The most important output of the ship routing and network design problem is the estimated arrival time of a ship to the seaports. We focus on these problems further in Chapter 3.

Containers are stacked on top of each other in docks of containerships and are accessible only from the top of the stack. In stowage planning, each group of containers is stored in containerships based on the size and destination port. The most important objectives for stowage planning are to maintain containership stability and minimize the number of reshuffling operations required to reach demanded containers in the destination CTs.

The most important output of the stowage planning problem is a primary plan for unloading and loading the containers in the CT. A brief description of the problem is reviewed in Chapter 4.

Ships are allocated a berthing time and a position, prior to the arrival at a seaport. The berth allocation problem (BAP) determines these decisions based on the available berthing area, size of the ship, load type of the ship and its estimated arrival time. The main objective of the BAP is to minimize delays in service time for a group of ships in a mid-term planning horizon.

Once a ship moors at the berth segment, a number of QCs or (un)loaders are assigned to the ship. In container terminals, a set of QCs are assigned to each ship, included in the berth plan, with a known volume of containers to be loaded and unloaded – the quay crane assignment problem (QCAP). The QCs move along the berth area on a rail and cannot overtake each other. The objective of the QCAP is to assign cranes to ships such that all required loading and unloading operations are performed before the expected departure time of the ship (i.e. ship due date). A detailed schedule for the QCs to unload and load containers to a containership is the main outcome of the quay crane scheduling problem (QCSP), in which the makespan of the entire ship's operations is minimized. Precedence relations between the containers are the most important constraints for the QCSP. The BAP, QCAP and QCSP, and the integrated planning and scheduling approach to these problems are reviewed in Chapter 4.

The imported loads from a ship need to be transferred from the berth area to the storage yard, while the exported loads need to be transferred from the storage yard to the berth area. In the vehicle scheduling problem, a set of vehicles is assigned to a ship and dispatched to the loading and unloading tasks. The prime objective of the vehicle scheduling problem is to minimize the total traveling time of the vehicles and the makespan for all the loading and unloading operations.

In the storage yard, which is a massive buffer area between the maritime transportation and the customers or other modes of transportation, temporary storage blocks are allocated to the imported/exporting loads; this allocation problem is known as the storage space allocation problem (SSAP). The main objective is to maintain a balanced workload of the blocks and to minimize the storage/retrieval time of loads. On the other hand, scheduling of the cranes in the storage yard is important to minimize total delayed workloads, and the total travel time of the cranes moving between blocks. The SSAP, the vehicle scheduling problem and yard crane scheduling problem are reviewed in Chapter 5.

Although the afore-mentioned problems are mainly approached as described, there are dependencies or even overlapping among some of the decisions involved. For example, the best routing may lead to a ship arriving at a port that cannot handle it, for instance, due to the unavailability of berth segments or cranes. Recently, such problems have started to attract some attention; however, integrated decision-making problems are still predominant research areas for future studies. Chapter 5 also reviews them.

1.6. Conclusion

In this chapter, we reviewed some facts and figures that show the important role of maritime transportation in global, regional and national economies, and the increasing demand for the loading/unloading capacity in seaports and maritime transportation. The ever-increasing need for maritime transportation pushes for better equipment and for improvements in the effectiveness and efficiency of its utilization.

As we have seen, there are many different problems, each involving many aspects that can be optimized in order to increase maritime transportation efficiency; both regarding ship operations and seaport operations. This way, giving a competitive edge to this transportation mode, which is already responsible for over 85% of the goods transported worldwide.

Most of the problems in the operational level are NP-hard, and thus mathematical exact methods are not capable of providing solutions in a timely manner. Thus, the majority of the research reported addressing these problems proposes heuristic and metaheuristic approaches capable of finding good quality solutions within a reasonable amount of time. In Chapter 2, we review some of the most popular metaheuristics regarding the optimization of maritime operations.

2

Metaheuristic Algorithms

Optimization methods aim to find an optimal or a near-optimal solution to a problem and can be divided into exact and (meta)heuristic methods. Exact methods are designed in a way that allows for finding an optimal solution in a finite amount of time; while (meta)heuristic methods cannot ensure optimality. However, exact methods are often too time (computational time) consuming, particularly in the presence of combinatorial problems of realistic dimension, as explicitly or implicitly enumeration is performed. Thus, unless the time requirements grow polynomially with the size of the problem or the instances being solved are of small size, a (meta)heuristic method should be used.

Heuristic methods and metaheuristic methods differ in the sense that while the former exploit problem properties, the latter is general and can be applied to any problem. Thus, heuristic methods are designed for a specific problem and incorporate its characteristics. In doing so, feasible and quite often reasonably good solutions are found very quickly; nevertheless, they tend to be too greedy and thus get trapped in local optima. Metaheuristics provide a general framework that can be used to solve different problems, like a black box. In addition, they also include a problem-specific module, many times referred to as heuristic, which allows for a problem-specific implementation of the aforementioned framework.

2.1. Basics of metaheuristics

A metaheuristic is a high-level iterative process that guides the search over the solution space and modifies solutions. It may consider complete or incomplete solutions and also a single solution or a collection of solutions at the time. The search process is stochastic in nature and its efficiency and effectiveness are closely related to the achievement of a good balance between exploration and exploitation. Exploration allows for searching new regions of the solution space, with the aim of finding areas with high-quality solutions and also avoiding getting trapped in local optima. Exploitation, on the other hand, intensifies the search in the promising areas found, i.e. looks for new solutions in the neighborhood of the best-known solutions. The main difference across the several metaheuristics that have been proposed over the years is the way in which this balance is sought [BIR 01]. A good and recent survey on the use and balancing of exploration and exploitation in the evolutionary algorithm can be found in [ČRE 13]. The authors also provide a discussion on misconceptions and misuse of these two concepts.

Metaheuristics have been categorized and classified in many different ways, e.g. Blum and Roli [BLU 03] distinguish metaheuristics according to the following five points: nature inspired, and non-nature inspired; population-based and single point search (trajectory methods); dynamic and static objective function; one and various neighborhood structures; and memory usage and non-memory usage. Other classification schemes have been proposed, see e.g. [TAL 02, BLU 03, LIU 09, CAS 09], among others.

Many metaheuristics have been proposed over the years. In the following sections, we introduce two trajectory methods, namely simulated annealing and tabu search, and two types of population base metaheuristics, namely evolutionary algorithms and swarm intelligence. Regarding evolutionary algorithms, we chose genetic algorithms as they are the most well known and most commonly used ones. Regarding swarm intelligence, although recently many techniques have been introduced, here only ant colony optimization and particle swarm optimization are discussed. The chapter is concluded by referring to some current trends regarding metaheuristics.

2.2. Simulated annealing algorithm

The simulated annealing (SA) method is a compact and robust technique that can be used both in single and multi-objective optimization problems. Simulated annealing is an adaptive local search method that borrows concepts from thermodynamics, more specifically, from the physical annealing of metals [MOK 15]. The annealing process involves heating the material to a high temperature and then slowly cooling it down to improve its crystalline structure and reach a low energy level. The liquid metal has a high level of energy and its atoms are free to move around and to change the structure of the metal. If the cooling process of a metal is slow enough (annealing), the atoms have the opportunity to find a state with a minimum level of energy and to form a pure crystal shape [SUM 06]. SA simulates the annealing process using the Metropolis algorithm [MET 53], a simple method to mimic the evolution of thermal equilibrium. The annealing process is transposed to a solution of an optimization problem by associating material states with problem solutions, material energy with the objective function, and the material temperature with a fictitious control parameter [KIR 83].

SA algorithm is a stochastic metaheuristic and stochasticity is introduced in SA in two different ways, namely in the generation of the initial solution, which can also be obtained by a constructive heuristic, and in the decision of accepting worse solutions. Thus, it performs a randomized local search to reach near-optimal solutions of combinatorial, as well as continuous, optimization problems [AAR 05]. Therefore, in addition to being a decent algorithm, it includes random ascent moves, which makes it possible to escape local optima that are not global optima. This way preventing premature convergence and making it possible to search other regions of the solution space.

The SA basic algorithm, which is illustrated in Figure 2.1, starts by initializing the temperature parameter and generating and evaluating an initial solution; then and until a certain "thermodynamic equilibrium" (usually, a certain number of iterations) is met, it iteratively finds a solution in the neighborhood of the current solution and decides on its acceptance as the new current solution. The temperature parameter is then decreased, and the iterative steps repeated; this is performed until some pre-specified criteria are met.

The acceptance of a neighbor solution to replace the current solution is based both on the quality of the solution and on the value of the temperature parameter; better solutions are always accepted, while there is an acceptance probability that is smaller for worse solutions and for lower temperature parameter values. The acceptance probability is, typically, computed as given in equation [2.1], in which Δf is the difference between the objective function value of the current solution and that of the neighbor solution.

$$P = EXP\left(\frac{\Delta f}{T_r}\right)$$ [2.1]

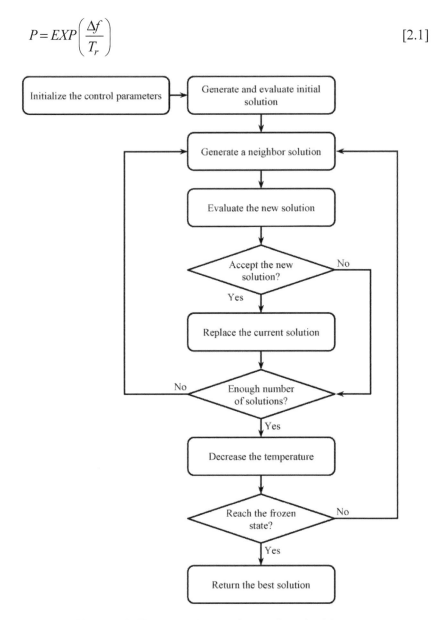

Figure 2.1. *The basic simulated annealing algorithm*

It should be noted that the worse the solution is, the less likely it is to be accepted and also that as the algorithm progresses the probability of accepting worse solutions decreases as the temperature parameter value is decreased. The choices of the point until which worse solutions are accepted and how much worse they can be are made in order to balance exploration (enlarge search space) and exploitation (intensification of the search around good solutions).

As can be seen from Figure 2.1, the SA algorithm has two loops: in the inner loop a neighbor solution is generated, evaluated and compared with the current solution, and a decision regarding its acceptance as a replacement of the current solution is made (at constant temperature); this loop is repeated several times. The outer loop controls the temperature parameter by decreasing it until a final value is reached, and usually, this is the SA algorithm stopping criterion.

The temperature cooling process is one of the most important factors regarding SA efficiency. On the one hand, if the temperature is decreased too quickly the algorithm converges to local optima, much like local search algorithms, as it does not accept worse solutions or only accepts the ones that are only slightly worse. This way, the exploration of the solution space is compromised. On the other hand, if the temperature is reduced very slowly, almost all solutions are accepted, and thus, not much exploitation around the best solutions is performed. It has been proved [GEM 84, HAJ 88] that if the temperature decreases according to equation [2.2] with an initial temperature T_0 sufficiently large convergence to a global minimum with probability one is ensured. However, pragmatically, a logarithmic decrease is too slow; thus, often in practice a linear decrease, as in equation [2.3], is used in the search for a suboptimal solution where alpha should be empirically determined for each problem.

$$T(t) = \frac{T_0}{\ln (t+1)} \qquad t = 1, 2, \ldots \qquad [2.2]$$

$$T_t = \alpha T_{t-1} \qquad t = 1, 2, \ldots; \ 0.85 \leq \alpha \leq 0.95 \qquad [2.3]$$

Several variants of the basic SA algorithm have been proposed. For example, the Microcanonic Annealing uses the Creutz algorithm [CRE 83] rather than that of Metropolis, the Threshold Accepting simulated annealing uses as acceptance criterion a threshold value for the solution quality loss [DEU 90], and many others [COL 88, SUM 06, TAN 08].

SA algorithms have shown very good performance in many optimization problems, both discrete and continuous; moreover, they are simple to develop and, usually, fast to run [JER 06]. Regarding maritime operations, some very recent works employing simulated annealing can be found. Here, we provide an elucidative, but not an exhaustive list of some applications in berth allocation [LIN 14b, LIN 17b], the ship routing problem [KOS 12] and integrated scheduling of handling operations [HOM 16].

2.3. Tabu search algorithm

Tabu search, similar to simulated annealing, enhances local search methods by allowing moves to a worse solution in order to avoid getting trapped into local optima and also to explore the search space. To do so, Tabu search (TS) explicitly uses information of the search history. Although the tabu search's origins date back to the 1960s [GLO 98, GLO 07], its present form was introduced by Glover [GLO 86] in 1986.

TS main distinctive characteristic is inspired by memory and thus it is able to learn from the "past". TS stores information of the solutions already tried in order to avoid going back to them, i.e. such solutions are classified as tabu[1]. This prevents cycling between solutions and, sometimes, forces the acceptance of worse solutions, if no improving solutions exist in the neighborhood or all are forbidden. There are three types of memory, namely short-term memory, intermediate-term memory and long-term memory.

The simplest version, short-term memory, uses a list of forbidden solutions. Since memory is not unlimited, only the last n solutions are forbidden. Once the list is full and a new solution is discovered, the first solution on the list, i.e. the one that has been in it the longest, is removed. Note that the balance between exploration and exploitation is obtained through the size of the list. If the list is small, just a few solutions are forbidden and thus the search favors exploitation as it is concentrated on a small area; on the other hand, if the list is large, a large number of solutions are forbidden, then TS needs to further explore the solution space in the search for new solutions. The flowchart of the basic TS algorithm is illustrated in Figure 2.2. The list size may be varied and adjusted during the search, reactive TS [GLO 89, GLO 90, BAT 94].

---

1 The origins of the word tabu can be traced to the Polynesian and it means "forbidden, prohibitive, disallowed, sacred".

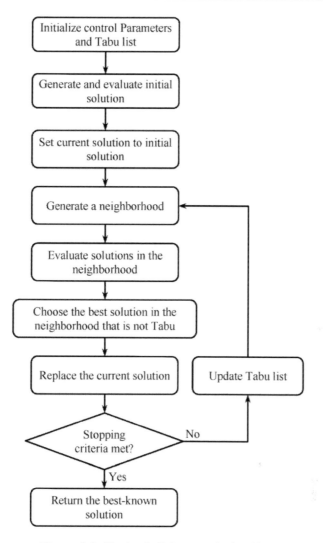

Figure 2.2. *The basic Tabu search algorithm*

More elaborate approaches store solution properties rather than solutions. In such cases, the number of forbidden solutions is much larger and thus there is the risk of "stagnation", that is by forbidding good solutions, which may not have been visited before or may lead to different areas of the solution space, TS may not be able to find any solution not forbidden. To prevent this from happening, an intermediate-term memory, known as aspiration criteria, is used. The aspiration criteria are a set of rules that establish the conditions in which tabu solutions are accepted, see e.g. [WER 89, HER 90]. For example, a solution that is better than the best-known solution may be forbidden; which obviously is unreasonable.

Looking into solution properties rather than solutions can also be advantageous in order to balance exploitation and exploration. In TS, this can be done by resorting to long-term memory. This mechanism records the frequency with which certain solution properties or characteristics have been encountered. Such information may be used to force searching for solutions with frequently encountered attributes (exploitation) or with rarely encountered attributes (exploration).

There is a large number of additional considerations, e.g. Rangaswamy and Glover [RAN 98] discuss candidate list strategies, Voß [VOß 96] discuss logical interdependencies, and Glover and Laguna [GLO 97] and Toth and Vigo [TOT 03] use probabilistic TS, which only considers a random sample of the neighborhood, to name but a few. For a detailed description of TS and its concepts, the reader is referred to [GLO 97], while surveys are provided in [GEN 03, GEN 14]. Although TS has been designed for combinatorial problems, where most of its applications lie, TS has also been used in continuous optimization [GLO 94, CVI 95, CHE 00].

TS algorithms have been used to solve problems in many different application areas. Here is a very brief list of some of the most recent ones involving scheduling [DAB 17], Cryptography [KAD 17], traveling salesman problem [BAS 17], resource planning [MOS 17] and molecular modeling [NAN 17]. Maritime optimization problems are no exception, e.g. the quay crane scheduling problem [SAM 07], yard crane scheduling [CHE 11] and vehicle routing problem [KOO 05].

2.4. Genetic algorithms

Genetic algorithms (GAs) were first proposed by Holland in the early 1970s as computer programs that mimic the evolutionary process in nature [HOL 92]. Since then, GAs have been demonstrating their efficiency and effectiveness by successfully being applied to many practical optimization problems in the few last decades. GAs are a powerful stochastic global search technique as the search is performed by exploiting information sampled from different regions of the solution space [GLO 93].

Owing to its origins from the study of genetics, GA principles and terminology are borrowed from the dynamics and biology of natural population genetics. As such, a GA evolves a population of chromosomes using natural selection and genetics along generations. In GAs, a population refers to a set of individuals (solutions to the problem). Each of these solutions is represented by a chromosome and is, usually, encoded as a string. Each string position is designated as a gene and its value as an allele. The population of strings is known as genotype; while the population of solutions is known as phenotype. The GA works in the genotype space, i.e. it evolves the population of chromosomes; however, to evaluate the fitness of a chromosome (suitability or quality of a solution), it needs to be converted into a solution to the problem being solved. This conversion is called decoding and should be fast as it is carried out for the whole population at each generation (iteration). The reverse transformation is called encoding. To evolve solutions, GAs use selection to choose, in the population, the chromosomes that will reproduce. Usually bias is introduced towards the best chromosomes, that is, better solutions are more frequently chosen to reproduce. Reproduction is mimicked by exchanging parts of two chromosomes to obtain new ones. Finally, random changes may occur to some gene values – mutation.

As said before, GAs evolve encoded parameters, or chromosomes, which represent solutions to the problem being addressed, thus GAs can be seen as a black box for which one only needs to specify the encoding (solution representation), decoding (solution construction) and fitness (solution quality evaluation), as illustrated in Figure 2.3.

The first step when developing a GA is the encoding of the possible solutions. This is a key factor and it heavily depends on the problem being studied. Many of the implemented GAs and theoretical studies are based on binary encoding. In this case, each chromosome is represented by a string of bits, each bit having a zero or one value. A gene consists of either a single bit or an association of adjacent bits. Most commonly, the strings have a fixed length, although it may be variable. Other encodings have been proposed over the years [SIN 08]. For example, Roque et al. [ROQ 14] and Fontes and Gonçalves [FON 13] use real numbers. Then, an initial population is generated. This can be done randomly or by resorting to heuristics in order to have, at least some, initial solutions of reasonable quality. From this initial population, a new one is generated using selection, crossover and mutation, hoping that the new population is better than the previous one and that this process leads to the generation of an individual that is an optimum solution or, at least, a good solution for the problem at hand.

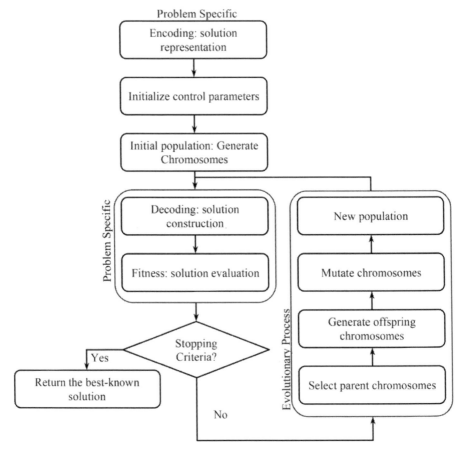

Figure 2.3. *The basic genetic algorithm*

Some of the most commonly used selection strategies are roulette-wheel, ranking and tournament. The roulette-wheel strategy aims at giving to each individual (solution) a chance of being selected based on its ability (fitness value); however, for small populations, the actual number of offspring an individual may have can be far from its expected number. The ranking strategy sorts individuals and then allocates offspring according to the individual position. It has the advantage of ignoring fitness values and thus avoids providing a very large number of offspring to a potentially very small number of individuals, reducing selection pressure when the fitness variance is high, while keeping it when the variance is low. However, in some cases, the magnitude of the fitness difference may be important. The tournament strategy randomly selects individuals from the whole population and then from these groups the best individual, i.e. the one with the best fitness value, is selected for reproduction. Selection pressure is adjusted by changing the number of individuals selected for the tournament. The smaller it is, the larger change is given less fit individuals.

Once solutions have been chosen, the crossover takes place, which combines multiple (usually two) selected individuals by exchanging part of their chromosomes. Although many strategies exist here, we refer to the single-point and uniform crossover. For the former, a position in the chromosome is selected randomly – crossover point – and two individuals are created by swapping the genes that lay after this point. In the uniform crossover, each gene is chosen from one of the parents according to a certain probability. After crossover, the mutation operator is applied in order to enforce diversity and avoid local optimal entrapment. Again, there are several ways in which mutation can be implemented; the most common one being randomly changing the value of a randomly chosen gene. Another possibility is to randomly generate some new solutions, following the idea of immigration [FON 13].

The new population may just be obtained by joining all the solutions generated by the genetic operators (just described). However, to avoid loss of information, there is the possibility of maintaining some of the best elements of the previous population; this strategy is designated by elitism, see e.g. [FON 07].

GAs are one of the most commonly used heuristics in many different problems: process planning and scheduling [CHA 17], inventory allocation [SHA 17], energy [ROQ 17], real options valuation [ZHA 12], optimal bearing placement [LIU 17], clinical decision support in oncology [FIT 15], production fuzzy control systems [HOM 09], project scheduling [KAD 18, FON 15] and network design [FON 13], to name but a few. Regarding maritime operations, some recent works employing GAs can be found: ship routing problem [LIN 11], vehicle scheduling problem [NG 07], quay crane scheduling problem [CHU 13] and integrated scheduling of handling operations [HOM 14].

2.5. Particle swarm optimization

Particle swarm optimization (PSO) is a population-based stochastic optimization technique developed by Eberhart and Kennedy [EBE 95] and it is inspired by the social group behavior of bird flocking or fish schooling.

In a PSO algorithm, a swarm, i.e. a population of solutions each termed particle, is stochastically generated in the search space and moves through it searching for good positions, i.e. good solutions to the problem at hand. Each of these particles is represented by a position and a velocity and has a memory of its best previous position. The particles move according to their own experience, the best previous position, the experience of their neighbors, and the best previous position in the neighborhood. The neighborhood may be defined as the entire population or as some subset of it, this way defining the particle or particles that have influence. Originally, the neighborhood considered was the entire population and as such the best previous position of all was to be considered; however, due to the tendency to converge too quickly [KEN 01], other neighborhoods have been investigated and proposed [KEN 02].

The basic PSO algorithm is illustrated in Figure 2.4. Initially, the positions and velocities for all particles (solutions) are randomly generated. Then, iteratively, particles adjust their positions and velocities using a cognitive-social compromise, i.e. balancing the individual's best and the neighborhood's best. The new particles are then evaluated and the best-known positions, of each particle and neighborhood, updated if needed.

The velocity update considers three components: the first one, known as *inertia* or *momentum*, prevents the particle from drastically changing its movement direction; the second component, the *cognitive* component, incorporates the particle experience using its best-found position; while the third component, the *social* component, incorporates the neighborhood best position. The particle position is updated by adding the velocity to the position.

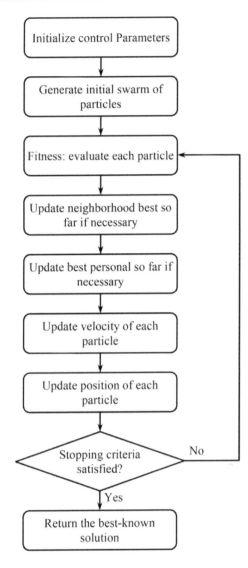

Figure 2.4. *The basic particle swarm optimization algorithm*

Over the years, some modifications have been introduced to this basic algorithm. For example, to overcome the problem of excessive convergence in [SHI 98], an inertia weight was proposed. This weight, which is included in the first velocity update component, is used to balance the local and global searches; larger weights lead to exploration (diversified search), while smaller ones lead to exploitation (intensified search in the current region). Eberhart *et al.* [EBE 96] propose the inclusion of upper and lower limits to the velocity to prevent the particles from searching outside of the solution space; however, the choice of the values for these limits needs to be done with care since they also affect the balance between exploration and exploitation [ANG 98].

More recently, PSO versions based on evolution operators have been proposed, see e.g. [FAT 16] for a PSO incorporating crossover and mutation proposed to solve a part feeding problem. Several recent surveys on PSO, its variants, and hybridizations, as well as PSO applications, can be found in [BON 17, ENG 16]. Some examples of recent works employing PSO in maritime operations are the green ship routing problem [DE 16], integrated berth allocation and quay crane assignment problem [HSU 16], and integrated storage space allocation and vehicle scheduling problem [NIU 16].

2.6. Ant colony optimization

Ant systems were first introduced by Dorigo and his colleagues [DOR 91, DOR 92] to solve the traveling salesman problem adapting the behavior of real ants. Ant colony optimization (ACO) is the most well-known and successful successor of the ant system. The idea behind ant algorithms is to adapt and use ants' communication style; thus, artificial ants can be seen and described as communicating agents sharing some characteristics of the real ants, but also incorporating other characteristics that do not have a parallel in nature.

Ants search for food in the vicinity of their nest and while doing it they deposit a chemical substance called pheromone in the ground. This is done with two objectives. On the one hand, it allows ants to find their way back to the nest and, on the other hand, it allows other ants to know the path they have taken. A path with a larger concentration of pheromone has been used more, most likely because it is shorter and thus ants travel through it more often, therefore with many more ants depositing pheromone on it. The trail-laying and trail-following behavior of ants is the base of ACO [DOR 04].

Some very interesting experiments have been performed with real ants to try to understand their path choices [DEN 90, GOS 89]: two bridges were set up between the nest and a food source, one being longer. Although several length ratios have been considered, the observation was always that, at first, the ants seemed to choose the path to follow at random; however, after a while, they converged to the shortest path. Dorigo and Stützle [DOR 04] interpreted this as a kind of exploration.

The basic ant algorithm, ant system (AS) algorithm, considers a single colony of cooperating (artificial) ants and has two main steps, namely solution construction and the pheromone update. The solution construction step is a specifically designed procedure that iteratively constructs a (feasible) solution to the problem at hand. This procedure is stochastic in nature since the choices are made using a "random proportional transition rule", which depends on the pheromone values, as well as on problem-specific information "heuristic information" or "visibility", since it can be interpreted as what ants can "see". The pheromones are updated by first being reduced, mimicking natural evaporation, and then increased by allowing each ant to "deposit" pheromone in its problem solution components, proportionally to the quality of the solution found. (Alternatives in which the deposit of pheromone is done while the solutions are being constructed have also been proposed, but typically performed worse.) These two steps are then repeated while the stopping criterion is not met.

Evaporation is used to prevent the algorithm from converging too quickly (all ants constructing the same tour), and thus, getting trapped into a local optimum. The balance between exploration and exploitation is, mainly, obtained through the value of the evaporation rate. On the one hand, by choosing a value close to 1, exploration is enforced as the pheromone trail will not have a lasting effect. On the other hand, if it has a small value, the importance of the pheromone is increased, leading to the exploitation of the search space near the current solution.

Changes to the AS algorithm have been proposed in order to improve the quality of the solutions obtained, mainly for large-sized problem instances. These improvements include, but are not limited to: elitist AS, rank-based AS, max–min AS and ant colony system (ACS). In Elitist AS [DOR 96], at each iteration, pheromone values are reinforced on all problem components used in the best-known solution, while in rank-based AS [BUL 97], the reinforcement is applied only to the components in the n best solutions. The max–min AS [STU 97] introduces the following changes: only iteration best and global best ants deposit pheromone; upper and lower limits are imposed to the pheromone values, i.e. when the updated value, due to either pheromone evaporation or pheromone deposit, falls out of the limit, it assumes the limit value; pheromones are initialized at the upper limit value; and pheromone values are reinitialized whenever no better solution is found for a certain number of iterations. ACS [DOR 97] changes include i) a new transition rule, which probabilistically uses one of the two ways of selecting a solution component during the constructing procedure: either randomly, although based on pheromone values, or deterministically as the one that maximizes the product between the pheromone trail and the heuristic information; ii) at the end of each iteration, pheromone values are reinforced only on the components used in the best-known solution; iii) during each iteration of the solution construction step, the pheromone is updated, this local update rule favors exploration by decreasing the desirability of incorporating the used components by the following ants; and iv) the use of a component candidate list, which, during the solution construction procedure, is to be considered first.

Following these improvements, ant colony optimization was proposed in 1999 [DOR 99a, DOR 99b] and the basic algorithm is illustrated in Figure 2.5. The main novelty is the introduction of a Daemon, which performs some problem-specific action after the solutions have been constructed, but before updating the pheromones. For example, the daemon can control the feasibility of each solution or give an extra pheromone quantity to the best-known solution, or even to the best solution in the current iteration. (This, of course, has no equivalence in nature.)

ACO algorithms have been proposed in several maritime problems, such as the ship routing problem [TSO 13], crude oil transportation network design [WAN 15], and the storage space allocation problem [SHA 13]. Some of these works are discussed in the chapter on the corresponding problem. Problems in many other application areas have been addressed by ACO algorithms, e.g. routing and transportation problems [HE 17, LI 17], scheduling problems [ELM 17], network problems [MON 13, MON 15], to name just few.

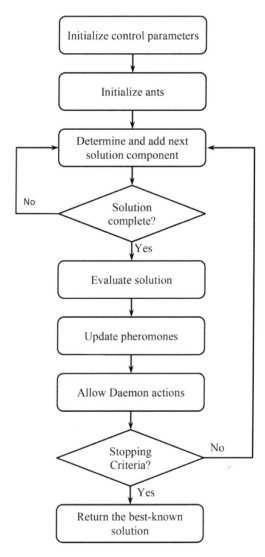

Figure 2.5. *The basic ant colony optimization algorithm*

2.7. Conclusion

This chapter reviews the principles of the metaheuristics that are an essential tool for complex and real-world optimization problems. They are particularly interesting for time-sensitive decision-making problems since, even for highly complex problem structures and very large-sized problem instances, metaheuristic algorithms are capable of finding near-optimal solutions in a reasonable amount of time.

Some of the most common and widely used metaheuristics are explained in detail. In addition, evidence of their applicability to maritime operations and other problems is demonstrated by providing references to works proposing their uses and reporting their efficiency and effectiveness.

3

Metaheuristics for Ship Operations

Expansion of the global economy highly depends on deep-sea transportation, which is the backbone of maritime transportation. An efficient decision on the ship operations (e.g. network design, routing, scheduling, stowage planning, etc.) increases the ship's productivity, and thus has impacts both on the local and on the global economies. The focus of this chapter is on the ship routing and scheduling problem, which is the major factor determining a ship's productivity. Section 3.1 reviews the ship routing problem, while energy-efficient transportation is discussed in section 3.2. Some conclusions are pointed out in section 3.3.

3.1. Ship routing problem

The ship routing problem (SRP) aims at allocating a fleet of ships (the number and type of ships are known) to the transportation requests. The generic SRP is a special case of the vehicle routing problem (VRP), which is known to be a strong NP-hard problem [LIN 11]. However, VRP and SRP are different in several ways [VIL 15], e.g. in VRP, the vehicles must return to the home depot, but the ships do not have to return to the starting point. In addition, some ships may not be able to transport some cargoes or to enter some ports, either due to physical reasons or due to political/cultural ones. Other differences include 24-hour operation, different starting times (i.e. the ships might have some jobs at the beginning of the planning horizon), compulsory and optional cargoes, among others.

Usually, the cargo ships are operated in one of the three possible modes, namely: industrial, tramp or liner [KJE 11]. In industrial shipping, the owner of the ships is also the owner of the cargoes, therefore the objective is to transport all cargoes from the ports to the destination ports at minimum cost. Tramp shipping is very similar to industrial shipping, differing from it only in the fact that the ships are hired by the cargo owner (the ship is chartered by the cargo owner to transport a specific route like a taxi cab). In many cases, the ship owners (tramp operators) have part of their capacity allocated under contracts that specify origin, destination, cargo types and quantities, prices, contract duration, etc. However, tramp operators may also consider transporting spot cargoes (if the time frame for the contracted cargoes and the remaining capacity of the ship allow it), that is cargoes they may decide to transport, but are not under any obligation to do so. These two approaches of shipping operation are most suitable for the companies with the known (or predicted) requests of transportation in pairs of origin-destination ports, e.g. for liquid bulk cargo, crude oil or dry bulk cargo.

Routing and scheduling decisions in industrial and tramp shipping are very similar [CHR 13]. For tramp shipping companies, the main concern is to plan routes and schedules for each individual ship in an efficient and continuous manner in order to be able to choose some optional cargoes. Therefore, the objective is to maximize the profit from the optional cargoes.

Similar to buses in urban public transportation, liner ships operate predefined routes with a fixed timetable and each cargo taken, typically, accounts for a small part of the ship capacity. A practical example of a timetable for the Southampton-Hong Kong route (known as AE1 Eastbound) by Maersk Line [MAE 18] is reported in Table 3.1. The liner shipping companies try to maximize their profit by establishing good routes, the sequence of ports, to which adequate ships, compatibility between ships and ports must be ensured, and adequate ship capacity is allocated. Profits are increased by attracting a larger market share. This type of shipping operation is most suitable for customers with smaller cargo volumes than a chartered ship, and/or non-frequent customers. Therefore, most likely the liner ships transport containers and break-bulk cargos.

The long-term decisions regarding the ship routing problem, especially for the liner shipping companies, are mainly about hub-and-spoke transportation versus direct shipment between origin-destination pairs. Obviously, the decision is affected by long-term prediction of the aggregate volume to be transported between, of the frequency of required trips between the ports, and the company's available fleet mix and size. For example, the hub-and-spoke transportation system is used in the main intercontinental liner routes (e.g. the Far East to Northern Europe), while for the intra-region transportation (e.g. between the Middle Eastern countries), a direct shipment system is in service.

Ports en route	Duration of the voyage (days)	Expected arrival time
Southampton, UK	4	24/1/2018
Bremerhaven, Germany	2	28/1/2018
Rotterdam, the Netherlands	5	30/1/2018
Port Tangier Mediterranee, Morocco	5	4/2/2018
The Suez Canal, Egypt	6	9/2/2018
Salalah, Oman	5	15/2/2018
Colombo, Sri Lanka	6	20/2/2018
Singapore, Singapore	7	26/2/2018
Ningbo, China	2	5/3/2018
Shanghai, China	0	7/3/2018
Yantian, China	4	7/3/2018
Hong Kong, Hong Kong	–	11/3/2018

Table 3.1. *Timetable for the Southampton–Hong Kong route by Maersk Line*

In a mid-term horizon, the company needs to decide which port will be the hub (based on the operational capacities and costs), the fleet size and mix to allocate to each route (based on the capacity of the ships and the governmental regulations), and the frequency of services. In the lowest level of decision-making, the sequence of ports to call and the timing of port calls is decided. In this problem, the company associates a specific ship type with a route to guarantee satisfactory cargo capacity (for customers in each port), and compatibility between the ships and the visiting ports. Ship–port compatibility has to account for issues like the ability of the ship to sail into the port, and the ability of the port to handle the cargo type and to perform all unloading and/or loading tasks of a ship in the given (or presumed) time interval. Although the timetables for the routes may change from time to time (e.g. due to seasonal change in demands), they are typically fixed for a long period of time.

3.1.1. *Formulation of the tramp SRP*

Since the tramp shipping companies do not frequently change the routes, and their operation is highly dependent on immediate orders (although they have some long-term contracts of affreightment), it is important to be able to make decisions regarding the acceptance or rejection of spot orders and to be able to update the fleet assignment in a timely manner. Thus, researchers have been working on improving the efficiency of solving the tramp SRP, see e.g. [LIN 11, NOR 11, LEE 15, WEN 16, VIL 17]. For a general classification of the studies published prior to 2011 in tramp SRP, we refer the reader to a recent and comprehensive review by Christiansen *et al.* [CHR 13].

An MILP model and a hybrid-GA were developed by Lin and Liu [LIN 11] for the tramp SRP. They evaluated the proposed approaches in a real-life case study for a shipping company operating handy-max dry bulk ships to transport various types of dry cargoes. Their work will be further discussed in section 3.1.2. Norstad *et al.* [NOR 11] developed a nonlinear mathematical formulation for the tramp ship routing and scheduling problem, considering the speed as a decision variable. Since the speed decision-making results in a nonlinear optimization problem, Norstad *et al.* [NOR 11] proposed two heuristic solution methods, namely a discretizing arrival times algorithm and a recursive smoothing algorithm. In the former, the arrival times are discretized within the time window of each port and the problem is solved as a "shortest path problem" on a cyclic graph; while in the latter the speed is assumed to be as low as possible and constant for the voyages to reach the ports within the time windows. A ship routing problem for a set of given origin–destination cargoes with soft delivery due times was formulated by Lee and Kim [LEE 15]. The cargoes can be shared between two or more ships (if the due times allow) and a ship can share its capacity between the cargoes in different ports. The problem considers a fleet of industrial and tramp ships simultaneously. The problem was also solved by an adaptive large neighborhood search method, which was tested on 11 problems instances; one being a real case study from a steel making company. The local search method solutions were compared with the optimal ones found by solving the MILP and they were found to be, on average, only 5% away of optimality.

Typically, the cargoes are categorized according to their volume as full ship-load and less-than-shipload. In the full ship-load, the cargo occupies the whole storage space of a ship, and thus the ship has a direct voyage between the origin and destination of the cargo. However, since the less than ship-load cargoes do not occupy the whole ship space, multiple cargoes are, usually, taken by the shipping company. In this, the problem is much harder as the ship needs to visit several ports (origin and destination ports) to load and/or unload the cargoes. Wen *et al.* [WEN 16] developed two mathematical models for the full-ship-load tramp ship routing and scheduling as a "three-index" formulation, in which the ship speed is a decision variable, and a "set packing" formulation, which is much more compact than the former. However, the set packing formulation is not good at handling further constraints for the speed optimization and/or the scheduling problems. Moreover, the set packaging model needs a list of all possible ship routes, which is unrealistic, even in the small-sized problem instances. The three-index formulation for the tramp SRP will be further discussed later in this section. In a recent research, Vilhelmsen *et al.* [VIL 17] considered the ship routing problem with voyage separation requirements that force a minimum time spread between some voyages. The incorporation of these separation requirements results in balancing the conflicting objectives of maximizing profit for the tramp operator and minimizing inventory costs for the charterer.

Wen *et al.* [WEN 16] address a tramp SRP considering full ship-load cargo in which the tramp shipping company has a fleet of ships with different sizes and fuel consumptions. It receives orders to load a full ship-load cargo at an origin port within a given time window and to transport it to a destination port. Although the assumption of receiving full ship-load cargo transportation simplifies the formulation of the problem, it is a realistic assumption. At least, for the transportation of the oil and gas products that tramp shipping companies frequently receive. The company decides whether to accept a cargo or not, assigns a compatible ship to the accepted cargoes, determines the starting time to load the cargoes and the ship average speed during the voyage, in order to maximize the profit. Since the ships (and cargoes) are of different types and sizes, not all cargoes can be transported by all the ships. The set of compatible ships to transport a cargo is known in advance. After a loaded voyage to transport a cargo, the ship does an empty voyage between the destination of the cargo to the origin of its next assigned cargo. In order to make a complete tour for each ship, a dummy destination port is assumed for each ship; however, the distance to this dummy destination (from any origin port) is assumed to be zero.

The ships can sail at various speed levels that have impact on the voyage time and fuel consumption. The fuel consumption to sail a unit of distance at a specific speed level depends on whether the ship is sailing empty or with a cargo; since, in the former case, it depends on the ship's deadweight and its speed level, while in the latter it also depends on the cargo weight. The MILP model for the tramp SRP developed by Wen *et al.* [WEN 16] is reproduced below with minor modifications in equations [3.1] to [3.11], together with the notation used.

Sets, indices and parameters:	
$\mathcal{R}$	set of cargoes;
$\mathcal{N}$	set of ships;
$\mathcal{V}$	set of speed levels;
p, q	cargo indices, $p, q \in \mathcal{R}$;
i	ship index, $i \in \mathcal{N}$;
v	speed level index, $v \in \mathcal{V}$;
o_i	origin of ship $i \in \mathcal{N}$ at the beginning of planning horizon;
d_i	destination (dummy) of ship $i \in \mathcal{N}$ at the end of planning horizon;
l_{pq}	distance between the destination of cargo $p \in \mathcal{R}$ and origin of cargo $q \in \mathcal{R}$;
w_p	beginning of the time window for loading cargo $p \in \mathcal{R}$;
w_p'	ending of the time window for loading cargo $p \in \mathcal{R}$;
h_p	total loading and unloading time of cargo $p \in \mathcal{R}$ at its origin and destination, respectively;
d_p	distance between origin and destination of cargo $p \in \mathcal{R}$;
c_{pi}^v	transportation cost per unit of distance of ship $i \in \mathcal{N}$ at speed $v \in \mathcal{V}$ with cargo $p \in \mathcal{R}$;
r_p	revenue for transporting cargo $p \in \mathcal{R}$;
f_i^v	fuel cost per unit of distance for empty ship $i \in \mathcal{N}$ at the speed level $v \in \mathcal{V}$;
z_{pi}	= 1 if cargo $p \in \mathcal{R}$ can be transported by ship $i \in \mathcal{N}$; and 0 otherwise;
s_v	time required to sail a unit of distance at speed $v \in \mathcal{V}$;
M	a sufficiently large positive number;

Decision Variables:	
X_{pqi}^v	$= 1$ if ship $i \in \mathcal{N}$ transports cargo $q \in \mathcal{R}$ immediately after transporting cargo $p \in \mathcal{R}$ at speed $v \in \mathcal{V}$; and 0 otherwise;
Y_{pi}^v	$= 1$ if ship $i \in \mathcal{N}$ transports cargo $p \in \mathcal{R}$ at speed $v \in \mathcal{V}$; and 0 otherwise;
T_{pi}	Starting time of loading cargo $p \in \mathcal{R}$ onto ship $i \in \mathcal{N}$.

$$Max\ Z = \sum_{p \in \mathcal{R}} \sum_{i \in \mathcal{N}} \sum_{v \in \mathcal{V}} r_p Y_{pi}^v - \sum_{p \in \mathcal{R}} \sum_{i \in \mathcal{N}} \sum_{v \in \mathcal{V}} c_{pi}^v d_p Y_{pi}^v - \sum_{p,q \in \mathcal{R}} \sum_{i \in \mathcal{N}} \sum_{v \in \mathcal{V}} f_i^v l_{pq} X_{pqi}^v, \quad [3.1]$$

Subject to

$$\sum_{q \in \mathcal{R}} \sum_{i \in \mathcal{N}} \sum_{v \in \mathcal{V}} X_{pqi}^v \leq 1 \qquad \forall p \in \mathcal{R}, \qquad [3.2]$$

$$\sum_{p \in \mathcal{R}} \sum_{v \in \mathcal{V}} X_{o_i p i}^v = 1 \qquad \forall i \in \mathcal{N}, \qquad [3.3]$$

$$\sum_{p \in \mathcal{R}} \sum_{v \in \mathcal{V}} X_{p d_i i}^v = 1 \qquad \forall i \in \mathcal{N}, \qquad [3.4]$$

$$\sum_{q \in \mathcal{R}} \sum_{v \in \mathcal{V}} X_{pqi}^v - \sum_{q \in \mathcal{R}} \sum_{v \in \mathcal{V}} X_{qpi}^v = 0 \qquad \forall p \in \mathcal{R}, \forall v \in \mathcal{V}, \qquad [3.5]$$

$$\sum_{q \in \mathcal{R}} \sum_{v \in \mathcal{V}} X_{pqi}^v - \sum_{v \in \mathcal{V}} Y_{pi}^v = 0 \qquad \forall p \in \mathcal{R}, \forall i \in \mathcal{N}, \qquad [3.6]$$

$$\sum_{v \in \mathcal{V}} Y_{pi}^v \leq z_{pi} \qquad \forall p \in \mathcal{R}, \forall i \in \mathcal{N}, \qquad [3.7]$$

$$w_p \leq T_{pi} \leq w_p' \qquad \forall p \in \mathcal{R}, \forall i \in \mathcal{N}, \qquad [3.8]$$

$$T_{pi} + h_p + \sum_{v \in \mathcal{V}} d_p s_v Y_{pi}^v + \sum_{v \in \mathcal{V}} l_{pq} s_v X_{pqi}^v - T_{qi} \leq M \left(1 - \sum_{v \in \mathcal{V}} X_{pqi}^v \right)$$

$$\forall p, q \in \mathcal{R}, \forall i \in \mathcal{N}, \qquad [3.9]$$

$$X_{pqi}^v, Y_{pi}^v \in \{0,1\} \qquad \forall p, q \in \mathcal{R}, \forall i \in \mathcal{N}, \forall v \in \mathcal{V}, \qquad [3.10]$$

$$T_{pi} \in \mathbb{R}^+ \qquad \forall p \in \mathcal{R}, \forall i \in \mathcal{N}. \qquad [3.11]$$

The objective function of the tramp SRP [3.1] maximizes the total profit, which is given by the total revenue of the company minus the transportation and fuel costs incurred with empty sailing. Constraints [3.2] guarantee that each cargo is transported by, at most, one ship. The ships must depart from their origin port (constraints [3.3]) and return to their (dummy) destination port after concluding all their transportation assignments (constraints [3.4]). Constraints [3.5] are the usual balance equations and they ensure that if a ship leaves a port with a cargo, then it has entered the port to pick up the cargo. Constraints [3.6] ensure the relationship between variables Y_{pi}^v and variables X_{pqi}^v. Cargoes can only be transported by compatible ships, which is stated by constraints [3.7]. On the one hand, the starting time to load cargoes onto ships has to be within the cargoes' time window, as imposed by constraints [3.8]. On the other hand, it can only occur after the ship's arrival at the port to perform the transportation assignment, as ensured by constraints [3.9]. Note that a ship arrives at a port to pick up a cargo after concluding the immediately previous cargo transportation assignment and sailing from the immediately previous cargo destination port; the time at which the ship can depart from the immediately previous cargo destination port is given by the summation of the loading and unloading time and the traveling time between its origin and its destination to the loading starting time. Finally, constraints [3.10] and [3.11] define the decision variables' nature.

3.1.2. *A simple GA for the tramp SRP*

A simple yet efficient GA for the tramp SRP has been proposed by Lin and Liu [LIN 11], in which the ship allocation, freight assignment and ship routing problems are considered, simultaneously. The tramp ship company may accept full-shipload or less-than-full-shipload cargoes (i.e. different cargoes can be shipped on the same ship). Customers usually ask for direct shipping (i.e. the cargoes are not transferred to other ships along the route), and non-split cargoes (i.e. the cargo of a single customer is not divided between various ships). Note that, the problem version considered by Lin and Liu [LIN 11] differs from that of Wen *et al.* [WEN 16] since the latter did not consider less-than-shipload cargoes. The GA is used to produce solutions that aim at maximizing total profit of the tramp shipping company in a given planning horizon.

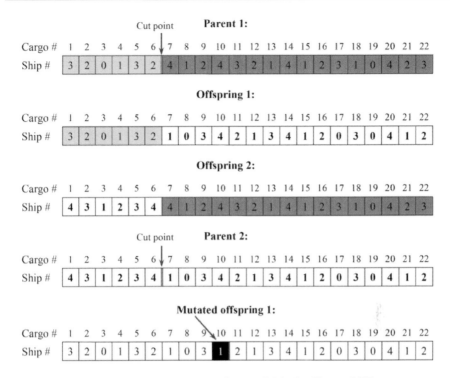

Figure 3.1. *A chromosome for the GA in the Tramp SRP*

The GA for the tramp SRP follows the basic GA procedure described in section 2.4. A chromosome represents a solution to the tramp SRP and it is defined as a string with as many elements as the number of cargo requests. Each element of the chromosome is filled with a random integer number between 0 and N (the number of available ships). Numbers from 1 to N indicate the ship assigned to transport a cargo, while the 0 means that the cargo is not transported. Note that tramp shipping companies may reject a request for transportation, e.g. if it is not a profitable one. A possible chromosome for a problem instance involving 22 cargoes and 4 ships is depicted in Figure 3.1. Looking at the first chromosome, we can see that cargo 1 is transported by ship 3, cargo 2 is transported by ship 2, cargo 3 is not transported, and so on. Although the chromosome provides the ship allocation, to construct a solution we also need to determine the ship's routing, that is the sequence in which the ship visits the ports. This is done using a constructive heuristic based on cargoes' pick-up and delivery dates. Consider that two cargoes are assigned to a ship and that the first cargo needs to be picked up on Day 1 from port p to be delivered to port q by Day 6, while the second cargo needs to be picked up on Day 3 from port p' and be delivered to port q' by Day 5; thus, a possible ship route would be $p \rightarrow p' \rightarrow q' \rightarrow q$. The heuristic routing attempts to find a route with the maximum profit for the tramp shipping companies (or with the minimum costs). However, the heuristic may construct an infeasible route, e.g. due to a violation of the ship capacity or of some pick-up/delivery time windows. In such cases, a penalty is added to the objective function value of the chromosome to reduce its future reproduction probability.

To construct the offspring chromosomes in the next generations, a single-point crossover operator is applied. Given a pair of parents, a random cut-point is selected, and two offspring are obtained: one by joining the right part of the first parent to the left part of the second parent and another by joining the left part of the first parent to the right part of the second parent. Refer to Figure 3.1 for an example. The mutation operator changes a randomly chosen gene by assigning to it a random integer value generated in the set 0 to N. This is also exemplified in Figure 3.1. The algorithm is run for a predetermined number of iterations.

The GA for the tramp SRP was computationally evaluated by finding solutions for six problem instances, each consisting of seven identical ships and 32 cargoes. The authors obtained an optimal solution for four instances by resorting to a commercial software (CPLEX) to solve the MILP model; however, for two of the instances, the MILP model was not solved within 30 hours. The GA was able to find an optimal solution for three of the four instances (that were optimized by CPLEX), and a solution close to optimal (within 2.47% of optimality) for the other instance; all with a reasonable computational time (always less than 254 seconds).

3.1.3. *An ACO for the liner SRP*

Liner shipping companies construct several routes with timetables (see Table 3.1 for an example), and it is common to have weekly departures at the ports of a route. Thus, they need to assign several ships to each route to respond to the weekly requests. In recent years, several studies considered the SRP in liner shipping networks; examples include, but are not limited to, [TSO 13, BRO 14, LIN 14a, BRA 15, DUL 17]. For a general classification of the studies published prior to 2012 regarding the liner ship routing problem, refer to the recent review by Meng *et al.* [MEN 14]. An ACO algorithm has been developed by Tsou and Cheng [TSO 13], in which the distance and speed of the ships are calculated using real data, obtained from the geographic information system (GIS). The ACO algorithm looks for the best routes for the ships in the fleet by considering a predetermined number of iterations. The proposed ACO will be described later in this section in more detail. Lin and Tsai [LIN 14a] developed an MILP model for the liner shipping routes with daily frequency operations. The number of ships in each route and the visiting ports in the routes are decided within the MILP model. This daily frequency liner shipping is in service for the customers at the major ports along both edges of the Pacific Ocean. A Lagrangian relaxation and a local search are proposed to efficiently find solutions; their computational times are, on average, 60% less than that of the MILP model. Brouer *et al.* [BRO 14] developed a metaheuristic algorithm for the liner SRP, which combines four main steps, namely construction, improvement, reinsertion and perturbation. Branchini *et al.* [BRA 15] developed an MILP model for the integrated liner SRP and fleet assignment problem, in which the liner shipping company benefits from the possibility of taking optional cargoes in addition to the contractual ones. The authors show the model to be suitable to address the tramp SRP, as well, by setting a single contractual or optional cargo to be loaded at each port and unloaded at another port. In a recent study, Dulebenets [DUL 17] extended the liner SRP to include the scheduling of perishable asset transportation. The perishable assets are transported in refrigerated containers, which allow maintaining a specific temperature; obviously incurring a higher transportation cost (i.e. refrigerated containers need an external power supply to stabilize the temperature). The problem has been formulated as a nonlinear mathematical model, in which the total route service cost and wasted assets are minimized.

An ACO algorithm for the liner SRP was developed by Tsou and Cheng [TSO 13], in which a ship is assumed as an artificial ant who selects its next destination (i.e. a port) according to the port probability. The port probability is updated progressively based on the navigation times. The shipping routes are evaluated according to their total navigation time, rather than simple total navigation distance, i.e. the shortest route between two ports is not necessarily the best one. Shorter navigation times result in smaller fuel consumption. The navigation time between any two ports p and q (T_{pq}) is estimated based on the geographical distance between the two ports and the average expected speed of the ship, which is estimated based on the weather/sea conditions and ocean currents (the necessary data are obtained from the GIS).

The ACO algorithm for the ship routing problem is reported in Algorithm 3.1; and it considers a set of K ants, each searching for an optimal shipping route. The algorithm is run for g^{max} iterations. Once an ant finishes a route, it can update the information of the route based on the route navigation time. The information en route between ports p and q at iteration g is denoted by τ_{pq}^{g} and is calculated through equation [3.12], where ρ is the residual information rate and Δ_{pq}^{k} is the information collected by the ant from traveling from port p to port q. The residual information rate is a constant between 0 and 1, and it represents the proportion of information kept from the previous iteration; or alternatively, $(1 - \rho)$ is the evaporation rate, i.e. information lost. The information collected by the ant between two ports, say p and q, is inversely proportional to the navigation time between the ports, if the ant travels between them or 0 otherwise, as given by equation [3.13], where moderating parameter Q is constant. The probability $P_{pq}^{g}(k)$ that ant k in port p selects port q to travel to next at iteration g is as given in equation [3.14], in which N_{p}^{k} is the set of ports not yet visited by the ant k and η_{pq} is heuristic information on the connection between ports p and q; in our case, the inverse of the time distance between them $\eta_{pq} = \frac{1}{T_{pq}}$.

$$\tau_{pq}^{g} = \rho . \tau_{pq}^{g-1} + \sum_{k \in K} \Delta_{pq}^{k} \qquad [3.12]$$

$$\Delta_{pq}^{k} = \begin{cases} \dfrac{Q}{T_{pq}}, & \text{If ant } k \text{ passes through } p \text{ to } q, \\ 0, & \text{else.} \end{cases} \qquad [3.13]$$

$$P_{pq}^{g}(k) = \begin{cases} \dfrac{\tau_{pq}^{g} . \eta_{pq}}{\sum_{q \in N_{p}^{k}} (\tau_{pq}^{g} . \eta_{pq})}, & \forall q \in N_{p}^{k} \\ 0, & \text{else} \end{cases} \qquad [3.14]$$

Initialize the control parameters,

Calculate the navigation time matrix,

For $g = 1: g^{max}$

    Set the initial port for all the ants,

    While there is an unvisited port in the list

        For $k = 1: K$

            Update the list of ports which can be visited by k^{th} ship (ant), at its current port,

            For $q \in N_p^k$

                Update the information for port q (τ_{pq}^g),

                Update the probability for visiting port q $(P_{pq}^g(k))$,

            End For % q

            Select the next visiting port for k^{th} ant,

            Update the current port for k^{th} ant,

        End For % k

    End While

End For % g

Return the best-known solution.

Algorithm 3.1. *The ACO algorithm for the liner shipping route design*

Computational experiments were conducted through the simulation of problem instances resorting to real data from a shipping route between Yokohama and San Francisco. The results have shown that a smaller number of ants (10 to 20 ants) lead to poor convergence and low-quality final solutions compared to a larger number of ants (200 ants or more).

3.2. Green maritime transportations

As said before, worldwide trade has had a tremendous growth, which in turn led to an increase in demand for maritime transportation. However, the benefits of this growth are unevenly distributed. In addition, environmental concerns have risen. Thus, it is needed to ensure sustainable maritime transport policies. Sustainable transportation means "meeting present transport needs without compromising the ability of future generations to meet their transport needs" [GIL 02]. Many researchers believe that maritime cargo transportation is the most fuel-efficient mode of transportation, e.g. in Shi *et al.* and in Wang *et al.* [SHI 08, WAN 16]. However, due to the high volume of maritime transportation, it is estimated that 3–5% of the world's anthropogenic CO_2 emissions come from global maritime transportation [TSO 13, KON 14]. Therefore, high public pressure is on the maritime transportation industry to reduce the greenhouse emissions. Pollution reduction by the maritime transportation has been emphasized in the 14th Goal of *United Nations 2030 Agenda for Sustainable Development*, to "conserve and sustainably use the oceans, seas and marine resources for sustainable development" [UNI 18]. Together with carbon dioxide (CO_2), other toxic substances in ship fuel are nitrogen oxide (NO_x) and sulfur oxide (SO_x). These are the most prevalent of greenhouse gases that are responsible for climate change [KON 11]. Shi *et al.* [SHI 08] believed that maritime transportation is efficient regarding CO_2 emissions; however, regarding SO_2 emissions, land-based vehicles have the advantage over cargo ships.

Four emission control areas (ECAs) have been defined in the MARPOL Convention (*the international convention for the prevention of pollution from ships*) by the International Maritime Organization (IMO) [IMO 18]. These areas are subject to stricter controls and include the Baltic Sea, the North Sea, and the English Channel (for SO_x control) and the North American and the US Caribbean coasts (for SO_x and NO_x control). Possible extensions in the near future will likely consider the Mediterranean Sea and the Norwegian, the Mexican, the Japanese and the Singaporean coasts. Since January 1, 2015, the ships are restricted to use a limit of 0.1% sulfur content in their fuel for voyages inside the ECAs. The EU region is already planning tighter restrictions. The IMO current agreements include a SO_x reduction to less than 0.5% by 2020 in the global maritime transportation industries [FAG 15].

Companies may reduce pollution emissions by using low-sulfur fuels (e.g. marine gas oil); however, such fuels are considerably more expensive than normal bunker fuel (heavy fuel oil). In addition, fuel costs can account for over 75% of the operational costs of larger ships, since they might consume up to 100,000 USD of bunker fuel per day, as estimated by Ronen [RON 11]. On the other hand, since there is a direct relation between the speed of the ship and its fuel consumption, a ship's speed may be lowered in order to save on fuel costs. Fuel consumption per unit of time can be estimated by a cubic function of the ship speed, within the practical speed range, see e.g. Ronen [RON 82]. Thus, "slow steaming", i.e. sailing at a lower speed, leads to a big reduction in fuel consumption, as well as in pollutant emissions, e.g. reducing the cruising speed by 20% leads to a reduction in bunker consumption by 50% [RON 11]. However, reducing the speed probably results in the need of additional ships in order to be able to maintain service frequency and service capacity. Therefore, in addition to observing emission control laws, shipping companies need to achieve a trade-off between the fuel costs and the service level, or the number of required ships. In practice, typically, a common speed is assumed for the ships in service to design the network; however, the speed is optimized en route to ensure service time windows compliance (i.e. speed up to catch a near due time or speed down to arrive later at a seaport or to save on fuel costs) [AND 15].

Some examples of studies on green ship routing problems (where speed optimization, inventory control and fleet deployment are considered as well) include, although are not limited to [AND 15, AGR 15, DE 16, DE 17, AYD 17]. Recent reviews on concepts and models for the ship routing-speed optimization problem can be found in Psaraftis and Kontovas [PSA 14] and on sustainability in maritime transportation in Mansouri et al. [MAN 15].

Andersson et al. [AND 15] developed a mathematical formulation and a rolling horizon heuristic algorithm for the ship routing and speed optimization problem. The solution approach was implemented in a RoRo shipping liner company. Agra et al. [AGR 15] developed a two-stage stochastic programming model for a ship routing and scheduling associated with the inventory management of oil products. In the first stage, the routing and loading and/or unloading decisions are made, and decisions on the scheduling and inventory levels are made in the second stage. In a recent study, Aydin et al. [AYD 17] considered the speed optimization and bunkering problem in liner shipping. They developed a dynamic programming model to determine the bunkering port, the bunkering quantity and the ship speed at each leg along the service route. De et al. [DE 16] developed a nonlinear mathematical formulation for the ship routing and scheduling problem with an emphasis on speed optimization and carbon emission control. They also proposed three metaheuristics (PSO, GA, PSO with composite particles) to solve the problem. The mathematical model and the PSO algorithm are further discussed in sections 3.2.1 and 3.2.2.

Later, in De *et al.* [DE 17], the authors added an inventory control policy to the problem.

3.2.1. *Mathematical formulation of GSRP*

The green ship routing and scheduling problem (GSRP) consists of designing the routes and schedules for a fleet of ships considering several ports such that the demand for loading and unloading operations is met. The problem can be translated as a multi-vehicle pick-up and delivery problem (m-PDPTW), which is known to be an NP-Hard problem [DE 16]. In this problem, ports supply some products types and have demand for some others. The mathematical model integrates decision-making for fleet deployment and speed optimization, while observing carbon emission allowances during the voyages and the docking, maneuvering of different types of engine fuel which are considered in this problem, "heavy fuel oil" – which is used during the voyages – and "marine gas oil" – which is used during the docking time at ports. The average fuel price for the former is 463.50 USD/ton, while for the latter it is 586 USD/ton. Moreover, the carbon emission can be estimated as a weighted (i.e. 3.021) cubic function of the ship speed, while it is sailing and as a weighted (i.e. 3.082) linear function of the docking maneuvering time and berthing or waiting time. The estimations for the fuel cost and carbon emissions are taken from Kontovas and Psaraftis [KON 11]. Obviously, the constant fuel prices and the emission coefficients can be updated from time to time according to the market conditions or fuel types.

The ships are initially berthed at a port, from where they might start a route to another port or end their route if there are no other loading and/or unloading operations that have been assigned to it. The travel time of each ship from one port to another depends on the distance between two ports and on the velocity of the ship. It is assumed that in a given time period, at the most one ship can be loaded and/or unloaded at a port. Each port has a specific time window for conducting the port operations within each period. Although the berthing time of a ship can be extended to more than one period, if the time window associated with a period is violated, then a penalty cost is incurred. The nonlinear programming model for the GSRP developed by De *et al.* [DE 16] is reproduced with minor modifications in equations [3.15]–[3.40], but before the notation used is described.

Sets, indices and parameters:	
$\mathcal{P}$	set of ports;
$\mathcal{N}$	set of ships;
$\mathcal{T}$	set of planning time periods;
$\mathcal{R}$	set of product types;
p, q	indices for the ports, $p, q \in \mathcal{P}$;
i	index for ships, $i \in \mathcal{N}$;
t, k	indices for the time periods, $t, k \in \mathcal{T}$;
r	index for product type, $r \in \mathcal{R}$;
p_i^*	origin port of ship $i \in \mathcal{N}$;
l_{pq}	distance between ports $p \in \mathcal{P}$ and $q \in \mathcal{P}$;
w_{pt}	beginning of time window for port $p \in \mathcal{P}$ in period $t \in \mathcal{T}$;
w'_{pt}	ending of time window for port $p \in \mathcal{P}$ in period $t \in \mathcal{T}$;
h_{pr}	handling time for a single unit of product $r \in \mathcal{R}$ in port $p \in \mathcal{P}$;
d_{ptr}	demand for product $r \in \mathcal{R}$ at port $p \in \mathcal{P}$ in period $t \in \mathcal{T}$;
c_{pqi}	transportation costs for a voyage between ports $p \in \mathcal{P}$ and $q \in \mathcal{P}$ for ship $i \in \mathcal{N}$;
c'_{pt}	delay penalty costs per hour for port $p \in \mathcal{P}$ in period $t \in \mathcal{T}$;
c''_{pr}	fixed setup cost for operations of product $r \in \mathcal{R}$ in port $p \in \mathcal{P}$;
s_{pr}	setup time for operations of product $r \in \mathcal{R}$ in port $p \in \mathcal{P}$;
y_{pr}	storage capacity for product $r \in \mathcal{R}$ at port $p \in \mathcal{P}$;
y'_i	storage capacity for ship $i \in \mathcal{N}$;
j_{pr}	$= \begin{cases} 1, \text{if port } p \in \mathcal{P} \text{ is a supplier of product } r \in \mathcal{R}, \\ -1, \text{if port } p \in \mathcal{P} \text{ has demand for product } r \in \mathcal{R}, \\ 0, \text{if port } p \in \mathcal{P} \text{ has no demand/suply for product } r \in \mathcal{R}, \end{cases}$
f_{pi}	fuel consumption per hour for ship $i \in \mathcal{N}$, while maneuvering at port $p \in \mathcal{P}$;
a_i	maximum allowed fuel consumption for ship $i \in \mathcal{N}$;
b_i	maximum allowed fuel costs for ship $i \in \mathcal{N}$;
co_i	maximum allowed carbon emission for ship $i \in \mathcal{N}$;
e	a constant.

Decision variables:	
X_{itk}^{pq}	= 1 if ship $i \in \mathcal{N}$ begins its operation at port $p \in \mathcal{P}$ in period $t \in \mathcal{T}$, and travel to port $q \in \mathcal{P}$ to start its operations there in period $k \in \mathcal{T}$; 0 otherwise;
Y_{itr}^{p}	= 1 if product $r \in \mathcal{R}$ is (un)loaded (from) to ship $i \in \mathcal{N}$ in period $t \in \mathcal{T}$ at port $p \in \mathcal{P}$; 0 otherwise;
Z_{it}^{p}	= 1 if ship $i \in \mathcal{N}$ ends its final voyage at port $p \in \mathcal{P}$ after an operation that started in period $t \in \mathcal{T}$; 0 otherwise;
T_{pt}	starting time of operations at port $p \in \mathcal{P}$ in period $t \in \mathcal{T}$;
T'_{pt}	ending time of operations at port $p \in \mathcal{P}$ in period $t \in \mathcal{T}$;
H_{pt}	total operating time outside the time window at port $p \in \mathcal{P}$ in period t;
V_{pqi}	velocity of ship $i \in \mathcal{N}$ in its voyage from port $p \in \mathcal{P}$ to port $q \in \mathcal{P}$;
S_{tr}^{p}	stock level of product $r \in \mathcal{R}$ at port $p \in \mathcal{P}$ at the end of period $t \in \mathcal{T}$;
Q_{itr}^{p}	quantity of product $r \in \mathcal{R}$ (un)loaded (from) to ship $i \in \mathcal{N}$ at port $p \in \mathcal{P}$ in period $t \in \mathcal{T}$;
I_{itr}^{p}	inventory level of product $r \in \mathcal{R}$ on ship $i \in \mathcal{N}$ after it departs port $p \in \mathcal{P}$ once it has accomplished its operations that started in period $t \in \mathcal{T}$.

$$Min\ Z = \sum_{p,q \in \mathcal{P}} \sum_{i \in \mathcal{N}} \sum_{t,k \in \mathcal{T}} c_{pqi} X_{itk}^{pq} + \sum_{p \in \mathcal{P}} \sum_{t \in \mathcal{T}} c'_{pt} H_{pt} + \sum_{p \in \mathcal{P}} \sum_{i \in \mathcal{N}} \sum_{t \in \mathcal{T}} \sum_{r \in \mathcal{R}} c''_{pr} Y_{itr}^{p}, \quad [3.15]$$

Subject to

$$\sum_{p \in \mathcal{P}} \sum_{i \in \mathcal{N}} \sum_{t \in \mathcal{T}} X_{itk}^{pq} \le 1 \qquad \forall q \in \mathcal{P}, \forall k \in \mathcal{T}, \qquad [3.16]$$

$$Z_{i1}^{p_i^*} + \sum_{q \in \mathcal{P}} \sum_{k \in \mathcal{T}} X_{i1k}^{p_i^* q} = 1 \qquad \forall i \in \mathcal{N}, \qquad [3.17]$$

$$\sum_{p \in \mathcal{P}} \sum_{t \in \mathcal{T}} X_{itk}^{pq} - \sum_{p \in \mathcal{P}} \sum_{t \in \mathcal{T}} X_{ikt}^{qp} - Z_{ik}^{q} = 0 \qquad \forall q \in \mathcal{P}, \forall k \in \mathcal{T}\backslash\{1\}, \forall i \in \mathcal{N}, \quad [3.18]$$

$$\sum_{p \in \mathcal{P}} \sum_{t \in \mathcal{T}} Z_{it}^{p} = 1 \qquad \forall i \in \mathcal{N}, \qquad [3.19]$$

$$w_{pt} \le T_{pt} \le w'_{pt} \qquad \forall t \in \mathcal{T}, \qquad [3.20]$$

$$\left(T_{qk} - T'_{pt} - \frac{l_{pq}}{V_{pqi}}\right) X_{itk}^{pq} \ge 0 \qquad \forall p,q \in \mathcal{P}, \forall t,k \in \mathcal{T}, \forall i \in \mathcal{N}, \quad [3.21]$$

$$T'_{pt} - T_{pt} - \sum_{i \in \mathcal{N}} \sum_{r \in \mathcal{R}} \left(s_{pr} Y^p_{itr}\right) - \sum_{i \in \mathcal{N}} \sum_{r \in \mathcal{R}} \left(h_{pr} Q^p_{itr}\right) = 0$$

$$\forall p \in \mathcal{P}, \forall t \in \mathcal{T}, \quad [3.22]$$

$$H_{pt} - T'_{pt} + w'_{pt} \geq 0 \qquad \forall p \in \mathcal{P}, \forall t \in \mathcal{T}, \quad [3.23]$$

$$T_{pt} - T'_{p(t-1)} \geq 0 \qquad \forall p \in \mathcal{P}, \forall t \in \mathcal{T} \setminus \{1\}, \quad [3.24]$$

$$y'_i Y^p_{itr} - Q^p_{itr} \geq 0 \qquad \begin{array}{l} \forall p \in \mathcal{P}, \forall t \in \mathcal{T}, \forall i \in \mathcal{N}, \\ \forall r \in \mathcal{R}, \end{array} \quad [3.25]$$

$$X^{pq}_{itk} \left(I^p_{itr} + j_{qr} Q^q_{ikr} - I^q_{ikr}\right) = 0 \quad \forall p, q \in \mathcal{P}, \forall t, k \in \mathcal{T}, \forall i \in \mathcal{N}, \quad [3.26]$$

$$y'_i \sum_{q \in \mathcal{P}} \sum_{k \in \mathcal{T}} X^{pq}_{itk} - \sum_{r \in \mathcal{R}} I^p_{itr} \geq 0 \qquad \forall p \in \mathcal{P}, \forall t \in \mathcal{T}, \forall i \in \mathcal{N}, \quad [3.27]$$

$$S^p_{(t-1)r} + \sum_{i \in \mathcal{N}} Q^p_{itr} - d_{ptr} - S^p_{tr} = 0 \qquad \forall p \in \mathcal{P}, \forall t \in \mathcal{T}, \forall r \in \mathcal{R}, \quad [3.28]$$

$$S^p_{tr} - y_{pr} \leq 0 \qquad \forall p \in \mathcal{P}, \forall t \in \mathcal{T}, \forall r \in \mathcal{R}, \quad [3.29]$$

$$Y^q_{ikr} - \sum_{p \in \mathcal{P}} \sum_{t \in \mathcal{T}} X^{pq}_{itk} \leq 0 \qquad \begin{array}{l} \forall q \in \mathcal{P}, \forall k \in \mathcal{T} \setminus \{1\}, \\ \forall i \in \mathcal{N}, \forall r \in \mathcal{R}, \end{array} \quad [3.30]$$

$$e \sum_{p,q \in \mathcal{P}} \left(l_{pq} V^3_{pqi}\right) + \sum_{p \in \mathcal{P}} \sum_{t \in \mathcal{T}} \left((T'_{pt} - T_{pt}) f_{pi}\right) \leq a_i$$

$$\forall q \in \mathcal{P} | q \neq p, \forall i \in \mathcal{N}, \quad [3.31]$$

$$463.5\, e \sum_{p,q \in \mathcal{P}} \left(l_{pq} V^3_{pqi}\right) + 586 \sum_{p \in \mathcal{P}} \sum_{t \in \mathcal{T}} \left((T'_{pt} - T_{pt}) f_{pi}\right) \leq b_i$$

$$\forall q \in \mathcal{P} | q \neq p, \forall i \in \mathcal{N}, \quad [3.32]$$

$$3.021 e \sum_{p,q \in \mathcal{P}} \left(l_{pq} V^3_{pqi}\right) + 3.082 \sum_{p \in \mathcal{P}} \sum_{t \in \mathcal{T}} \left((T'_{pt} - T_{pt}) f_{pi}\right) \leq co_i$$

$$\forall q \in \mathcal{P} | q \neq p, \forall i \in \mathcal{N}, \quad [3.33]$$

$$X^{pq}_{itk} \in \{0,1\} \qquad \begin{array}{l} \forall p, q \in \mathcal{P} | q \neq p, \forall t, k \in \\ \mathcal{T} | t < k, \forall i \in \mathcal{N}, \end{array} \quad [3.34]$$

$$Z_{it}^p \in \{0,1\} \qquad\qquad \forall p \in \mathcal{P}, \forall t \in \mathcal{T}, \forall i \in \mathcal{N}, \qquad [3.35]$$

$$Y_{itr}^p \in \{0,1\} \qquad\qquad \begin{aligned}&\forall p \in \mathcal{P}, \forall t \in \mathcal{T}, \forall i \in \\ &\mathcal{N}, \forall r \in \mathcal{R},\end{aligned} \qquad [3.36]$$

$$V_{pqi} \in \mathbb{R}^+ \qquad\qquad \forall p, q \in \mathcal{P} | q \neq p, \forall i \in \mathcal{N}, \qquad [3.37]$$

$$S_{tr}^p \in \mathbb{R}^+ \qquad\qquad \forall p \in \mathcal{P}, \forall t \in \mathcal{T}, \forall r \in \mathcal{R}, \qquad [3.38]$$

$$I_{itr}^p, Q_{itr}^p \in \mathbb{R}^+ \qquad\qquad \begin{aligned}&\forall p \in \mathcal{P}, \forall t \in \mathcal{T}, \forall i \in \\ &\mathcal{N}, \forall r \in \mathcal{R},\end{aligned} \qquad [3.39]$$

$$T'_{pt}, T_{pt}, H_{pt} \in \mathbb{R}^+ \qquad\qquad \forall p \in \mathcal{P}, \forall t \in \mathcal{T}. \qquad [3.40]$$

The objective function is to minimize total transportation, penalty and setup costs as represented by expression [3.15]. Constraints [3.16] ensure that, in a given period k at port q, at most one ship can start its loading and/or unloading operations. Constraints [3.17] guarantee that ship i either travels from its initial port (p_i^*) to another one, or it ends the route there (port p_i^*), after its loading/unloading operations started in the first period at port p_i^*. Similarly, constraints [3.18] ensure that when a ship arrives at a port, it either moves on to another port or stays there, i.e. it is its final destination, regardless of the time period this occurs, except if it is the first one, which has been dealt with by equations [3.17]. Constraints [3.19] state that each ship must end its route in a port. The starting time of operations at a port in any time period must be within the port time window, as imposed by Constraints [3.20]. If ship i travels from port p to port q, the starting time of the operations at port q must occur after the ending time of the operations at port p plus the ship travelling time from port p to port q (which is the distance of the two ports divided by the velocity of the ship), stated in Constraints [3.21]. The operations ending time at the ports is calculated by Constrains [3.22] as the summation of the operations starting time of each port and the total time required for setup and handling all loading and/or unloading operations in that period. Constraints [3.23] determine the amount of operation time used at each port outside of the port time windows. A ship can start its operation at port p in period t once the port operations in the previous period have been finished, and this is ensured by Constraints [3.24]. Constraints [3.25] guarantee that the product (un)loaded (from) to each ship does not violate the capacity limit of the ship. Constraints [3.26] are balance equations and they ensure that every ship departs from a port with an inventory level given by the inventory level with which it arrived plus/minus the quantity loaded/unloaded at the current port, for every product type. In addition, as stated by Constraints [3.27], the total amount of all products in a ship during a voyage is at most its capacity. This constraint also prevents the departure of an empty ship. The demand for each product at each port and in each time period must be satisfied, as stated in Constraints [3.28]. Stock level of a product at a port must be less than the port capacity to store that product in each period, see Constraints [3.29]. Constraints [3.30] ensure that ships are only operated at ports in their respective route.

Constraints [3.31] assure that total fuel consumption by a ship in its voyages (estimated as $e \sum_{p,q \in \mathcal{P}} (l_{pq} V_{pqi}^3)$) together with the consumption while docked at the ports in its route (estimated as $\sum_{p \in \mathcal{P}} \sum_{t \in \mathcal{T}} ((T'_{pt} - T_{pt}) f_{pi})$) is not more than the maximum allowed fuel consumption. For a ship with no voyages in the planning horizon (i.e. $\sum_{p,q \in \mathcal{P}} \sum_{t,k \in \mathcal{T}} X_{itk}^{pq} = 0$), the constraint is replaced by $\sum_{p \in \mathcal{P}} \sum_{t \in \mathcal{T}} ((T'_{pt} - T_{pt}) f_{pi}) \leq a_i$. Similarly, the total fuel cost for a ship must be no more than the maximum allowed budget for the fuel costs, as stated by Constraints [3.32]. As was the case for the fuel consumption, if a ship has no voyages in the planning horizon, then the Constraint is replaced by $586 \sum_{p \in \mathcal{P}} \sum_{t \in \mathcal{T}} ((T'_{pt} - T_{pt}) f_{pi}) \leq b_i$. Constraints [3.33] set an upper limit for the carbon emissions by each ship. The carbon emission is estimated as $3.021e \sum_{p,q \in \mathcal{P}} (l_{pq} V_{pqi}^3)$ during the voyages and as $3.082 \sum_{p \in \mathcal{P}} \sum_{t \in \mathcal{T}} ((T'_{pt} - T_{pt}) f_{pi})$ during the dock maneuvering time. Again, for a ship with no voyages during the planning horizon, the Constraint for carbon emissions is replaced by $3.082 \sum_{p \in \mathcal{P}} \sum_{t \in \mathcal{T}} ((T'_{pt} - T_{pt}) f_{pi}) \leq co_i$. Finally, Constraints [3.34] to [3.40] determine the decision variables' nature.

3.2.2. A PSO for the GSRP

De *et al.* [DE 16] propose a PSO algorithm, which follows the general procedure described in section 2.5, to address the GSRP. A solution is encoded as a string (particle) with as many elements as the number of variables (denoted as n) defined for the mathematical formulation they developed for the GSRP and reproduced in the previous section. Particle i in the swarm ($i = \{1, ..., S^{max}\}$) is denoted by $X_i = [x_{i1}, x_{i2}, ..., x_{ij}, ..., x_{in}]$

and each of its elements is a number in the interval $[0, 1]$, initially uniformly distributed random numbers. Then, and in order to construct a solution, the uniform random numbers are converted into the defined range for each variable. For the binary variables (i.e. X_{itk}^{pq}, Y_{itr}^{p}, and Z_{it}^{p}), random numbers greater than or equal to 0.5 become 1 and 0, otherwise; and for real variables (i.e. T_{pt}, T_{pt}', H_{pt}, V_{pqi}, S_{tr}^{p}, Q_{itr}^{p}, and I_{itr}^{p}), the random numbers are decoded in the predefined range of the variables as follows $Min + (Max - Min)x_{ij}$, where Min and Max are, respectively, the lower and upper bound values of the variable, and x_{ij} is the particle element associated with the variable. The solution obtained from decoding a particle is then evaluated through the objective function of the mathematical formulation (expression [3.15]). If the decoding of a particle results in an infeasible solution, then although the solution is still considered, a penalty is added to the objective function value. This way allows for the possibility of moving to other regions of the search space and therefore favors diversification.

Let us consider an example in which there are three ports with demand for two types of products in the next three periods and two ships to perform the transportation. A solution is then encoded by a particle with 213 elements; an example is provided in Figure 3.2. Note that some variables are set to zero as they do not represent "real possibilities". For instance, all X_{itk}^{pq} variables with $q = p$ or $t > k$ are set to 0; therefore, the number of particle elements associated with the X variables comes down to 36, for the aforementioned example.

X_{itk}^{pq}	Y_{itr}^{p}	Z_{it}^{p}	T_{pt}	T_{pt}'	H_{pt}	V_{pqi}	S_{tr}^{p}	Q_{itr}^{p}	I_{itr}^{p}
36	36	18	9	9	9	6	18	36	36
1... ...36	37... ...72	73... ...90	91... ...99	100. ..108	109. .117	118. .123	126. ..141	142. .177	178. .213

Figure 3.2. *Representation of the solution for GSRP in the PSO algorithm*

The authors consider a swarm with 100 particles and evolve it for g^{max} iterations. The velocity (v_{ij}^{g}) and position of each particle (x_{ij}^{g}) are updated using equations [3.41] and [3.42], respectively, where p_{ij} denotes the element j value of particle i best position, and p_{bj} represents element j value of the historically best particle of the neighborhood; r_1 and r_2 are two uniform random numbers between 0 and 1; and c_1 and c_2, the self-learning factor and social learning factor, respectively, take values 0.1, and 0.98, respectively [DE 16], and are used to decide whether particles prefer learning from personal best experience or best experience of the neighborhood. The inertia term $w \, v_{ij}^g$ is used to take into account the previous direction and the value of w, the inertia weight, takes 0.9 [DE 16]. Large inertia weight values allow the PSO to explore new areas of the solution space as the other terms of the equation take negligible values, while smaller inertia weight values favor exploitation of the solution space around high-quality solutions.

$$v_{ij}^{g+1} = w \, v_{ij}^g + c_1 \, r_1 \left(p_{ij} - x_{ij}^g \right) + c_2 \, r_2 \left(p_{bj} - x_{ij}^g \right) \qquad [3.41]$$

$$x_{ij}^{g+1} = x_{ij}^g + v_{ij}^{g+1} \qquad [3.42]$$

In order to enhance the performance of the PSO, a composite particle process (known as PSO-CP) has been added to the PSO [DE 16], in which the search algorithm is manipulated to improve the quality of the worst particle in composites of particles. As reported in Algorithm 3.2, after the main typical steps of the PSO algorithm, the swarm is copied directly into a new repository (termed $List$), sorted in ascending solution quality order. The $List$ is indexed so that we can match its particles with the corresponding particles in the swarm and clustered into N_c ($N_c = \left\lceil \frac{S^{max}-1}{3} \right\rceil$) composites, each of which with three particles and further, the N_p, ($N_p = S^{max} - 3N_c$) best particles are excluded from the CP process. For instance, if $S^{max} = 100$, there are 33 composites and one particle (the best one) is excluded from the CP process. The composite construction procedure gives higher priority to the weakest particles in the $List$ (denoted as $L^{\blacksquare}$) and selects from it the two particles with the smallest Euclidean distance to the weakest particle to construct a composite. Note that the $List$ is updated after each step in the CP process, by removing the $L^{\blacksquare}$ and the other members of the current composite from it.

Two operators are introduced in this PSO, namely scattering and velocity-anisotropic reflection (VAR). The scattering operator deals with low local diversity (i.e. when the Euclidean distance between the two weakest particles in a composite is below a threshold, $D\left(C_k^1, C_k^2 \right) \leq \theta$) by scattering the two worst particles in the direction of the best particle in the same composite (i.e. $C_k^1 = (1 + \varphi)C_k^3 - \varphi C_k^1$, $C_k^2 = (1 + \varphi)C_k^3 - \varphi C_k^2$, where φ is a uniform random vector); this way avoiding excessive local convergence. The VAR operator replaces the worst particle in each composite with a new particle randomly generated as a reflection point in the direction of the two better particles (to explore the promising search space.). In order to do so, first a mediator particle (denoted as $\tilde{C}$) is randomly generated on the straight line connecting the two best particles, $\tilde{C} = \varphi C_k^2 + (1 + \varphi)C_k^3$, where φ is a uniform random vector. Then, the worst particle is replaced with a new particle generated as a reflection of the mediator particle (i.e. $\tilde{C} + R\,\gamma\left(C_k^1 - \tilde{C}\right)$, where γ is a uniform random vector and R is the reflection step size that controls the degree that the worst particle moves away from the mediator particle. In the final step of the CP process, the swarm is updated by replacing the matching composite particles; then the algorithm moves on to the next iteration. This is repeated for g^{max} iterations.

Performance of the PSO and the PSO-CP algorithms was evaluated by De *et al.* [DE 16] in a set of six small-sized problem instances, each with three ports, three periods, two ships and two types of products. The PSO-CP shows better performance than that of PSO since, on average, the solutions found by the PSO-CP are 17% better than the ones found by the PSO, although the average CPU time requirements of the PSO-CP algorithm are 33% higher than those of the PSO algorithm, which is not a problem since the PSO-CP time requirements are always less than 390 seconds. In addition, the authors also solve these instances without considering the carbon emission constraints. In the latter case, the total cost goes up by 4% up to 10%.

3.3. Conclusions

In this chapter, we discussed the ship routing and scheduling problem in industrial, tramp and liner shipping networks. This is a complex combinatorial problem to which further complexities are being added, mainly due to environmental concerns. Given the relationships between air emissions and fuel consumption and also between fuel consumption and speed, all decisions are interrelated, and thus, the problem becomes even more complex.

Initialize the parameters for the PSO-CP, $(FV(P_i) = FV(P_b) = M$, M is a big positive number)

Generate initial *Swarm*,

For $g = 1: g^{max}$,

    For $i = 1: S^{max}$, %*The PSO algorithm*

        Calculate the *Fitness Value* (*FV*) for the particle i,

        If $FV(X_i^g) \leq FV(P_i)$, then $P_i = X_i^g$,

        If $FV(X_i^g) \leq FV(P_b)$, then $P_b = X_i^g$,

        Update velocity of elements of particle i ([3.41]),

        Update position of elements of particle i ([3.42]),

    End For % i

    $List = Swarm_g$

    For $k = 1: N_c$ %*Construction of the composite particles*

        Sort the *List* according to the objective value in descending mode,

        $C_k^1 = L_1$ (i.e. first particle in sorted *List*),

        Update the *List* by removing particle $L^\blacksquare$ from it,

        Sort the *List* according to the Eucleadian distance to C_k^1 in ascending mode,

        For $l = 1: 2$

            $C_k^{(l+1)} = L_1$ (i.e. first particle in sorted *List*),

            Update the *List* by removing particle L_1 from it,

        End For %l

        Sort k^{th} composite according to the objective value in descending mode,

        IF $D(C_k^1, C_k^2) \leq \theta$, % *Scattering operation*

            $C_k^1 = (1 + \varphi)C_k^3 - \varphi C_k^1$,

            $C_k^2 = (1 + \varphi)C_k^3 - \varphi C_k^2$,

            Sort k^{th} composite according to the objective value in

            descending mode,

        End IF

        % *VAR operation*

        $\tilde{C} = \varphi C_k^2 + (1 + \varphi)C_k^3$,

        $C_k^1 = \tilde{C} + R \gamma (C_k^1 - \tilde{C})$,

    End For % k

    Update the $Swarm_g$ by replacing the matching composite particles,

End For % g

Return the best-known solution.

Algorithm 3.2. *The PSO-CP algorithm for the GSRP*

As the main observation, given the nature and complexity of the problem, the number of proposed metaheuristic approaches is quite a bit smaller than expected. This is most likely due to the fact that the decisions are mainly seen as strategic decisions; therefore, the decisions are not made frequently and do not need to be found quickly, allowing for other types of approaches.

Another observation concerns the lack of benchmark problem instances to test and compare the proposed methods. This should include smaller and lab instances, as well as real-world case studies in order to measure real improvements with respect to the current operations.

Finally, methods developed for road transportation problems may prove to be useful for this problem as well. It should be noticed that research in vehicle routing problems is in a much more mature stage, specifically in what concerns green ship routing and scheduling problems; see the parallel body of research known as "pollution routing problem", "emissions VRP" and "Green VRP", among other designations.

4

Optimization of Seaside Operations

Once a ship arrives at a seaport, exporting cargoes are loaded into it and/or imported cargoes unloaded from it. Importing cargoes (e.g. dry bulks, liquid bulks or containers) are transferred to the storage yards, from where they are delivered to the final customer. In a reverse direction, the exporting cargoes are delivered by the customers to the storage yard, from where they are loaded onto a ship to be transported. The berthing area and time, and the cranes needed for loading and/or unloading are among the most critical resources in seaports, sometimes even being the bottleneck ones. Penalty costs due to the late berthing time of incoming ships are among the most expensive costs for port authorities. Thus, it is necessary to provide a reliable and timely berth allocation plan. This chapter is dedicated to the use of metaheuristic algorithms to optimize seaside operations. In section 4.1, the important problem of berth allocation is reviewed for container terminals whilst section 4.2 is dedicated to the berth allocation problem in bulk seaports. Section 4.3 is dedicated to the optimization of handling operations of quay cranes and the following section to the integrated scheduling and/or allocation problem for the berth area and the quay cranes. Concluding remarks are provided in section 4.5.

4.1. Berth allocation problem

Berth space is one of the most important resources in seaports, and its assignment to the incoming ships is commonly known as the berth allocation problem (BAP) on the berth scheduling problem. Berth allocation is the process of assigning and scheduling incoming ships to berthing positions of a seaport. Objectives for the BAP include minimizing total flow time, the ships' total tardiness and the containers' delivery distance. The outcomes of the BAP are ships' service time schedule and ships' position in the berth area of the seaport. The service time is the amount of time a ship is in the seaport from its arrival to its departure, including the time required by the unloading and loading operations, as well as any waiting time. BAP is, most likely, the maritime operations problem that deals with the most unreliable information, as the ships arrival time can be affected by weather conditions and mechanical issues. Furthermore, some contracts are for berth-on-arrival, which gives ship operators the right to quick and prompt berthing upon arrival. Therefore, normal functioning of a seaport can be disrupted, thus requiring quick on-line re-allocation algorithms.

Another complicating issue in the BAP is that not every ship can be located in any berth as ships have different sizes and depth requirements. The space requirements are related to ship size, particularly its length, while the depth requirements are determined by the vertical distance between the waterline and the ship keel [BIE 15]. Among all possible locations, we wish to choose, for each ship, one that optimizes a certain performance metric. Many different metrics have been used in the literature. Here, following the works by Cordeau et al. [COR 05] and Imai et al. [IMA 07], three measures are considered and minimized, namely unused berth time, unused berth space and ship service time. The longer the berthing horizon (as long as the accurate arrival time of ships is available), the better the berth allocation plan.

Several variations in the BAP have been considered in the literature regarding the type of berth layout (discrete, continuous, hybrid), as well as regarding ship arrival (static and dynamic). In discrete berthing, the berth area is divided into predefined berth segments of various sizes. Each ship is assigned to one berth segment and only one ship is allowed per berth segment at any given time. Thus, the whole berth segment is occupied by the ship during the time required by its loading and unloading operations. On the other hand, in continuous berthing, there are no segments and ships can dock at any empty berthing area. Thus, a better occupation ratio may be achieved at the expense, however, of more complex planning. Finally, hybrid berthing layouts consider predefined berth segments as in a discrete layout, allowing large ships to use more than one berth segment and small ships to share a berth segment, thus following a continuous berth strategy. Figure 4.1 provides a schematic view of the three layout configurations. The arrival time can be considered static or dynamic. In the former, ships are already at the port and whenever berths become available they are assigned to the ships. Alternatively, ships that are nearby can be ready to berth whenever berths become available by speeding up, although at a cost. Therefore, the arrival time is a soft constraint for the static BAP. In the dynamic case, ships' arrival times are known but subject to unexpected changes.

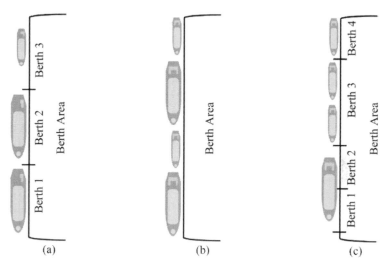

Figure 4.1. *Types of berth layout in seaports:*
a) discrete, b) continuous, c) hybrid

The continuous BAP can be seen and modeled as a two-dimensional packing problem or as a two-dimensional cutting problem, where one dimension is the time and the other is the ship size. On the other hand, the discrete BAP can be seen as an unrelated parallel machine-scheduling problem, where ships are jobs and berths are machines [BIE 15]. Both of these BAP versions have been addressed over the years and several models have been reported in the literature, differentiating themselves in the assumptions made, in the mathematical formulations given, and in solution approaches proposed. Nevertheless, and since these problems are NP-hard [GUA 05, LEE 09a, BUH 11] to solve realistic size instances in a reasonable computational time, heuristics and metaheuristics are required. According to

Bierwirth and Meisel [BIE 15], evolutionary algorithms are the most common types used, accounting for approximately 40 percent of such approaches. Examples of the GAs developed for the BAP include, but are not limited to [HU 15, LAL 14, GAN 10, IMA 07, NIS 01]. In sections 4.1.2, 4.1.3 and 4.1.4, the works by Imai *et al.* [IMA 07], Nishimura *et al.* [NIS 01], and Hu [HU 15] are, respectively, discussed in more detail. The remaining methods comprise other metaheuristics such as TS (e.g. [LAL 12, ZEN 11, COR 05]), SA (e.g. [LIN 17b, LIN 14b]), and PSO (e.g. [TIN 14]) among others and problem-specific heuristics such as local search and greedy rules (e.g. [XU 12, GUA 10]). For further details, the reader is referred to the comprehensive literature reviews of [BIE 15, BIE 10].

Given that the BAP is highly dependent on the availability of port equipment, many studies have been dedicated to the integrated planning and scheduling of berth and other port equipment allocation. Ignoring the interrelations between various scheduling and planning problems in seaside operations may lead to poor-quality solutions for the overall problem and even to each individual problem. Metaheuristic approaches for these problems are reviewed in section 4.4.

4.1.1. *Formulation of the BAP*

Here, a mixed integer linear programming (MILP) model for the discrete BAP with dynamic arrival times in container terminals is presented. The problem was originally translated and modeled as a heterogeneous vehicle routing problem with time windows (HVRPTW) by Cordeau *et al.* [COR 05]; and later, improved by Buhrkal *et al.* [BUH 11]. Buhrkal *et al.* [BUH 11] discussed modeling the BAP as a generalized set partitioning problem (GSPP) model, originally developed by Christensen and Holst [CHR 08]. From the computational tests performed on the instances by Cordeau *et al.* [COR 05], Buhrkal *et al.* [BUH 11] were able to conclude that the GSPP model was superior to all other models, followed by the HVRPTW model, to produce solutions in lower CPU time. However, the GSPP model is not good at handling precedence constraints that result from considering several ships, e.g. when the ship service time depends on the ship served immediately before. Thus, here we present the HVRPTW model developed by Cordeau *et al.* [COR 05] and later improved by Buhrkal *et al.* [BUH 11], with minor modifications. The notation used is introduced immediately before.

Sets, indices and parameters:	
$\mathcal{N}$	set of ships;
$\mathcal{B}$	set of berth segments;
$\{f\}, \{l\}$	first and last berth (dummy) tasks;
i, j	ship indices $i, j \in \mathcal{N}$;
b	berth segments index $b \in \mathcal{B}$;
α_i	relative importance of ship $i \in \mathcal{N}$ (objective function weight);
a_i	arrival time of ship $i \in \mathcal{N}$;
d_i	ship $i \in \mathcal{N}$ departure time;
s^b	time at which berth $b \in \mathcal{B}$ is available to start its service;
e^b	time at which berth $b \in \mathcal{B}$ should finish its service;
h_i^b	estimated handling time for ship $i \in \mathcal{N}$ in berth $b \in \mathcal{B}$;
m_{ij}^b	$= \max\{d_i + h_i^b - a_j, 0\}$; a constant for the possible sequence of ships $i, j \in \mathcal{N}$ at berth $b \in \mathcal{B}$.
Decision variables:	
X_{ij}^b	=1 if ship $j \in \mathcal{N}$ docks at berth $b \in \mathcal{B}$ immediately after ship $i \in \mathcal{N}$; 0 otherwise;
T_i^b	service starting time of ship $i \in \mathcal{N}$ at berth $b \in \mathcal{B}$.

$$Min\ Z = \sum_{i \in \mathcal{N}} \sum_{b \in \mathcal{B}} \alpha_i \left((T_i^b + h_i^b - a_i) \sum_{j \in \mathcal{N} \cup \{l\}} X_{ij}^b \right), \qquad [4.1]$$

Subject to

$$\sum_{b \in \mathcal{B}} \sum_{j \in \mathcal{N} \cup \{l\}} X_{ij}^b = 1 \qquad \forall i \in \mathcal{N} \cup \{f\}, \qquad [4.2]$$

$$\sum_{j \in \mathcal{N} \cup \{l\}} X_{fj}^b = 1 \qquad \forall b \in \mathcal{B}, \qquad [4.3]$$

$$\sum_{i \in \mathcal{N} \cup \{f\}} X_{il}^b = 1 \qquad \forall b \in \mathcal{B}, \qquad [4.4]$$

$$\sum_{j \in \mathcal{N} \cup \{l\}} X_{ij}^b = \sum_{j \in \mathcal{N} \cup \{f\}} X_{ji}^b \qquad \forall b \in \mathcal{B}, \forall i \in \mathcal{N}, \qquad [4.5]$$

$$T_i^b + h_i^b - T_j^b \leq (1 - X_{ij}^b) m_{ij}^b \quad \forall b \in \mathcal{B}, \forall i, j \in \mathcal{N}, \qquad [4.6]$$

$$a_i \leq T_i^b \qquad \forall b \in \mathcal{B}, \forall i \in \mathcal{N}, \qquad [4.7]$$

$$T_i^b + h_i^b \sum_{j \in \mathcal{N} \cup \{l\}} X_{ij}^b \leq d_i \qquad \forall b \in \mathcal{B}, \forall i \in \mathcal{N}, \qquad [4.8]$$

$$s^b \leq T_f^b \qquad \forall b \in \mathcal{B}, \qquad [4.9]$$

$$T_l^b \leq e^b \qquad \forall b \in \mathcal{B}, \qquad [4.10]$$

$$X_{ij}^b \in \{0,1\} \qquad \forall b \in \mathcal{B}, \forall i, j \in \mathcal{N}, \qquad [4.11]$$

$$T_i^b \in \mathbb{R}^+ \qquad \forall b \in \mathcal{B}, \forall i \in \mathcal{N} \cup \{f, l\}. \qquad [4.12]$$

The objective function of the discrete BAP minimizes the weighted sum of the ship's service time (presented in equation [4.1]). Constraint [4.2] ensures that each ship i is assigned to exactly one berth b. Constraints [4.3] and [4.4] guarantee that each berth services exactly one first and one last ship, respectively. Constraint [4.5] ensures that all other ships serviced at each berth have one other ship being serviced before and one other ship being serviced afterward. Constraint [4.6] ensures that the service of a ship only starts after concluding the service of the previous ship at the same berth. Constraints [4.7]–[4.10] ensure ship and berth time windows, respectively. Finally, constraints [4.11] and [4.12] define the nature of the decision variables.

4.1.2. Representation of the BAP solution

Nishimura *et al.* [NIS 01] developed a simple GA for the hybrid BAP with dynamic ship arrival time. They use two permutation representations for the problem, each determining the order in which ships are allocated to berths. The berth schedules are then calculated based on this berthing order. In the so-called longer presentation, there is a gene associated with each ship for each berth segment, thus there are $N \times B$ genes, where N is the number of ships and B the number of berth segments. N random genes, out of the $N \times B$ existing ones, are filled with a random number between 1 and N, and no repetitions are allowed. The remaining genes are set to zero. Non-zero valued genes are of interest and they provide the order in which ships should be serviced. Figure 4.2(a) illustrates this representation for an instance considering 10 ships and 3 berthing sections. The first gene in the first berth segment is 7, which means that ship 7 is the first one to be allocated to the first berth segment. The second one is zero and thus it is ignored. The other non-zero gene values for the first section are 3, 2 and 8, meaning that ships

3, 2 and 8 will also be serviced in the first berth and in this order. Using the same reasoning, we can see that ships 1, 9 and 6 will be serviced, in this order, in berth segment 2, and finally, ships 10, 4, 8 and 5 will be serviced in berth segment 3, in this order. The remaining genes exist to allow for the possibility that all ships are serviced in the same berth segment, and thus, the whole solutions space is represented.

The shorter representation works in a similar way except that ships in different berths are separated by a zero. Thus, there are $N + (B - 1)$ genes; N genes are used to represent the N ships and thus will have a value between 1 and N and $(B - 1)$ are used to represent a berth change, and thus, will be zero. Figure 4.2(b) shows the shorter representation of the same solutions of Figure 4.2(a). The first four genes have non-zero values and thus represent the ships to be serviced in berth segment 1 in the order in which they appear; the fifth gene has a zero value, representing the fact that the next non-zero values will represent ships to be serviced in berth segment 2. Genes six to eight represent the ships and ship order to be serviced in berth segment 2. Gene nine is a separator gene, as it has a zero value, and the rest of the genes provide the ships and ship order to be serviced in the last berth segment.

The shorter representation is more popular and has been used by many researchers in different metaheuristic approaches, e.g. by Lalla-Ruiz and Voß [LAL 16] in a POPMUSIC algorithm and by Lin and Ting [LIN 14b] in an SA algorithm. Moreover, Imai et al. [IMA 07] used this representation to address the hybrid BAP.

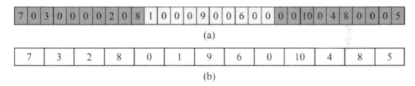

(a)

(b)

Figure 4.2. *A permutation representation for the BAP*

Solutions using the representation and construction procedure introduced above are feasible as long as no precedence relations exist between the ships, and any ship can be serviced in any berth segment. Nishimura et al. [NIS 01] consider draft constraints, thus ships can only be serviced at berth segments that satisfy the water depth requirements. They handled infeasible solutions by setting the objective function to an unfavorable value. Since the objective function has been converted into a maximization one (see equation [4.13]), infeasible solutions are given a zero objective function value. Unfeasible solutions may also be generated through reproduction, depending on the crossover operator used

$$f(x) = \frac{1}{1 + e^{y(x)/10000}}$$ [4.13]

Nishimura *et al.* [NIS 01] have developed a mathematical formulation for the BAP, and a Lagrangian relaxation-based heuristic to find lower-bound solutions for the problem. They have concluded that the overall performance of the GA is acceptable compared with the lower bounds for the BAP. The GA with a longer chromosome yields better results than those of the GA with the shorter chromosome. However, the GA with a longer chromosome requires larger CPU times and thus it cannot handle large and real applications.

4.1.3. *An SA algorithm for the BAP*

Here we review the work by Lin and Ting [LIN 14b], since they address both the discrete and the continuous BAP using an SA algorithm and produce state of the art results. Consider that there are N ships to be berthed in B berthing areas and that each ship has a known dynamic arrival time. The representation used is the short one explained above, in which $N + B - 1$ genes are used to represent the sequence of berthing ships in the berth segments, as depicted in Figure 4.2(b). The objective function they consider is to minimize total service time for all ships. For the discrete dynamic BAP, the completion berthing time of each ship can be calculated by knowing the sequence of ships in the berth and their arrival time. The service time for each ship is the difference between its completion time and its arrival time (including its waiting time before berthing). A large penalty is added to the objective function if a solution violates any constraint (i.e. is infeasible).

An initial solution is generated by resorting to the simple and well-known first-come, first-served (FCFS) heuristic rule. The ships that arrive earlier are assigned first and each one of them is assigned to the berth that results in its shortest completion time. If a tie occurs, then the ship with the smallest waiting time is chosen. Remaining ties are resolved by choosing the berth with the smallest number.

Two operators are used to generate neighbor solutions, namely swap and insertion operators. The swap operator interchanges two randomly selected ships. Note that the selected ships may be served in two different berths or in the same berth. In the insertion operator, one ship is randomly removed from its position and inserted immediately before another randomly selected ship. To decide on the operator to use, a random number between 0 and 1 is generated. If the number is less than 0.4, then the swap operator is used, while if the number is between 0.4 and 0.8, then the insertion operator is used [LIN 14b]. Finally, if the generated number is above 0.8, the specific move producing the best neighbor in the last g iterations is selected, among the swap moves if below 0.9 and among the insertion moves otherwise. Let us consider the following example, and assume the random number to be 0.86 and the best swap move of the past g-neighbors to involve ships in 8th and 15th genes, following which the current 8th and 15th genes are swapped.

The linear cooling process used is given in equation [2.3] and the parameter values (i.e. initial temperature, cooling rate, local search duration in each temperature, etc.) have been selected after carrying out numerical experiments. An alternative acceptance probability function, namely the Cauchy function (equation [4.14]), has been used in this SA algorithm, since [LIN 14b] believe it to be better at escaping local entrapment, in comparison to the Boltzmann function (equation [2.1]).

$$P = \frac{T_r}{T_r^2 + \Delta f^2} \qquad\qquad [4.14]$$

In discrete dynamic BAP, the length of a ship is not important, other than to check feasibility, as the berth segment has a fixed length. However, in the continuous BAP, the length of a ship should be taken into account to prevent overlapping between the ships' handling times and the berth length. For the continuous dynamic BAP, a similar representation for the allocation and sequencing of ships to the berth segments can be used. However, the position of the ships is not predetermined and will only be fixed in a further assignment process. The assignment procedure considers the spatial constraints for the berth segments. In this procedure, the ships are assigned to the corresponding berth in order of appearance in the solution string. The earliest time to start berthing a ship is the largest among its arrival time, the completion time of the previous ship at the same berth segment, and the earliest available time for the berth segment.

The performance of the SA algorithm for discrete and for continuous BAP was evaluated by solving the benchmark problem instances proposed by Cordeau *et al.* [COR 05] and by Lin and Ting [LIN 14b]. The SA algorithm was capable of finding an optimal solution for all discrete BAP instances, and improving on the best-known solution for 27 out of 30 continuous BAP instances. The authors were able to conclude that longer local search cycles, at each temperature level, are required for the continuous dynamic BAP.

4.1.4. *A bi-objective GA for the BAP*

A bi-objective optimization of the discrete BAP with dynamic ship arrival time has been proposed by Hu [HU 15], based on the principles of the NSGA-II algorithm. The objective function includes minimizing delayed services and duration of services during the night. In this problem, it is assumed that daytime services are preferred by the port authorities because of comfort, safety and energy-saving in services. Ships arriving in the berthing horizon are sorted according to their estimated arrival time in the ascending mode, and numbered 1 to N. A two-part chromosome of total length $2N$ is used to represent a BAP solution. The first part consists of a permutation string with N elements that determine the ships' mooring priority in the berth segments. The second part contains random values in the interval [0, 1] and represents the ships relative berthing time. This allows the values of any two genes to be exchanged without violating the boundaries of the ships' berthing time windows.

In a heuristic berth allocation algorithm, the ships are selected to moor according to their priority (larger numbers) within an assessment window. With reference to Figure 4.3, if the length of the priority assessment window is 3 then, among the first three ships, ship 3 has a higher priority to moor. Next, the corresponding value in the second part of the chromosome is proportionally converted to the real berthing starting times by considering 0 as the maximum time between the ship's estimated arrival time and the berth ready time and 1 as the ship departure due time; the berth with minimum estimated departure time (real berthing starting times plus ship operation time at berth) is allocated to the ship. The berth ready times are updated, and the ship is eliminated from the berthing allocation string, after each step of the berth allocation algorithm.

The multi-objective GA follows the typical flow of a GA. The GA finds several solutions in each generation. Then, the population is sorted by a non-dominated ranking method, rather than the typical ascending order. The population ranking method used to determine the fronts is reported in Algorithm 4.1. A tournament selection scheme with two randomly selected chromosomes is then performed. If one chromosome dominates the other, then it is the tournament winner, while if none is dominated, the one in the less crowded front is the winner. The procedure is repeated to select as many chromosomes as required by the crossover and mutation operators.

Identify the non-dominated chromosomes from the current population to constitute the first non-dominated front.
Set fitness values for chromosomes in the first non-dominated front equal to "1".
Exclude the individuals in the first front from the population and identify the non-dominated chromosomes to form the second non-dominated front.
Set fitness values for chromosomes in the second non-dominated front equal to "1/2".
Repeat steps 3 and 4 until all the chromosomes in the population are non-dominated, and set the fitness values for chromosomes in the dth front equal to "1/d".

Algorithm 4.1. *Ranking procedure for the multi-objective GA for the BAP*

Hu [HU 15] used two identical crossover and mutation operators for each part of the chromosome. A simple position-based crossover is used for the first part of the string; one offspring is created by randomly choosing some genes to be copied from the first parent and then filling the remaining ones from the second parent, in the order they appear, and ignoring genes having repeated values. The same procedure is used for the second offspring, but this time the randomly chosen genes come from the second parent. The second part of the string uses a two-point crossover, in which the genes in between two randomly selected positions are interchanged between two parents to create the offspring. An example is depicted in Figure 4.3. The mutation operator selects two positions in the first part of the chromosome and inverts the string between them, while in the second part a gene is randomly selected, and its value is replaced by a new randomly generated value.

Computational experiments evolving a population of 100 individuals over 300 generations were conducted on a proposed test dataset of practical scale with four berth segments and 100 incoming ships in a planning horizon of 180 hours, which is divided into 180 equal segments. The estimated arrival times, expected departure due time and the ship operation times were generated randomly. The results reported that the overnight workload was minimized while keeping the delayed services as low as possible. Generally, for the solutions in Pareto front, the weighted overnight workload is in [500, 800], and the weighted delays are in [14000, 21000]. Nevertheless, the overnight workload can be reduced to less than 500 with an additional 25% delayed workloads.

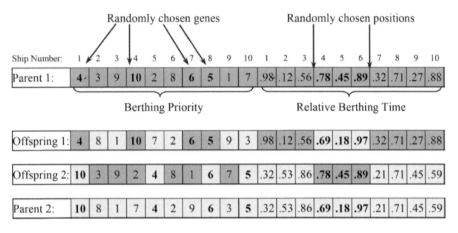

Figure 4.3. *Example of the crossover operator used in the multi-objective GA in the BAP*

4.2. BAP in bulk seaports

Although much of the work in the BAP is related to the operations in the CTs, most of the algorithms and method for the CTs can be implemented in bulk ports as well [UMA 11]. However, BAP in CTs differs from BAP in bulk seaports mainly due to the difference in the services required to handle containerships and to handle bulk ships. While standardized mobile equipment with known handling times is in service in CTs (because of the standard shape and weight of the loads), many different fixed specialized (un)loader equipment is in service in bulk ports [UMA 14]. For example, pipelines, which are required to (un)load liquids (e.g. crude oil), and conveyors (for ores) are installed in certain sections of a bulk seaport. Thus, berth segments are distinct, in the sense that they have different equipment available. Therefore, in the BAP for bulk ports, the berth assignment has to take into account the type of bulk ship, i.e. equipment requirements, in addition to the usual CTs limitations (berthing time and space) [UMA 13].

On the other hand, since bulk ships are generally larger and heavier than containerships, a loaded bulk ship cannot depart during a low tide [ERN 17]. Thus, besides all other constraints in the BAP, departure time of a bulk ship depends on the high tide window, as well.

BAP optimization in bulk ports is rarely found in the literature. Barros et al. [BAR 11] considered tidal conditions for the bulk seaports. In some seaports, the movement of ships is restricted to high tide time intervals. Moreover, the stock level of bulk cargoes is taken into account, where the higher priority goes for the bulk ships related to the most critical bulk cargo stock level at the seaport. Note that, for some bulk cargoes (e.g. mineral grains), a safety level must be kept at the seaports, mainly due to the continuous nature of the consumption or production process of those cargoes. The discrete BAP for one berth segment is modeled as a transportation problem, in which N ships are allocated to the next t time intervals (duration of time intervals depends on the high and low tide conditions). Barros et al. [BAR 11] address this problem using SA, and details of this work are provided in section 4.2.2. The tidal restrictions have recently been considered by Ernst et al. [ERN 17], who propose two new mathematical formulations for the continuous BAP in bulk seaports. The problem is defined for the largest coal exporting bulk terminal based in the Newcastle region of Australia and its focus is on enabling maximum exporting flow of coal based on the stocks stored to serve the arriving ships. However, both Barros et al. [BAR 11] and Ernst et al. [ERN 17] restrict the scope of the problem to a single-type bulk cargo. On the other hand, Umang et al. [UMA 13] address the BAP problem in bulk ports handling several types of bulk cargoes. Their work is reviewed in section 4.2.1.

4.2.1. Formulation of the BAP in bulk seaports

Umang et al. [UMA 13] developed two MILP models for a seaport that serves bulk ships handling a variety of different bulk cargoes with dynamic arrival times. The berthing area is divided into small berth segments with variable berth length and a ship can moor in one or more berth segments (as defined for hybrid BAPs). Although a ship may use only a part of a berth segment, berth segments cannot be occupied by more than one ship (or part of it) at the same time. Continuous berthing is not considered since it may result in several nonlinearities associated with the calculation of ship handling times, which are dependent on the berthing location of the ships.

The first model is adapted from the HVRPTW and the second is based on the GSPP approach. However, since, in the GSPP base model, the feasible assignments are explicitly enumerated, the model size is much larger and thus it may lead to computational issues such as running out of memory. Thus, here, we only reproduce the model based on the HVRPTW. Note that, to be consistent throughout the book, the notation is not exactly the same as the one used in [UMA 13].

As said before a ship may occupy one or more berth segments, thus a parameter $(t_i^{\ell b})$ is defined based on the ship size and berth segment size. This parameter takes the value 1 if, when ship i is allocated to berth segment ℓ, it also requires segment b, regardless of needing all of it or just part. Note that this is an input to the model. In addition, and since the ship may occupy several berth segments, another parameter $p_i^{\ell b}$ is needed to specify the percentage of the cargo that is handled by each of the berth segments the ship is in and, therefore, the resources needed at each berth segment. Another prior calculation is required to find out the expected service time for a unit load. The full notations are provided below and, just after it, the MILP model is stated by the mathematical expressions [4.15] through [4.27].

Sets, indices and parameters:	
$\mathcal{N}$	set of ships;
$\mathcal{B}$	set of berth segments;
i, j	indices for ships, $i, j \in \mathcal{N}$;
b, ℓ	indices for berth segments, $b, \ell \in \mathcal{B}$;
a_i	arrival time of ship $i \in \mathcal{N}$;
d_i	draft of ship $i \in \mathcal{N}$;
l_i	length of ship $i \in \mathcal{N}$;
q_i	quantity of cargo on ship $i \in \mathcal{N}$;
h_i^b	handling time per unit of cargo on ship $i \in \mathcal{N}$ in berth $b \in \mathcal{B}$;
d^b	water depth in berth $b \in \mathcal{B}$;
l^b	length of berth $b \in \mathcal{B}$;
c^b	starting coordinate of berth $b \in \mathcal{B}$;
L	total length of the port;
$t_i^{\ell b}$	=1, if ship $i \in \mathcal{N}$ mooring starts at segment $\ell \in \mathcal{B}$ and also uses berth segment $b \in \mathcal{B}$, 0 otherwise;
$p_i^{\ell b}$	percentage of the cargo of ship $i \in \mathcal{N}$ handled at berth segment $b \in \mathcal{B}$ (its only not

	zero if ship $i \in \mathcal{N}$ mooring starts at berth segment $\ell \in \mathcal{B}$ and also uses berth segment $b \in \mathcal{B}$);
M	a sufficiently large positive number.
Decision variables:	
T_i	starting time for the services of ship $i \in \mathcal{N}$;
C_i	total handling time for ship $i \in \mathcal{N}$;
B_i^b	=1 if berth segment $b \in \mathcal{B}$ is the starting segment of ship $i \in \mathcal{N}$; 0 otherwise;
X_i^b	=1 if ship $i \in \mathcal{N}$ occupies, even if partially, berth segment $b \in \mathcal{B}$; 0 otherwise;
Y_{ij}	=1 if ship $i \in \mathcal{N}$ is berthed immediately to the left of ship $j \in \mathcal{N}$ without overlapping; 0 otherwise;
Z_{ij}	=1 if service for ship $i \in \mathcal{N}$ finishes before the start of service to ship $j \in \mathcal{N}$; 0 otherwise.

$$Min\ Z = \sum_{i \in \mathcal{N}} (T_i + C_i - a_i), \qquad [4.15]$$

Subject to

$$T_i - a_i \geq 0 \qquad \forall i \in \mathcal{N}, \qquad [4.16]$$

$$\sum_{b \in \mathcal{B}} (B_j^b c^b) + M(1 - Y_{ij}) \geq \sum_{b \in \mathcal{B}} (B_i^b c^b) + l_i \quad \forall i,j \in \mathcal{N}, i \neq j, \qquad [4.17]$$

$$T_j + M(1 - Z_{ij}) \geq T_i + C_i \qquad \forall i,j \in \mathcal{N}, i \neq j, \qquad [4.18]$$

$$Y_{ij} + Y_{ji} + Z_{ij} + Z_{ji} \geq 1 \qquad \forall i,j \in \mathcal{N}, i \neq j, \qquad [4.19]$$

$$\sum_{b \in \mathcal{B}} B_i^b = 1 \qquad \forall i \in \mathcal{N}, \qquad [4.20]$$

$$\sum_{b \in \mathcal{B}} (B_i^b c^b) + l_i \leq L \qquad \forall i \in \mathcal{N}, \qquad [4.21]$$

$$\sum_{\ell \in \mathcal{B}} (t_i^{\ell b} B_i^{\ell}) = X_{ib} \qquad \forall i \in \mathcal{N}, \forall b \in \mathcal{B}, \qquad [4.22]$$

$$(d^b - d_i)X_i^b \geq 0 \qquad \forall i \in \mathcal{N}, \forall b \in \mathcal{B}, \qquad [4.23]$$

$$h_i^b p_i^{\ell b} q_i X_i^b \leq C_i \qquad \forall i \in \mathcal{N}, \forall b, \ell \in \mathcal{B}, \qquad [4.24]$$

$$B_i^b, X_i^b \in \{0,1\} \qquad \forall i \in \mathcal{N}, \forall b \in \mathcal{B}, \qquad [4.25]$$

$$Y_{ij}, Z_{ij} \in \{0,1\} \qquad \forall i, j \in \mathcal{N}, \qquad [4.26]$$

$$T_i, C_i \in \mathbb{R}^+ \qquad \forall i \in \mathcal{N}. \qquad [4.27]$$

The objective is to minimize total service time of the ships in the berthing horizon, as stated by equation [4.15]. The service starting time of a ship can only occur after its arrival, as expressed by inequality [4.16]. Space and time overlaps are avoided through constraints [4.17] to [4.19]. Ships have only one starting berth segment (constraint [4.20]) and the ships entire length must be within the berth segment (constraint [4.21]). Constraint [4.22] determines which other berth segments are occupied by a ship. Draft limitations of the ships are ensured by constraint [4.23]. The ship's handling time at each berth segment is ensured to be within the ship allowed service time by constraints [4.24]. Finally, constraints [4.25] to [4.27] determine the nature of the decision variables.

4.2.2. SA for the BAP in bulk seaports

Since bulk ships are heavier and generally larger than containerships, tidal conditions are more important for their arrival to and departure from seaports. At low tide, available depth in some ports is not adequate for the movement of these ships. Thus, even if a berth segment is available, ships may need to wait for appropriate tidal conditions before being able to berth. An SA algorithm for the BAP in the bulk seaports that accounts for tidal conditions was developed by Barros *et al.* [BAR 11], aiming at minimizing total costs of the ships service time. The berthing horizon is divided into several time intervals according to the tidal conditions (usually a 12-hour time interval). Then, a number of incoming ships are allocated to the berth segments in each time interval based on two main criteria. First and for importing cargoes, priority is given to bulk cargoes for which a safety stock in the seaport has been imposed. Regarding exporting cargoes, the first consideration is the availability of the bulk cargo to load the ship. Then, ships are prioritized according to demurrage costs, which are incurred by the port operator whenever a ship is not loaded on time.

The demurrage cost for each ship is calculated through equation [4.28]; in which, α_i is the demurage cost for the ith ship, and a_i, h_i, w_i are its arrival time interval, estimated berthing time (in terms of time intervals) and the number of time intervals it is allowed to remain in the seaport, respectively. Moreover, T_i is the starting time for the ship berthing, which is associated with the ship priority and only known after a solution is found. A solution with the minimum total demurrage cost for the ships is of interest.

$$\text{Demurrage Cost}_i = \max(\alpha_i(T_i + h_i - a_i - w_i), \quad 0) \qquad [4.28]$$

The simulated annealing algorithm for the BAP in bulk seaports follows the basic SA algorithm presented in section 2.2, in which the incoming ships are numbered consecutively from 1 to N. A solution string is a random sequence of the ships, and the incoming ships are prioritized (the second criterion) for berthing according to their order of appearance in the solution string. However, the exact berthing times for the ships are determined according to both criteria, and the arrival time of the ships. Evidently, subsequent ships in the solution string can have a berth conflict with previous ones. Once a berth conflict happens, the low-priority ship is delayed, which may result in demurrage costs.

To create a neighbor solution for the problem, a greedy swap operator exchanges the position of two ships in the solution string. The choice is greedy as it is based on the demurrage costs of individual ships. A ship with a positive demurrage cost is randomly selected. Then, a second ship is randomly chosen among the ones with higher priority than that of the first chosen (i.e. to the left of the selected ship) and that has a lower demurrage cost. These two ships are exchanged in the solution string as depicted in Figure 4.4. Note that if a ship with high demurrage costs swapped with another low-priority ship, its demurrage cost would increase due to the delays in its expected departure time.

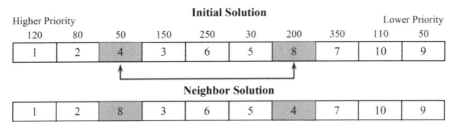

Figure 4.4. *An example solution string, and its neighbor for the SA in bulk seaport BAP*

The SA algorithm was computationally evaluated by solving 21 proposed problem instances corresponding to real scenarios. Optimal solutions for these instances were obtained by solving the mathematical model [BAR 11]. The SA was able to find an optimal solution for 18 of the 21 instances attempted with much smaller computational time requirements. The average CPU time was about 30 seconds, ranging from less than a second to 2.5 minutes; while the commercial used to solve the mathematical model required 3570 seconds on average (ranging from less than a second to over 13 hours) to find an optimal solution for any of the 21 instances.

4.3. Quay crane scheduling problem

Quay cranes are an interface between landside and seaside operations in container terminals. In CTs, the loading/unloading tasks related to the QCs are the bottleneck operations, and their performance affects the throughput of a CT [LEE 08]. Usually, even with high capital investments in QCs, their number is insufficient which may cause long delays in the loading/unloading tasks.

Precedence relationships between transshipment operations are the most important constraint for the problem. For example, unloading of a container should be performed before loading a container in the same place or ship. Another very important constraint for the QCSP is stacking the containers according to the stowage planning of the ship. On the other hand, QC schedules should follow the overall QC assignment plan for each ship. Moreover, QCs work on the same track, and thus, they cannot cross; in addition, QCs can operate only one task at the time. Several objectives have been defined for the QCSP, including minimizing the makespan of the entire ship operations, minimizing the QC movements, and maximizing QC utilization. In QCSP, the sequence and time for a set of loading/unloading tasks of a containership are optimized.

In containerships, containers are stacked on top of each other in columns, termed stacks. The ship area where rows of similar stacked containers are located is called a bay and ships have several bays (see Figure 4.5 for one bay in a containership). In QCSP, loading/unloading tasks of a cluster of containers are considered and the clusters may refer to a group of connected bays (i.e. bay areas), a single bay, a stack (light grey colored cells in Figure 4.5), a group of containers stored in adjacent slots of a bay (dark grey colored cells in Figure 4.5) or single containers. Usually, these tasks have near destinations in the storage area and are assigned to a single QC and are collectively performed without pre-emption. However, in some cases, preemption is allowed, and thus, the cluster of task may be divided among several QCs. As the containers usually carry heavy materials, ships might face instability if all the QCs operate on one side of the bays. Therefore, decisions on the loading/unloading tasks sequence have to take into account ship stability and ensure weight distribution along the ship, e.g. through the minimization of the weight differences between the stacks of containers loaded on the ship bays (e.g. look at [ALD 15]).

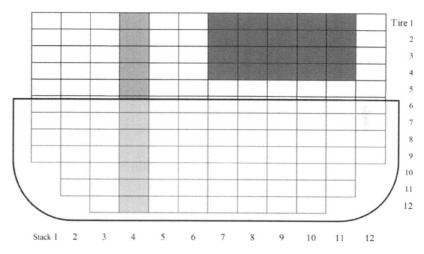

Figure 4.5. *Structure of a bay of storage locations in a containership*

The QCSP can be interpreted generally, as an m-parallel machine-scheduling problem. Thus, the QCSP can be generally classified as an NP-hard problem. However, precedence relationships among the containers and spatial constraints required in the QCSP to avoid QCs crossing one another are not involved in the machine-scheduling problem, which makes the QCSP even harder to solve. To avoid conflicts and owing to safety issues, the tasks cannot be performed simultaneously if, on one hand, the clusters of containers are very close to each other (usually, they cannot be adjacent), and on the other hand, the storage locations of two containers are served by the same yard crane.

During the last two decades, many researchers studied the QCSP, as it is a daily decision-making problem for the CT operators. Examples include two heuristic algorithms by Zhang *et al.* [ZHA 17] that minimize the makespan of the ship subject to the non-crossing constraints between the QCs. A simulation-based GA approach has been developed by Al-Dhaheri *et al.* [ALD 16], in which the handling time of the containers is uncertain. Ship stability is addressed in [ALD 15] by minimizing the differences between the container loads stacked over a number of bays and by maintaining a balanced load across the bays, and in [ALD 16] by explicitly considering changes in the ship's center of gravity. The interested reader is referred to the recent and comprehensive review by Bierwirth and Meisel [BIE 15].

4.3.1. *An MILP for the QCSP*

One of the first models for the QCSP was proposed by [KIM 04], which was then extended by Moccia *et al.* [MOC 06], Sammarra *et al.* [SAM 07], and Bierwirth and Meisel [BIE 09]. The extension devised by [BIE 09] is considered here. Consider scheduling a set of identical containers with precedence relationships. QCs work in a specific row and cannot cross one another; further let their earliest available time be known. Some of the tasks cannot be performed simultaneously, and these constraints can arise due to practical situations, such that the two containers are on the same stack. No preemption is allowed for un/loading tasks of a cluster of containers. The QCs and location of containers are numbered increasingly in one direction according to the bay numbers. This assumption, although not introducing any limitation to the scope of the problem, is important for the setting of constraints to avoid conflict between QCs. The safety distance between two adjacent QCs should be at least one bay. The crossing of the lower QC should be eliminated if a task located after the current position of an upper QC is assigned to a lower QC. Therefore, determination of a suitable distance/time span (Δ_{ij}^{vw}) between any two tasks is important to involve safety margins between the tasks, and to avoid crossing of cranes (refer to [BIE 09], for more details). The notation used in the MILP model is presented below and the mathematical model follows, given in equations [4.29] to [4.46].

Sets, indices and parameters:	
$\mathcal{K}$	set of QCs;
$\mathcal{N}$	set of tasks;
k, v, w	index for QC, $k, v, w \in \mathcal{K}$;
i, j, u	index for (un)loading tasks, $i, j, u \in \mathcal{N}$;
$\{f\}, \{l\}$	first and last tasks of the QCs;
$\mathcal{W}$	set of pairwise tasks (i and j) that cannot be performed simultaneously; $(i, j) \in \mathcal{W}$ and $i, j \in \mathcal{N}$;
$\mathcal{U}$	set of pairwise tasks (i and j) with a precedence relationship, $(i, j) \in \mathcal{U}$, and $i, j \in \mathcal{N}$;
$\mathcal{S}$	the set of all combinations of tasks (i, j) and QCs (v, w) that may lead to crane interference, $\left(i, j, v, w \in \mathcal{N}^2 \times \mathcal{K}^2 \mid i < j \ \& \ \Delta_{ij}^{vw} > 0\right)$;
p_i	handling time of task $i \in \mathcal{N}$;
l_i	location of task $i \in \mathcal{N}$ (expressed by the bay number);
l_k^f	the starting position of QC $k \in \mathcal{K}$ expressed by a bay number;
l_k^l	the final position of QC $k \in \mathcal{K}$ expressed by a bay number;
t_{ij}^k	travel time of QC $k \in \mathcal{K}$ between the location of task $i \in \mathcal{N}$ (l_i) and the location of task $j \in \mathcal{N}$ (l_j). Note that t_{fj}^k and t_{jl}^k represent QC $k \in \mathcal{K}$ traveling time from its starting position l_k^f to task $j \in \mathcal{N}$ (l_j) and from task $j \in \mathcal{N}$ (l_j) to its final position l_k^l, respectively;
Δ_{ij}^{vw}	minimum required time difference between two tasks $i \in \mathcal{N}$ and $j \in \mathcal{N}$, being processed by QCs $v \in \mathcal{K}$ and $w \in \mathcal{K}$, respectively;
r_k	ready time for QC $k \in \mathcal{K}$;
α_1	weight associated with the makespan (the maximum completion time);
α_2	weight associated with the total completion time;
M	a sufficiently large positive number.
Decision variables:	
Y_k	completion time of QC $k \in \mathcal{K}$;
C_i	completion time for task $i \in \mathcal{N}$;
C_{max}	time at which all tasks are completed;
X_{ij}^k	=1, if task $j \in \mathcal{N}$ is performed immediately after task $i \in \mathcal{N}$ by QC $k \in \mathcal{K}$, 0 otherwise;
Z_{ij}	=1, if task $j \in \mathcal{N}$ starts later than the completion time of task $i \in \mathcal{N}$; 0, otherwise.

$$Min \ Z = \alpha_1 C_{max} + \alpha_2 \sum_{k \in \mathcal{K}} Y_k, \qquad [4.29]$$

Subject to

$$Y_k \leq C_{max} \qquad \forall k \in \mathcal{K}, \qquad [4.30]$$

$$\sum_{j \in \mathcal{N}} X_{fj}^k = 1 \qquad \forall k \in \mathcal{K}, \qquad [4.31]$$

$$\sum_{j \in \mathcal{N}} X_{jl}^k = 1 \qquad \forall k \in \mathcal{K}, \qquad [4.32]$$

$$\sum_{k \in \mathcal{K}} \sum_{i \in \mathcal{N} \cup \{f\}} X_{ij}^k = 1 \qquad \forall j \in \mathcal{N} \cup \{l\}, \qquad [4.33]$$

$$\sum_{j \in \mathcal{N} \cup \{l\}} X_{ij}^k = \sum_{j \in \mathcal{N} \cup \{f\}} X_{ji}^k \qquad \forall k \in \mathcal{K}, \forall i \in \mathcal{N}, \qquad [4.34]$$

$$C_i + t_{ij}^k + p_j - C_j \leq M(1 - X_{ij}^k) \quad \forall k \in \mathcal{K}, \forall i, j \in \mathcal{N} \cup \{f, l\}, [4.35]$$

$$C_i + p_j \leq C_j \qquad \forall i, j \in \mathcal{U}, \qquad [4.36]$$

$$C_i - C_j + p_j \leq M(1 - Z_{ij}) \qquad \forall i, j \in \mathcal{N}, \qquad [4.37]$$

$$C_j - C_i - p_j \leq M Z_{ij} \qquad \forall i, j \in \mathcal{N}, \qquad [4.38]$$

$$Z_{ij} + Z_{ji} = 1 \qquad \forall i, j \in \mathcal{W}, \qquad [4.39]$$

$$\sum_{u \in \mathcal{N} \cup \{f\}} X_{ui}^v + \sum_{u \in \mathcal{N} \cup \{f\}} X_{uj}^w \\ \leq 1 + Z_{ij} + Z_{ji} \qquad \forall i, j, v, w \in \mathcal{S}, \qquad [4.40]$$

$$C_i + \Delta_{ij}^{vw} - C_j + p_j \leq M\left(3 - Z_{ij} - \sum_{u \in \mathcal{N} \cup \{f\}} X_{ui}^v - \sum_{u \in \mathcal{N} \cup \{f\}} X_{uj}^w\right) \\ \forall i, j, v, w \in \mathcal{S}, \qquad [4.41]$$

$$C_j + \Delta_{ij}^{vw} - C_i + p_i \leq M\left(3 - Z_{ji} - \sum_{u \in \mathcal{N} \cup \{f\}} X_{ui}^v - \sum_{u \in \mathcal{N} \cup \{f\}} X_{uj}^w\right) \\ \forall i, j, v, w \in \mathcal{S}, \qquad [4.42]$$

$$C_j + t_{jl}^k - Y_k \leq M(1 - X_{jl}^k) \qquad \forall k \in \mathcal{K}, \forall j \in \mathcal{N}, \qquad [4.43]$$

$$r_k - C_j + t_{fj}^k + p_j \leq M\left(1 - X_{fj}^k\right) \qquad \forall k \in \mathcal{K}, \forall j \in \mathcal{N}, \qquad [4.44]$$

$$x_{ij}^k, Z_{ij} \in \{0,1\} \qquad \forall k \in \mathcal{K}, \forall i, j \in \mathcal{N} \cup \{f, l\}, [4.45]$$

$$Y_k, C_i \in \mathbb{R}^+ \qquad \forall k \in \mathcal{K}, \forall i \in \mathcal{N}. \qquad [4.46]$$

The objective of the MILP model (presented in equation [4.29]) consists of minimizing the weighted sum of the makespan and the total usage time of QCs. The makespan is given by the largest completion time among all QCs (as in constraints [4.30]). First and last tasks of each QC are determined through constraints [4.31] and [4.32], respectively. Constraint [4.33] ensures each container is assigned to exactly one QC. Constraint [4.34] states that each container operation has a previous operation and a following operation in the same QC, except the first and the last that only have a following and a previous operation, respectively. Constraint [4.35] ensures the consistency of the scheduling network and determines the completion time for each task. Constraint [4.36] imposes precedence constraints by forcing a task to be completed no earlier than the completion of all preceding tasks plus its own handling time p_j. Constraints [4.37] and [4.38] ensure the definition of the auxiliary variables Z_{ij}, which take the value 1 if and only if task j is completed after task i; while constraint [4.39] forces either task i to be done after the completion of task j or vice versa if tasks i and j have been predefined as non-simultaneous tasks, i.e. $(i, j) \in \mathcal{W}$). Constraint [4.40] identifies the scheduled assignments of tasks to QCs, in which $\sum_{u \in \mathcal{N} \cup \{f\}} X_{ui}^v = 1$ if task i is processed by QC v, and $\sum_{u \in \mathcal{N} \cup \{f\}} X_{uj}^w = 1$ if task j is processed by QC w; however, if both assignments take place, the left-hand side takes two, meaning that the tasks are not allowed to be processed simultaneously. In constraints [4.41] and [4.42], the minimum temporal distance between the completion time of task i and the starting time of task j is enforced for all task combinations. The completion time of each QC is calculated in constraints [4.43] and [4.44], assuring that the first task of each QC is started only after the earliest available time of that QC, and also taking into account the QC travelling time from its starting position. Finally, constraints [4.45] and [4.46] define the nature of the decision variables.

4.3.2. Genetic algorithms for the QCSP

Lee *et al.* [LEE 08] proved that QCSP is an NP-complete problem and proposed the first GA to solve it. Like for most scheduling problems, the authors used a permutation-encoded chromosome to represent the solution string for the QCSP, with length N — the number of tasks. The tasks sequence is determined by the order of appearance in the chromosome. This representation has also been used by Nguyen *et al.* [NGU 13]. An example is provided in Figure 4.6, according to which the tasks are allocated to QC in the following order: 5, 8, 4, 9, 6, 2, 7, 1, 10 and 3. The decoding procedure used to construct a feasible solution starts by identifying all QCs that can perform the first task. If there is more than one available, the QC resulting in the earliest completion time of the task is selected. Ties are broken by choosing the QC closer to the task location and persisting ties are resolved by selecting the QC with a smaller identification number. Nguyen *et al.* [NGU 13] have used a similar, yet more flexible heuristic method to construct the QC schedule. The priority for the QCs is calculated according to the earliest completion time of a task and ready times of the QCs. In both papers, possible conflicts are eliminated from the final schedule using a heuristic method.

1	2	3	4	5	6	7	8	9	10
5	8	4	9	6	2	7	1	10	3

Figure 4.6. *Representation of chromosomes for the GA by [LEE 08] and [NGU 13] in QCSP*

A two-part permutation string was presented by Chung and Choy [CHU 12] (see Figure 4.7). In this chromosome, the first part (grey-colored) indicates the sequence of tasks and the second part (white-colored) indicates the QCs assigned to the corresponding tasks in the first part. In the example provided, the QC 1 performs the sequence of tasks corresponding to the third, fifth, seventh, eighth and tenth gene values, in this case, tasks 4, 6, 7, 1 and 3, while QC 2 performs the sequence of tasks 5, 8, 9, 2 and 10. In the case of violation of the precedence constraints, the genes corresponding to the violated tasks are swapped and the respective genes in the second part are also swapped.

To generate new offspring, two parents are selected from the current population, and an order-based crossover is performed as follows: a segment of connected genes in the first part of Parent 1 is copied onto the corresponding genes of offspring 1. Then, the other tasks (tasks not present in the segment copied from Parent 1) are chosen from Parent 2, in the order they appear. Similarly, and using Parent 2, offspring 2. This is illustrated in Figure 4.7. The segments including genes 4, 5 and 6 were copied (in bold). The first task in Parent 2 not in the segment is task 8, which is in the third gene of the first part. Thus, the first gene of the first part of the offspring takes the value 8, while the first gene of the second part takes the value 2, which is the value of the third gene of the second part of Parent 2. This is then repeated until all genes have been filled. Feasibility issues may arise in the presence of precedence constraints.

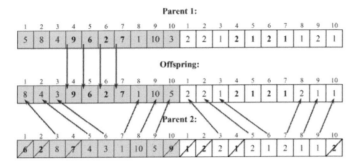

Figure 4.7. *Representation of chromosomes and order-based crossover by* Chung and Choy *[CHU 12] for the QCSP*

Chung and Chan [CHU 13] proposed a different representation. To start, the tasks are numbered according to their location in the ship in one direction (e.g. from left to right). The chromosome is a string with N elements which is filled with random integer numbers in the interval $[1, K]$ (K is the number of QCs). The tasks are performed in a sequence from left to right in the chromosome. For example, in Figure 4.8, QC 1 performs the sequence of tasks 3, 5, 7, 8 and 10 and QC 2 performs the sequence of tasks 1, 2, 4, 6 and 9. A unidirectional search approach is applied, in which higher priority to perform its set of tasks goes to the QC with a larger number (i.e. the right QC performs the set of tasks earlier than the left one). In case of violation of the precedence constraints, violated genes are swapped. A simple two-point swap crossover was used, as shown in Figure 4.8. In the mutation operator, a randomly selected gene has the assigned QC changed. The new value is either $k + 1$ or $k - 1$. The reason behind this conditional change is twofold: first, to reduce the interference constraints, and second, to guide the mutation process to balance the workload of adjacent QCs. Thus, the choice between $k + 1$ and $k - 1$ is done in order to have the QCs with an equal number of tasks.

Task Number:	1	2	3	4	5	6	7	8	9	10
QC Number:	2	2	1	2	1	2	1	1	2	1

Figure 4.8. *Representation of chromosomes for the GA by Chung and Chan [CHU 13] in QCSP*

4.3.3. *Tabu search for the QCSP*

Sammarra *et al.* [SAM 07] proposed a Tabu search approach to solve the QCSP. In it, the QCSP is viewed as a vehicle routing-scheduling problem. In the routing subproblem, the sequence of tasks on each QC is determined; and in scheduling subproblem, the completion time of each task belonging to a route is calculated. The sequence of tasks handled by the QC k is denoted by a route, σ_k. Thus, a solution for the QCSP can be represented as $\sigma = (\sigma_1, \dots, \sigma_K)$. The left and right adjacent routes for a given QC (σ_k) are σ_{k-1} and σ_{k+1}. It is obvious that, for the QC 1, only the right adjacent route can be defined, and there is no right adjacent route for the QC K.

Neighborhood solutions are obtained by resorting to swap and insertion operators. The swap operator's any two adjacent tasks of a specific QC can be swapped, as long as no infeasibilities are introduced. In the insertion operator, a task currently assigned to QC k is inserted into the tasks of one of the adjacent QCs. According to Sammarra *et al.* [SAM 07], the best insertions are those that limit crossing between QCs. Four kinds of insertion operators are considered:

– Insert a task of QC k ($k = 1, \dots, K - 1$) as the first task of QC ($k + 1$);

– Insert a task of QC k ($k = 1, \dots, K - 1$) as the last task of QC ($k + 1$);

– Insert a task of QC k ($k = 2, \dots, K$) as the first task of QC ($k - 1$);

– Insert a task of QC k ($k = 2, \dots, K$), as the last task of QC ($k - 1$).

The aforementioned insertions are allowed as long as no infeasibilities are introduced, e.g. if task i from QC k is being inserted into QC ($k + 1$) or QC ($k - 1$) and in it there is at least a task j such that $(j, i) \in \mathcal{W}$, the insertion is not performed.

The Tabu search algorithm is shown in Algorithm 4.2, in which the current solution and its makespan are denoted by σ and C_{max}, and the best-known solution and its makespan are σ^* and C^*_{max}, respectively. The neighborhood of the current solution σ is designated by $N(\sigma)$ and the set of non-Tabu neighbors by $M(\sigma)$. The best solution in $M(\sigma)$ and its makespan are denoted by $\hat{\sigma}$ and $\hat{C}_{max}$, respectively. The algorithm is run for λ_{max} iterations. For any solution, $B(\sigma)$ is the set of (i, j, k) attributes, stating that task j is done immediately after task i and both are performed by QC k.

Generate Initial solution (σ), and its makespan (C_{max}),

Set $\sigma^* = \sigma$, and $C_{max}^* = C_{max}$,

Initialize short and long term tabu lists ($\beta_{ij}^k = \delta_{ij}^k = 0$); and the aspiration level ($\alpha_{ij}^k = \infty$),

Set $\alpha_{ij}^k = C_{max}, \forall (i, j, k) \in B(\sigma)$,

For $\lambda = 1, \dots, \lambda_{max}$

    $M(\sigma) = \emptyset$;

    Update the non-tabu neighbors list,

$$M(\sigma) = M(\sigma) \cup \{\bar{\sigma}\}, \forall \bar{\sigma} \in N(\sigma), \forall (i, j, k) \in B(\bar{\sigma}) \setminus \left(\beta_{ij}^k < \lambda \text{ or } \bar{C}_{max} < \alpha_{ij}^k \right)$$

    Penalize the non-improving solutions,

$$\forall \bar{\sigma} \in M(\sigma), if \ \bar{C}_{max} \geq C_{max} \text{ then}$$

$$g(\bar{\sigma}) = \bar{C}_{max} + \frac{C_{max} + \Sigma_{i,j,k \in B(\bar{\sigma}) \setminus B(\sigma)} \delta_{ij}^k}{\lambda}, \text{else } g(\bar{\sigma}) = \bar{C}_{max}$$

    Find the best solution in non-tabu neighbors list ($\hat{\sigma}$),

    Set $\hat{\sigma}$ as the current best solution, such that $\hat{C}_{max} = \min_{\bar{\sigma} \in M(\sigma)} g(\bar{\sigma})$

    Update the short term memory, $\forall (i, j, k) \in B(\sigma) \setminus B(\hat{\sigma}), \beta_{ij}^k = \lambda + \theta$

    Update the long term memory, $\forall (i, j, k) \in B(\hat{\sigma}) \setminus B(\sigma), \delta_{ij}^k = \delta_{ij}^k + 1$

    If $\hat{C}_{max} < C_{max}^*$ then $\sigma^* = \hat{\sigma}$, and $C_{max}^* = \hat{C}_{max}$

    Update the aspiration level, $\forall (i, j, k) \in B(\hat{\sigma}), \alpha_{ij}^k = \min\{\alpha_{ij}^k, \hat{C}_{max}\}$

    Set $\sigma = \hat{\sigma}$, and $C_{max} = \hat{C}_{max}$

End for %λ

Return the best-known solution.

Algorithm 4.2. *Tabu search algorithm for the QCSP*

The algorithm uses both short-term and long-term memories; the first is implemented through a short-term list, in which an attribute (i, j, k) remains forbidden for β_{ij}^k iterations. Attributes are removed for the list whenever the makespan of the Tabu neighbor solution is less the current aspiration level (α_{ij}^k). At each iteration, the aspiration level is set to the minimum between its current value and $\hat{C}_{max}$. On the other hand, non-improving solutions have a penalty (depending on the frequency that an attribute has been added to a solution, δ_{ij}^k) added to the makespan and the corresponding move is added to the long-term Tabu list. This mechanism leads the search into an unexplored region of the solution space and maintains its diversification.

The performance of the Tabu search algorithm has been computationally evaluated by solving in 37 problem instances, first proposed in [KIM 04]. Optimal solutions for these instances have been found by solving the MILP model using a branch-and-cut algorithm [MOC 06]. The instances are divided into small (ten instances), medium (twenty instances) and large (seven instances). The TS algorithm was capable of finding an optimal solution for all small-sized instances, for seven out of the 20 medium-sized instances, and four out of the seven large-sized ones. Regarding computational time requirements, the branch-and-cut algorithm is faster for the small sized and some of the others (four out of the 27); however, the TS was faster for the remaining 23 instances.

4.3.4. *Double cycling QCSP*

For easier practical scheduling in container terminals, it is common among port operators to first unload all the import containers from the ship, and then load all the export containers into the ship. Generally, it is supposed that single cycling of QCs results is a less complicated problem both for the seaside and the yard side operations. However, in almost all the operations, the QCs, vehicles and the storage equipment perform one empty travel after each loading or unloading operation. For example, suppose two unloading tasks are assigned to a QC. The spreader of the QC moves from its current dwell point to the top of the deck (where the import container is located), grabs it and moves back to the quayside to put down the container in the buffer area. Next, it must have another empty move from the quayside to the top of the ship to grab the next import container. The same happens with the vehicles and the storage equipment.

In double cycling, however, loading and unloading tasks for a single ship are addressed simultaneously. Therefore, the empty moves of the crane (and other handling equipment) are converted, at least partially, into productive ones. A cycle is a complete round-trip of the QC trolley from ship to quayside and back to ship, or vice versa. It is expected that a double cycling strategy results in a higher level of productivity for handling operations at the ports and it can be achieved by appropriate operations planning and scheduling (double cycling in the scheduling of QCs, transportation and storage tasks is discussed in section 5.5.). Goodchild and Daganzo [GOO 07] claim that, by using double cycling, it is possible to accomplish a 10% reduction in the turnaround operating time of a ship. However, not many works have been reported regarding double cycling and very few existing ones are recent (mostly in the last decade).

Generate Pop_1 (QCs operation sequence)

For $g_1 = 1, ..., g_1^{max}$

    Generate Pop_2 (Stowage plan)

    For $g_2 = 1, ..., g_2^{max}$

        Calculate fitness function ($S = Min(\sum_{i \in N} Y_i)$)

        Generate the new Pop_2 (Selection → Crossover → Mutation)

    End %For g_2

    Obtain stowage plan, calculate yard crane operation time

    Calculate fitness of upper level ($Min(C_{max} + S)$)

    Generate the new Pop_1 (Selection → Crossover → Mutation)

End %For g_1

Return the best-known solution.

Algorithm 4.3. *Two-layer GA for the QCDCP*

When compared with the QCSP, the double cycling QC scheduling problem is more complex and challenging. Next, we review a two-layer GA for the containers in a bay of a ship served by a QC on top of the ship and one yard crane in the storage yard due to [ZEN 15]. The problem definition and formulation can be found in [GOO 07, ZHA 09, LIU 15, ZEN 15, ZHA 16]. The algorithm for a two-layer GA by Zeng *et al.* [ZEN 15] for the QCDCP is shown in Algorithm 4.3. In the inner layer, the stowage plan of exporting containers is decided, i.e. the storage position for each individual container in the rows of the bay is determined. In the outer GA, the unloading and loading operations are decided. It should be noticed that the stowage plan decisions, in the inner GA, affect both the operational time of the yard crane and the number of stored containers in the bay.

It is assumed that a stowage plan with lower operational time for the yard cranes (due to less reshuffling operations) is more efficient. In the inner layer, the objective function is to minimize total operational time of the storage yard cranes for the N exporting containers ($S = \sum_{i \in N} Y_i$). The chromosome in the inner layer is a vector with N (i.e. the number of exporting containers) elements, filled with non-repetitive integer numbers from 1 to N. The gene position provides the order of operations and the gene value of the operation to be done. Figure 4.9 depicts two chromosomes (Parent 1 and Parent 2) and the offspring generated from them. The solution corresponding to chromosome Parent 1 requires the exporting containers to be loaded in the following order: 9, 3, 5, 1, 6, 2, 8, 10, 4 and 7. In this layer, the offspring are produced by a one-point crossover operator. In the example in Figure 4.9, the first part, i.e. genes 1 until the crossover point (grey color in Figure 4.9), is copied from Parent 1 and the remaining genes are filled with the non-repetitive gene values of Parent 2 according to the order of appearance. Mutation is done by a simple swap operator. The initial population is randomly generated.

In the outer GA, the objective function is to minimize the weighted sum of the makespan (QCs largest service time considering both loading and unloading operations) and the operational time (S) of the yard cranes, calculated previously in the inner GA. The chromosome is a two-section string; the first section represents the sequence of rows for unloading operations, and the second one the sequence of rows for loading operations. The initial population for the outer GA is randomly generated, by non-repetitive row numbers from 1 to R (total number of rows in a bay), for both chromosome sections. Figure 4.10 shows a chromosome example. A one-point crossover operator is used for each chromosome section; thus, two random points are generated and the genes in each section to the left of the generated points are copied to the offspring. As was the case in the inner GA, the remaining genes take their value from the second parent in the order they appear in it; obviously disregarding repeated rows. A swap mutation operator is applied to each section of the chromosome.

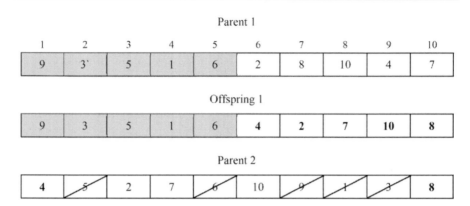

Figure 4.9. *Example chromosomes and crossover operator for the inner GA in QCDCP*

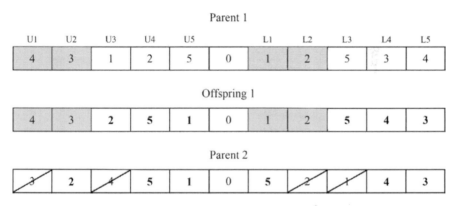

Figure 4.10. *Example chromosomes and crossover operator for the outer GA in QCDCP*

Numerical experiments by Zeng *et al.* [ZEN 15] indicate that double cycling can reduce the operation time of QCs in comparison to scheduling loading and unloading tasks separately.

4.4. Integrated berth allocation problem

Decisions made for the berth plans are highly dependent on the availability of the equipment to load/unload the ships. Without knowing the exact number of available cranes or the required yard operations, setting the due dates for the ship is hard. On the other hand, in almost all the problems related to the crane scheduling or assignment problem, it is simply assumed that the workload on a ship and its available time is known in advance. However, due to the natural interrelation of the operations in the quayside, and regarding integrated berth allocation, two main problems have been investigated in the literature, namely the integrated berth allocation and QC assignment (B&CAP) and the integrated berth allocation and QC scheduling (B&CSP).

Typical objectives of the QCAP include minimizing crane productivity losses, by reducing the number of crane setups at ships, and crane travel times. In the QCAP, it is common to either determine only the number of assigned QCs, or determine the specific set of QCs assigned to a ship. Simple heuristic rules can help the port operators to decide on the number of assigned QCs to an arriving ship. For example, in many real practices, a minimum number of assigned QCs are specified in the contact between the port and the ship operators. In some discrete BAP applications, for each berth segment, the number of QCs is fixed. This way, when the planner selects a berth, he can assign the QCs, as well. Thus, in these applications, an explicit assignment of QCs to the ships is not necessary. On the other hand, two major approaches to assigning QCs in practice are either time-invariant, in which the number of assigned QCs is not changed over the ship berthing time, or time-variant, in which the number of QCs assigned to a ship can be further adjusted over the berthing time [BIE 10]. With the time-variant QC assignment, the port operators can use the QCs at a higher utilization number, and they can give more attention to the incoming ships with higher priorities (e.g. with higher workloads), although, at a higher degree of complexity for the problem and the cost of more QC setups and movements.

Although the QCAP is one of the most important optimization problems in seaside operations of the ports, as far as we are aware of, no works have been reported in the literature addressing this problem on its own. All studies we were able to find address it as a part of a larger topic in seaside operations.

Although the early works for the integrated planning and scheduling problems date back to 1989 [DAG 89], most of the studies for these problems are recent and have been done in the last ten years, as reviewed by Bierwirth and Meisel [BIE 15]. For the B&CAP, either the number of the assigned QCs is a decision variable or the exact QCs among a fleet are assigned to a ship, in addition to its berth plan. The B&CAP was studied by

Imai *et al.* [IMA 08] who developed a mathematical formulation of the problem, and a GA to solve the problem more efficiently. Later, Chang *et al.* [CHA 10] developed a parallel GA for the B&CAP. The berthing location and time and the number of allocated QCs are determined first. The algorithm then calculates the exact times and eliminates infeasibilities. This algorithm is reviewed in detail, in section 4.4.1. Hsu [HSU 16] proposed a PSO and a GA using real encoding for the berth scheduling and time-variant QC assignment plan. The PSO algorithm is reviewed in more details in section 4.4.2. Other recent studies for the B&CAP include [TÜR 14] for B&CAP with time-invariant QC assignment, and [TÜR 16] for the B&CAP with time-variant QC assignment. Two of the most recent studies propose a biased random-key GA for the time-invariant B&CAP [COR 17] and an MIP model and a rolling horizon heuristic algorithm [AGR 18].

In recent years, an increasing interest to include green objectives in the seaside operation can be observed in the literature. For example, Hu *et al.* [HU 14] considered the fuel consumption and emissions from ships in a nonlinear multi-objective integer programming model for the B&CAP. Moreover, emission of the ships during their waiting time in the seaport and the impact of the number of allocated QCs on the operational costs and the energy consumption are also considered. More recently, He [HE 16] developed an MILP model and a memetic algorithm for the B&CAP to study trade-offs between time-saving and energy-saving. Despite the typical random mutation operators used in the GA and memetic algorithms, they proposed to use a local search algorithm based on the SA algorithm to find a so-called good swap mutation operator for the memetic algorithm.

In the B&CSP, the berth plan and the sequence of workloads for the assigned QCs are decided. Despite the expectations, there are not that many studies related to the integrated berth allocation and QC scheduling (B&CSP). Song *et al.* [SON 12] developed a bi-level programming model for the B&CSP, and a heuristic approach to solve the problem in realistic instances, in which a GA finds a solution for the BAP, and a heuristic procedure finds the QC scheduling. The other example is the work by Lee *et al.* [LEE 10], in which a two-layer MILP model and a GA were developed for the B&CSP. This problem is discussed in more details in section 4.4.3.

4.4.1. *A parallel GA for the B&CAP*

A parallel GA (PGA) for the B&CAP with continuous berth area and time-variant QC assignment was developed by Chang *et al.* [CHA 10]. A fixed-time rolling planning technique is used and thus the algorithm is performed for a fixed number of periods (e.g. 6) and, at the end of each period, the plan is updated for the following, say 6, periods. The objectives of the PGA are to minimize the total deviation between the actual and ideal berth locations of the ships, total penalty costs for the delayed ships and total energy consumption by the QCs.

The PGA independently evolves n populations, each with m individuals. In fact, every population is optimized on an individual processor to speed up the optimization process. For retaining diversity of population and taking advantage of the best known solutions in each population, after a predefined number of generations (empirically determined), some of the best individuals of each population migrate to the other populations. An individual is represented by a matrix chromosome with 3 rows and N (the number of ships in berthing horizon) columns. The rows indicate the *berth location*, the *berth time* and the number of *assigned QCs*. Three sample chromosomes are depicted in Figure 4.11.

The initial chromosomes are created using the heuristic algorithm reported in Algorithm 4.4. This algorithm produces only feasible chromosomes. In this algorithm, all the ships that have already arrived (but not departed), or will arrive during the berthing horizon are considered for the berth planning. The *available berth length* is the total berth area (L) subtracted net off all previously assigned berthing lengths. The required berthing length of a ship in period t is denoted by l_{it}. This length changes over time, because of the safety length required between the ship and its adjacent ships. The ideal location to berth a ship is the closest location to the storage yard dedicated to the ship (x_{it}^*). The heuristic algorithm tries to find the nearest *berth location* for a ship compared with its best berth location. If $l_{it} >$ *available berth length*, it means that there is not enough berth area for the ship in this period. Nevertheless, a berthing location is allocated to the ship, which must wait until it becomes available. This location (and the berth location for other ships) is later optimized with the PGA. The heuristic also assigns to each ship a random *berth time* within the ship service time window (greater than or equal to its arrival time a_{it} and less than its expected departure time d_{it}). The assignments made ensure no overlapping, both regarding berthing time and location. Finally, the number of *QCs assigned* to a ship, say i, is a uniformly generated random number between the minimum number of QCs available for ship i in period t (Q_{it}^{Min}) and the minimum between the best number of QCs for ship i (q_{it}^*) and the maximum available QCs for ship i in period t (Q_{it}^{Max}), that is between Q_{it}^{Min} and $min\{q_{it}^*, Q_{it}^{Max}\}$.

In the crossover operator, two individuals are chosen according to the roulette wheel operator, and one offspring is generated by mating them. For the *berth location*, the number of *assigned QCs* of the offspring is generated through an arithmetic crossover (Offspring $= \lambda$ Parent 1 $+ (1 - \lambda)$ Parent 2), in which λ is a random number between 0 and 1. For the *berth time*, a single-point crossover is applied to generate the offspring. A random cell (in the *berth time* row) is selected in Parent 1, and its left-hand side is directly copied into the same cells of the offspring. The right-side cells of the offspring are filled with the same cells of Parent 2. An example of the crossover operator can be seen in Figure 4.11.

1. For $t = 1$: *Berth Horizon*	
2.	N_t is the number of ships arriving (arrived) at the terminal during period t,
3.	For $i = 1$: N_t
4.	If $l_{it} \le$ *available berth length*, then
5.	Allocate the nearest berth location to i^{th} ship (*i.e.*, Minimize $\|x_{it} - x_{it}^*\|$),
6.	else
7.	Randomly allocate berth location (x_{it}) to i^{th} ship,
8.	End %if
9.	Randomly assign a feasible berth time (y_{it}) in $[a_{it}, d_{it}]$,
10.	Compute the number of assigned QCs, $$q_{it} = rand\left(Q_{it}^{Min}, Min\left(q_{it}^*, Q_{it}^{Max}\right)\right),$$
11.	End For % i

Algorithm 4.4. *Heuristic algorithm to create feasible random chromosomes for the parallel GA in the B&CAP*

A non-uniform mutation operator is applied as follows: a column (Col) is randomly selected, and its cells are mutated (Col') using equation [4.47], where A and B are the minimum and maximum allowed limits for the mutation, r is a random number between 0 and 1, g is the current generation, g^{max} is the maximum number of generations, and β is a parameter used to adjust mutation steps. The lower and upper limits for the berth location, berth time, and number of assigned QCs are $\left[\frac{l_{it}}{2}, L - \frac{l_{it}}{2}\right]$, $[a_{it}, d_{it}]$, and $\left[Q_{it}^{Min}, Min(q_{it}^*, Q_{it}^{Max})\right]$, respectively.

$$
Col' = \begin{cases} Col - (B - A) \times \left(1 - r^{\frac{(1-g)\beta}{g^{max}}}\right), & r < 0.5 \\[4mm] Col + (B - A) \times \left(1 - r^{\frac{(1-g)\beta}{g^{max}}}\right), & r \geq 0.5 \end{cases} \tag{4.47}
$$

Although the initial chromosomes are feasible, during the crossover and mutation operations some infeasibilities may be introduced. The infeasibilities, if any, are repaired through the following set of rules.

– if the *berth location* is feasible, and the *berthing time* is not in the range $[a_{it}, d_{it}]$, go to step 9 of Algorithm 4.4;

– if the *berthing time* is feasible, and the *berth location* is not in the range $\left[\frac{l_{it}}{2}, L - \frac{l_{it}}{2}\right]$, perform steps 4 to 8 of Algorithm 4.4;

– if both berth location and time have overlaps with other ships and if the latest departure time of the ships occupying the berth location of the ith ship in period t exceeds $1/10$ p_{it}, ($p_{it} = d_{it} - a_{it}$) perform steps 4 to 9 of Algorithm 4.4 to generate a new feasible berth location and time; otherwise, go to step 9 of Algorithm 4.4 to adjust berth time;

– if the number of assigned QCs is not in the range $\left[Q_{it}^{Min}, Min(q_{it}^*, Q_{it}^{Max})\right]$, go to step 10 of Algorithm 4.4.

The performance evaluation of the PGA resorted to a real B&CAP application involving 21 ships in a 7-day berthing planning horizon. The results were compared with those of the heuristic approach proposed in [CHA 08]. The PGA was able to decrease the total deviation between the actual and the ideal berth locations of the ships from 1286 meters in

[CHA 08] to 642 meters (more than 100%), the penalty costs decreased from 3581 USD to 396 USD (more than 800%), the total turnaround times decreased from 172.26 hours to 165.88 hours (3.8%), and the total energy consumption by the QCs decreased from 102,497.3 to 99,957.5 kWh (2.5%).

Parent 1

Arriving Ship	1	2	3	4	5
Berth Location	110	210	300	400	650
Berth Time	10:15	11:30	13:20	15:35	16:10
Assigned QCs	2	4	4	2	3

Offspring

Arriving Ship	1	2	3	4	5
Berth Location	305	170	261	275	
Berth Time	10:15	11:30	15:10	16:32	17:45
Assigned QCs	2	3	4	2	3

Parent 2

Arriving Ship	1	2	3	4	5
Berth Location	500	130	223	150	360
Berth Time	11:35	12:45	15:10	16:32	17:45
Assigned QCs	3	2	4	2	4

Figure 4.11. *Sample chromosomes and the crossover example for the PGA in the B&CAP*

4.4.2. PSO for the B&CAP

Although PSO is a powerful tool for the optimization problems in the continuous search spaces, some applications of the PSO have been reported for the discrete application, e.g. the storage space allocation problem [NIU 16] and B&CAP [HSU 16]. In this section, a PSO algorithm for the B&CAP with time-variant QC assignment, proposed by Hsu [HSU 16], is reviewed. This is an interesting application of converting a continuous search space into a discrete one. The smallest position value (SPV) rule, originally devised by Tasgetiren *et al.* [TAS 06] in a random key GA, is used by Hsu [HSU 16]. The objective function aims at minimizing the total waiting, delay and operation costs.

The approach proposed by Hsu [HSU 16] hybridizes a PSO with two heuristic procedures, which are used to convert the continuous solution space into a discrete solution space and, thus, it is termed HPSO. The HPSO is reported in Algorithm 4.5 and its first step, after parameter initialization, is to create a random swarm of particles. A swarm consists of S^{max} particles, each with $2N$ elements, where N is the number of ships, denoted $X_i^g = \left[x_{i1}^g, x_{i2}^g, \dots, x_{ij}^g, \dots, x_{i(2N)}^g \right]$, $\forall i = 1, \dots, S^{max}$; $\forall g = 1, \dots, g^{max}$, g^{max} being the maximum number of iterations. Since a random key encoding is used, the value of each element of X_i^g is a number in the interval $[0,1]$, initially randomly generated. Figure 4.12 illustrates one sample particle for the HPSO. The *BAP segment* of the solution representation is used to determine the ship berthing sequence by the berth planning heuristic, while the *QCAP segment* is used to determine the ship sequence in the QC assignment heuristic. In each iteration, particles are converted to a B&CAP solution. In the *BAP segment* of the solution, the sequence of the jth ship in the berth planning heuristic algorithm is assigned; and the sequence of the jth ship in the QC assignment heuristic algorithm is determined in the $(j + N)^{th}$ cell (in the *QCAP segment* of the solution). Details of the two heuristic procedures to construct a solution to the B&CAP will be discussed in the next paragraphs of this section.

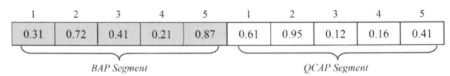

1	2	3	4	5	1	2	3	4	5
0.31	0.72	0.41	0.21	0.87	0.61	0.95	0.12	0.16	0.41

BAP Segment   *QCAP Segment*

Figure 4.12. *An example solution (particle) for the HPSO in the B&CAP*

The fitness value (FV) is given by the weighted summation of the ships' total waiting time, the ships' total delayed time and the total operational cost of the QCs. In the following steps, the best position of the ith particle P_i and the best-known position of the swarm P_b are updated and then the velocity and position of each particle are updated as given in equations [4.48] to [4.53], where p_{ij}, and p_{bj} denote the jth element in P_i and P_b, respectively.

equations [4.49]–[4.51] include the current iteration FV of each particle to update its next velocity and, therefore, its new position, which differs from the PSO original and commonly used equations. The reasoning behind it is that if a particle has a lower (better) FV at the current iteration, then it should have a smaller move (lower velocity) in the next iteration to further exploit the neighborhood; while otherwise, a higher velocity is calculated so that the particle moves further away looking for good solutions elsewhere, this way reinforcing the exploration capabilities.

$$v_{ij}^{g+1} = w_1^g v_{ij}^g + w_2^g \left(p_{ij}^g - x_{ij}^g\right) + w_3^g \left(p_{bj}^g - x_{ij}^g\right) \quad 1 \le j \le 2 \times N \qquad [4.48]$$

$$w_1^g = \frac{1}{1 + e^{-T^g/FV(P_b)}} \qquad\qquad [4.49]$$

$$w_2^g = \frac{2}{1 + e^{-1/FV(X_i) \times T^g}} \qquad\qquad [4.50]$$

$$w_3^g = \frac{2}{1 + e^{-1/FV(P_b) \times T^g}} \qquad\qquad [4.51]$$

$$T^{g+1} = \alpha T^g \qquad\qquad 0 < \alpha < 1 \qquad [4.52]$$

$$x_{ij}^{g+1} = x_{ij}^g + v_{ij}^{g+1} \qquad\qquad 1 \le j \le 2 \times N \qquad [4.53]$$

As said before, two distinct heuristics are used, one for the *BAP segment* and another for the *QCAP segment*. To decide the berthing sequence, the random keys are sorted in ascending order, and their values are replaced by rank values (1 to N). In the case of a tie, a lower rank is given to the ship with a lower identification number. The ships assignment sequence is then given by their ranks and the berth they are assigned to is the one with the least workload (smaller expected handling time for the assigned ships), with ties being broken by berth identification number.

Initialize the parameters for the HPSO ($FV(P_i) = FV(P_b) = M$, M is a big positive number,

Generate the dataset for the problem,

Generate initial *Swarm*,

For $g = 1: g^{max}$,

       For $i = 1: S^{max}$,

              Convert *BAP segment* of particle i into the berth plan,

              For $t = 1: (2 \times N - 1)$, % QC assignment algorithm

                    Identify the next event,

                    Update the list of berthed ships in current stage,

                    Rank the berthed ships according to the *QCAP segment* of particle i,

                    Assign QCs to the berthed ships based on their rank & remaining workload,

              End For % t

              Calculate the *Fitness Value* (FV) for the particle i,

              If $FV\left(X_i^g\right) \leq FV(P_i)$, then $P_i = X_i^g$,

              If $FV\left(X_i^g\right) \leq FV(P_b)$, then $P_b = X_i^g$,

              Update velocity of elements of particle i (Equation [4.48]),

              Update position of elements of particle i (Equation [4.53]),

End For % i

End For % g

Return the best-known solution.

Algorithm 4.5. *Hybrid particle swarm optimization algorithm for the B&CAP*

The QC assignment heuristic simulates the berthing process in stages denoted by t. Stages are defined as the time between two consecutive events, either the arrival of a ship to the terminal or the departure of a ship from the terminal, whichever happens first. In total, there are $2N$ events in a berthing planning horizon. At each stage t, the berthed N_t ships are ranked based on the *QCAP segment* in a similar way as described for the BAP segment. All other ships not yet in the port are ranked 0. Let K denote the total number of available QCs in the berthing horizon and q^{min} and q^{max} denote the minimum and maximum allowed number of QCs to serve a ship, respectively. The number of QCs q_{jt} assigned to a ship in stage t is given by equation [4.54], where R_j is the rank of the jth berthed ship (according to the *QCAP segment* of particle i) and w_{jt} its remaining workload calculated according to equation [4.57], while the initial workload (w_{jt}^*) of a ship, at the first stage it moors at a berth, is declared by the ship operator.

Since this is a time-variant QCAP, the number of assigned QCs may change from stage to stage. At each stage, the serving QCs are assigned to the berthed ships according to their remaining workload relative to the total remaining workload of the ships in that time stage (i.e. $w_{jt}/\sum_{j \in N_t} w_{jt}$). However, any number of QCs that have not been assigned to the ships with lower rank are assigned to the last ranked ship (i.e. the one with the largest random number in the *QCAP segment*). Obviously, the minimum and maximum allowed QCs for each ship should be observed in this procedure.

$$
q_{jt} = \begin{cases} Min\left\{Max\left\{q^{min}, \left\lfloor \dfrac{w_{jt}}{\sum_{j \in N_t} w_{jt}} \times K \right\rfloor\right\}, q^{max}\right\}, & 1 \leq R_j < N_t \\[2em] Min\left\{Max\left\{q^{min}, K - \left(\sum_{R_j=1}^{N_t-1} q_{jt}\right)\right\}, q^{max}\right\}, & R_j = N_t \end{cases}
$$

[4.54]

To identify events in the simulation process of the QC assignment algorithm, the expected departure time (EDT) of the ships is also required. EDT is calculated based on the number of QCs assigned to serve a ship. However, EDT changes whenever the number of assigned QCs changes; thus ships' EDT needs to be calculated at each stage. The first time a ship berths the EDT is calculated as given in equation [4.55] and then in the following as given in equation [4.56]. In these equations, C is the capacity of the QCs in terms of TEUs per hour. Any time that the number of assigned QCs is changed there would be a setup time (denoted by S) for the QCs to start/continue their handling process. The remaining workload of a ship at the end of this stage relative to its workload at the beginning of the time stage is given by equation [4.57], where D_t denotes the duration of stage t.

$$
EDT_{jt} = S + \frac{w_{jt}^*}{q_{jt} \times C} \quad \text{if this is the first stage of the berthed ship} \tag{4.55}
$$

$$
EDT_{jt} = S + \frac{w_{jt}}{q_{jt} \times C} \quad \text{if this is not the first stage of the berthed ship} \tag{4.56}
$$

$$w_{jt} = \left(1 - \frac{D_{(t-1)}}{EDT_{(j-1)}}\right) w_{j(t-1)} \quad \begin{array}{l}\text{if this is not the first stage of the}\\\text{berthed ship}\end{array} \qquad [4.57]$$

Let us illustrate the algorithm by solving a small example, in which five ships are incoming to moor at three berths. The expected arrival time of the ships (hours from time 0 in berthing horizon) and their workload (in TEUs) are reported in Table 4.1. The whole berth area is served by 8 QCs; each of which can handle 25 TEUs per hour. The minimum and a maximum number of allowed QCs per ship are 1 and 4, respectively; and the setup time for the QCs to start their handling process is 0.25 hour.

	Ship j				
	1	2	3	4	5
Arriving time	0.5	1.5	2	2	4
Workload	200	100	75	100	50

Table 4.1. *Data for the example for the B&CAP*

Figure 4.13 shows the steps for the berth planning heuristic algorithm, in which the initial random numbers (Figure 4.13(a)) are converted into ranked numbers (Figure 4.13(b)). Then, the fourth ship is assigned to berth 1 (because all the berths have 0 assigned workload, the berth with the smallest number is selected), and the first and third ships are assigned to berths 2 and 3, respectively. Next, because the current workload of the third ship (and berth 3) is the smallest among the three ships, the second ship is also planned to moor at berth 3. The next berth with the smallest assigned workload is berth 1, where the fifth ship will moor. The final berth plan is shown in Figure 4.13(c).

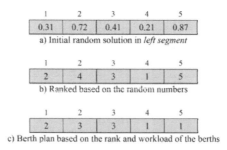

Figure 4.13. *Steps of berth planning heuristic algorithm for the B&CAP example*

The heuristic QC assignment algorithm has been performed for the example presented in Table 4.1, and its stages are depicted in Figure 4.14. Although ship 4 has the highest ranking, in the first stage ship 1 is moored at berth 2, since it is the first one to arrive (smallest expected arrival time). After one hour, ship 2 docks at berth 3. Therefore, ships 1 and 2 got the ranked numbers 1 and 2 according to the random numbers in *QCAP segment* of the solution. In this stage, because the remaining workload of both ships is almost the same and the number of required QCs for both ships is less than the maximum allowed QCs, four QCs are assigned to each ship. The procedure is continuous to assign QCs in the next three stages. The Gantt chart for the B&CAP example is illustrated in Figure 4.15. Time horizon is in hours, and for each ship, the number of assigned QCs in each stage (in parentheses) and the number of handled containers in that stage (above the bar) are reported. It should be noticed that whenever a new ship arrives at the berth area or the number of assigned QCs is changed, setup times are required for the QCs to start their work. Obviously, at times 1.5 and 4.25, there are no required setup times for ships 1 and 3 because the number of assigned QCs is not changed. Events 1, 2, 3, 7 and 8 are the earliest possible start time of ships; and events 4, 5, 6, 9 and 10 are departure times of ships 1, 2, 4, 3 and 5, respectively. Note that ship 3 must wait for the previous ship (ship 2) to finish its service time as they use the same berth; and because the arrival time of ship 5 is later than the completion time of the first berth, there is an idle time for that berth.

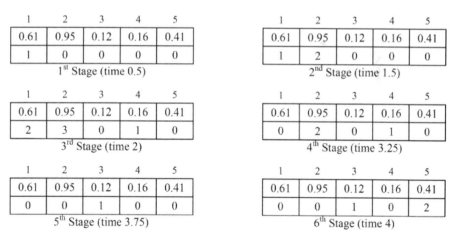

1	2	3	4	5
0.61	0.95	0.12	0.16	0.41
1	0	0	0	0

1st Stage (time 0.5)

1	2	3	4	5
0.61	0.95	0.12	0.16	0.41
1	2	0	0	0

2nd Stage (time 1.5)

1	2	3	4	5
0.61	0.95	0.12	0.16	0.41
2	3	0	1	0

3rd Stage (time 2)

1	2	3	4	5
0.61	0.95	0.12	0.16	0.41
0	2	0	1	0

4th Stage (time 3.25)

1	2	3	4	5
0.61	0.95	0.12	0.16	0.41
0	0	1	0	0

5th Stage (time 3.75)

1	2	3	4	5
0.61	0.95	0.12	0.16	0.41
0	0	1	0	2

6th Stage (time 4)

Figure 4.14. *Stages for the heuristic QC assignment in the B&CAP example*

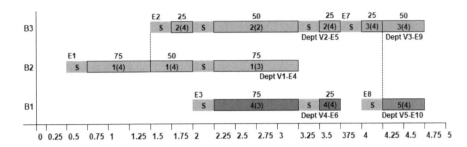

Figure 4.15. *Gant chart for the B&CAP example*

In addition to the HPSO just described, a GA and a hybrid GA have been proposed by Hsu [HSU 16]. The performance of all three algorithms was evaluated through 50 problem instances (with 20 up to 100 ships in the berthing horizon for three berth segments). The HPSO best solutions are 5% and 15% better than those of the HGA and of the GA, respectively. However, from the CPU time point of view, the algorithms' rank is GA, HGA and HPSO. Nevertheless, the HPSO approach computational times were still very low, always below 1829 seconds.

4.4.3. *A simple hybrid GA for the B&CSP*

As already highlighted in section 4.1, the berthing time of a ship is highly dependent on the number of QCs assigned to it and on the scheduling of these QCs. A two-layer MILP model for the B&CAP was proposed by Lee *et al.* [LEE 10], in which the BAP is solved in the first layer and then QC schedules are determined in the second layer. The objective function of the B&CSP is to minimize the makespan of handling all containerships. However, due to the NP-hardness of the problem, a hybrid GA is used to find solutions.

In the discrete BAP, the berth area is divided into some berth segments. The berth segments are numbered from left to right (i.e. the smallest numbered berth segment is the most left one), and for each berth segment, the number of QCs is fixed (although, it is different for various berth segments). This way, when the planner selects a berth, he can assign the QCs as well. QCs operate on the same track and cannot cross one another; in addition, once allocated, no preemption is allowed until all operations of the ship have been concluded [LEE 10]. Ship bays are numbered from left to right (as illustrated in Figure 4.16) and ships approximated processing time (P_j) is known in advance. A ship can depart the terminal once processing in all its bays has been completed. Thus, the completion time of a ship is given by the time of the longest processing time of its bays or by the time of the last finishing QC.

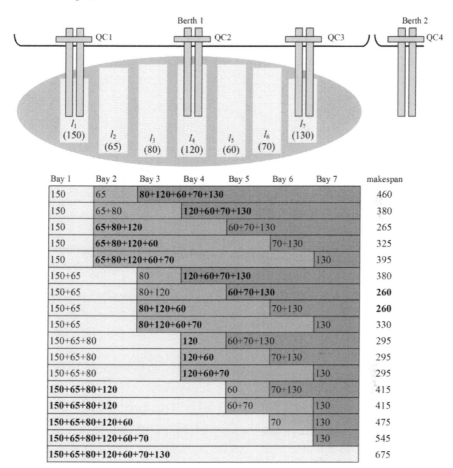

Figure 4.16. *An example of the heuristic algorithm for QC scheduling in the B&CSP*

In the GA developed for the B&CSP, a chromosome is a string with N elements (N being the number of arriving ships), filled with random generated permutation numbers between 1 and N. The chromosome defines the sequence of the ships to be assigned to the berth segments. A heuristic algorithm is applied for the berth planning and an approximation algorithm based on dynamic programming calculates the ship processing time. In this GA (shown in Algorithm 4.6), the offspring chromosomes for the next generation are produced through an order crossover, and a simple swap operator mutates the population to maintain population diversity and thus the exploration abilities of the GA.

Initialize the parameters for the GA,

Generate initial *Population*,

For $g = 1: g^{max}$,

    For $i = 1: Popsize$

        For $j = 1: N$

            Allocate ship in j^{th} cell to a suitable berth (using heuristic algorithm),

            Schedule the QCs in the allocated berth (using dynamic programing),

            Calculate the approximated handling time of the ship,

            Update the earliest completion time of the berth,

        End For % j

        Calculate the *fitness value* for i^{th} chromosome,

    End For % i

    Generate next *Population* using the *Order crossover* operator,

    Mutate the *Population* using *Swap mutation* operator,

End For % g

Return the best-known solution.

Algorithm 4.6. *GA algorithm for the B&CSP*

In the berth planning heuristic algorithm, the chromosome is considered from left to right and the corresponding ships are allocated to idle berths, one at a time. If no such berth exists, then the ship waits until the berth with the earliest completion time becomes available. If there is more than one idle berth (or more than one berth with the same earliest completion time), then the berth with the largest number of QCs is chosen. Ties are broken by choosing the most left located berth. Once a ship has been allocated to a berth, the second algorithm determines the schedule of the berth QCs and returns the processing time of the ship. The berth completion time (which is calculated in the QC scheduling algorithm) is then updated and another following ship is considered, i.e. the berth allocation heuristic is applied to the ship corresponding to the next gene in the chromosome.

The QC scheduling algorithm is a dynamic programming-based heuristic and it supposes that a ship with B bays is allocated to a berth with K QCs. $T[l, l']$ is the total processing time required for bays l to l' (equation [4.58]), and $C[1, l]$ is the minimum latest completion time of the first QC when it operates on bays 1 to l (equation [4.59]). Note that, due to the interference constraints of the QCs, the first QC in the berth should start its operation from bay 1. For the remaining QCs (other than the first one), the minimum latest completion time of the QC k can be calculated through equation [4.60]. In Figure 4.16, all possible options for the QC scheduling for a sample ship assigned to a berth with 3 QCs are reported. Note that the processing time for each bay is shown in parentheses in this figure. The best makespan for this ship is obtained when QC 1 is scheduled to operate on the first and second bays, QC 2 works on the third and fourth bays, and QC 3 on the fifth, sixth and seventh bays. The makespan is 260 minutes.

$$T[l, l'] = \sum_{j=l}^{l'} P_j \tag{4.58}$$

$$C[1, l] = T[1, l] \qquad\qquad \forall l, 1 \leq l \leq B \tag{4.59}$$

$$C[k, l] = \min_{k-1 \leq l' \leq l-1} (\max(C[k-1, l'], T[l'+1, l])) \quad \forall k, 2 \leq k \leq K; \forall l, k \leq l \leq B \tag{4.60}$$

4.5. Conclusions

Chapter four was dedicated to the major planning and scheduling problems for seaside activities. Berth space and time as the two most important resources of the seaports are allocated to the incoming ships in the BAP, which was reviewed for the container terminals and bulk seaports in the first two sections. However, most of the scheduling and planning solutions for the CTs can be implemented in the bulk seaports with minor modifications. Since the QCs are a bottleneck for increasing throughput of the CTs, the QC scheduling is a highly pressuring problem for the seaport operators. The problem and its newer version, the double cycling operations by the QCs, were also reviewed. While the BAP is related to a weekly decision-making level, the QC assignment and scheduling are daily problems. The quality of QC schedule and assignment plans has a great impact on the berthing time of a ship. Thus, berth scheduling and equipment assignment decisions should be integrated; this type of problem has also been reviewed.

5

Problems in Yard Operations

The last chapter of this book is dedicated to the problems related to the transferring area and the storage yard operations. Most of the problems reviewed in this chapter are the most challenging ones for the port operators as they need to be solved on a daily basis. Moreover, for most of the problems, a prompt and reliable solution is needed. The operations start with the allocation of a suitable storage location for the importing and exporting containers, addressed in section 5.1, followed by the operation scheduling for the yard cranes, in section 5.2, while vehicle scheduling problems are reviewed in section 5.3. However, the planning and scheduling problems in the storage yard and the transferring area are interdependent. In the last two sections of this chapter (sections 5.4 and 5.5), some solution methods for these problems are reviewed, and the concluding remarks are highlighted in section 5.6.

5.1. Storage space allocation problem

The storage yard is a temporary destination for importing loads from ships and a departure point for exporting loads. Storage yards are used as an essential massive buffer area between ships and customers who will take the loads in another mode of transportation. Typically, a large portion of the seaport is allocated to the storage yard area; thus, a major part of the seaport workload deals with the operations in this area. Apart from the strategic decision-making processes, such as yard layout design and handling equipment selection, there are tactical and operational decisions that must be made every day: allocating storage space to the loads (especially for the containers) and crane dispatching/scheduling are among the most important ones. The storage yard is divided into yard blocks, where containers are laid side by side (several rows of containers) and are stacked on top of each other or on the ground. Figure 5.1 shows two blocks, each with three rows of containers. These are usually stored in six stacks of up to six tiers. A storage slot for a container can thus be indicated by tier, stack, row and block numbers.

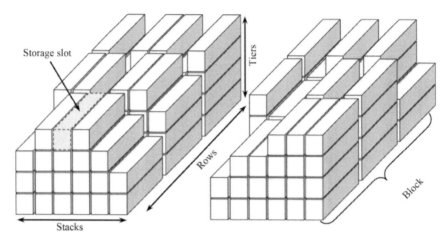

Figure 5.1. *Typical storage yard layout in container terminals*

In fact, the performance of the storage yard operations influences the overall performance of seaport operations. All decisions potentially influence each other mutually and thus a major part of the efforts has been referred to the integrated planning and scheduling methods. This section reviews the storage space allocation problem (SSAP), in which storage spaces are assigned to importing and exporting containers. Finding the best storage space for the importing and exporting containers is an important daily problem in CTs.

The SSAP has been solved for individual containers, determining their allocation to a precise slot (*e.g.* [PAR 11] and [GUL 11]), and for groups of containers, distributing them among the yard blocks (*e.g.* [BAZ 09] and [SHA 13]). The studies on SSAP for individual containers generally use heuristic rules validated by simulation studies. These rules are applied to online decision-making processes when data for the incoming ships are not precise or not available. However, studies associated with the allocation of groups of containers use optimization methods for offline decision-making problems. Evidently, precise data about the arrival/departure times of the importing/exporting containers have a great impact on the quality of the solutions found for the offline SSAP. As an optimization problem, the SSAP can be formulated as a generalized assignment problem and, therefore, it belongs to the NP-hard problems category [BAZ 09].

The objectives of the online SSAP include, but are not limited to, minimizing the storage yard operations cycle time (*i.e.* storage/retrieval and reshuffling times) and the total expected number of reallocations. For online SSAP, Lin and Chiang [LIN 17a] proposed a rule-based heuristic, which allocates slots to containers on a first-come-first-serve basis (the best storage to minimize the service time); however, future digging activities required to reach a container also affect the storage space allocated to the container. Since the time to solve the SSAP is less than 1 s and the practical applications are extremely large and in uncertain environments, the approaches need to be of a heuristic nature. Readers can refer to [CAR 14b] for a review of the studies published on online SSAP before 2012.

For offline SSAP, the most important objective is to balance workload among the yard blocks, followed by the minimization of the traveling time of the handling equipment (cranes and/or vehicles). It is important to minimize workload imbalances, mainly because they force the CT operator to move yard cranes to the block with higher workloads, which is a time-consuming process and leads to unproductive moves by the yard cranes. On the contrary, balanced workloads lead to less congestion of vehicles in the transferring area, because they become evenly distributed among the yard blocks. We note that the berthing time of a containership directly depends on the maximum processing time of the parallel yard cranes working on unloading and/or loading the containership [ZHA 03]. Thus, the balanced workloads can reduce the average container handling time.

A mathematical model and a heuristic rule to solve the SSAP for the exporting containers were developed by Kim and Park [KIM 03], aiming at minimizing travel time from the blocks to the quayside. In the heuristic rule, a container with shorter duration of stay has a higher probability to be allocated to the storage locations. The SSAP of groups of containers was formulated by Zhang *et al.* [ZHA 03], in which a rolling-horizon planning approach is implemented. They decompose the problem into two levels: the first level determines the number of containers allocated to each yard block to balance the workload of the blocks; the second level allocates a specific group of containers associated with the containerships with the objective of minimizing the traveling time between the blocks and the containership. The final objective of the study is to minimize the storage/retrieval time of the containers. Obviously, the decisions in the second level are constrained by the outcomes of the model in the first level. This model was extended by Bazzazi *et al.* [BAZ 09] to include independent decision variables for various types of importing containers. However, the SSAP only involves the first-level decision, *i.e.* allocating the number of containers being stored in the yard blocks. Decisions on the specific storage slot for the containers are made during an online process. They have developed a meta-heuristic algorithm to solve the problem. Both the model and the meta-heuristic algorithm are reviewed in sections 5.1.1 and 5.1.2.

The offline SSAP for the importing containers was studied by Yu and Qi [YU 13], aiming at minimizing the expected waiting time for the customers to reach their containers. The study focused on the SSAP of the importing containers and overnight remarshaling operations (idle time of the yard cranes) to re-organize the block space allocation after some containers are retrieved. Moreover, an ant-based algorithm for the SSAP of importing and exporting containers was developed by Sharif and Huynh [SHA 13], in which the containers are dynamically allocated to the storage spaces once they arrive at the terminal (after unloading from the containerships or received from the customers to load on the containerships). Similar to [BAZ 09], they studied SSAP to determine the number of containers being imported to the block, aiming to minimize the workload imbalances among blocks and the travel times of the yard vehicles during the loading and unloading of the containerships.

It is important to note that the SSAP is strictly associated with the scheduling/dispatching problem of vehicles and yard cranes; thus, some researchers studied the integrated scheduling of vehicles and SSAP. The integrated scheduling allocation problems are reviewed in section 5.4.

5.1.1. *Formulation of the SSAP*

In the following paragraphs, an MIP model for the mid-term SSAP is presented, which is modified from that of [BAZ 09]. The model considers the allocation of importing containers to the storage yard, after dividing them into the following two identical subsets: containers with and containers without a known delivery time to the customer. The model extends the one developed by Zhang *et al.* [ZHA 03], by considering different decision variables for various types of containers (different size or weight; empty or refrigerated containers) and their distribution among the blocks. However, allocation of a specific slot for a container within the block remains a decision of the operators in the operational level. The planning horizon for the SSAP can be the next 24 h, being updated at the end of that duration with the available data from the incoming containerships.

The containers without a known delivery time to the customers are assumed to be stored in the yard at least until the end of the planning horizon. Thus, these containers are distributed to the blocks in proportion to their available storage capacity at the beginning of the planning horizon, so as to balance the block densities. Therefore, a portion of the block capacity is dedicated to these containers based on the available data from the incoming containerships during the planning horizon. It is, of course, expected that, for the majority of the importing containers, the delivery time to the customers is known and lies within the planning horizon.

The objective of the MIP for the SSAP is to balance the workload between yard blocks in order to minimize the storage/retrieval times of the containers; it calculates how many containers of each type should be stored in each block. The data required for the SSAP include the type of containers and the allowable blocks for each container type. Moreover, the expected time for a container to be unloaded from the containership and the expected time for it to be delivered to the customers should be determined. Notations for the MIP model of the SSAP are as follows; the model is presented in equations [5.1]–[5.8].

Sets, indices and parameters:	
$\mathcal{B}$	Set of blocks in the storage yard,
$\mathcal{R}$	Set of types of containers,
$\mathcal{T}$	Set of planning periods on the horizon,
b	Index for the blocks in the storage yard, $b \in \mathcal{B}$,
r	Index for the type of containers, $r \in \mathcal{R}$,
t, k	Indices for the periods, $t, k \in \mathcal{T}$,
d_{tkr}	Number of containers of type $r \in \mathcal{R}$ being imported during period $t \in \mathcal{T}$ that will be delivered to customers in period $t + k, (t, k \in \mathcal{T})$,
$\tilde{d}_{btr}$	Number of containers of type $r \in \mathcal{R}$ being imported in block $b \in \mathcal{B}$, during period $t \in \mathcal{T}$, without a known delivery time to the customer,

z_{btr}^0	Number of containers of type $r \in \mathcal{R}$, previously located in block $b \in \mathcal{B}$, to be delivered to customers during period $t \in \mathcal{T}$,
c_b	Storage capacity of block $b \in \mathcal{B}$,
s_{br}	=1, if container type $r \in \mathcal{R}$ can be allocated to block $b \in \mathcal{B}$, and 0 otherwise,
η	Allowed density for the storage blocks,
M	A big positive number.
Decision Variables:	
X_{btkr}	Number of containers of type $r \in \mathcal{R}$ being imported in block $b \in \mathcal{B}$ during period t that will be delivered to customers in period $t + k$, $(t, k \in \mathcal{T})$,
Y_{btr}	Number of containers of type $r \in \mathcal{R}$ being imported in block $b \in \mathcal{B}$ during period $t \in \mathcal{T}$,
Z_{btr}	Number of containers of type $r \in \mathcal{R}$ being delivered to customers during period $t \in \mathcal{T}$ from block $b \in \mathcal{B}$,
V_{btr}	Number of containers of type $r \in \mathcal{R}$ remaining in block $b \in \mathcal{B}$ at the end of period $t \in \mathcal{T}$.

$$Min\ Z = \sum_{t \in \mathcal{T}} \sum_{r \in \mathcal{R}} \left(w_1 \left[\max_{b \in \mathcal{B}}\{Y_{btr}\} - \min_{b \in \mathcal{B}}\{Y_{btr}\} \right] + \right. $$
$$\left. w_2 \left[\max_{b \in \mathcal{B}}\{Y_{btr} + Z_{btr}\} - \min_{b \in \mathcal{B}}\{Y_{btr} + Z_{btr}\} \right] \right), \qquad [5.1]$$

Subject to

$$\sum_{b \in \mathcal{B}} X_{btkr} = d_{tkr} \qquad \forall r \in \mathcal{R}, \forall t \in \mathcal{T}, \forall k \in \{0, ..., (|\mathcal{T}| - t)\}, \quad [5.2]$$

$$Y_{btr} = \tilde{d}_{btr} + \sum_{k=0}^{|\mathcal{T}|-t} X_{btkr} \quad \forall b \in \mathcal{B}, \forall r \in \mathcal{R}, \forall t \in \mathcal{T}, \qquad [5.3]$$

$$Z_{btr} = \sum_{k=0}^{t} X_{b(t-k)kr} + z_{btr}^0 \qquad \forall b \in \mathcal{B}, \forall r \in \mathcal{R}, \forall t \in \mathcal{T}, \qquad [5.4]$$

$$V_{btr} = V_{b(t-1)r} + Y_{btr} - Z_{btr} \qquad \forall b \in \mathcal{B}, \forall r \in \mathcal{R}, \forall t \in \mathcal{T}, \qquad [5.5]$$

$$\sum_{r \in \mathcal{R}} V_{btr} \leq \eta c_i \qquad \forall b \in \mathcal{B}, \forall r \in \mathcal{R}, \forall t \in \mathcal{T}, \qquad [5.6]$$

$$Y_{btr} \leq M\, s_{br} \qquad \forall b \in \mathcal{B}, \forall r \in \mathcal{R}, \forall t \in \mathcal{T}, \qquad [5.7]$$

$$X_{btkr}, Y_{btr}, Z_{btr}, V_{btr} \in \mathbb{W} \quad \forall b \in \mathcal{B}, \forall r \in \mathcal{R}, \forall t, k \in \mathcal{T}. \qquad [5.8]$$

The objective of the model (equation [5.1]) minimizes unbalances in the workload of the blocks for all types of container in the whole planning horizon. The first term calculates the unbalances for the importing containers, while the second term calculates unbalances for both importing containers and containers being delivered to the customers. Although the objective function is nonlinear, it can be easily converted to a linear function by adding some constraints to the model (the interested reader is referred to [ZHA 03]). Constraint [5.2] assures that all the importing containers with known delivery time to customers are allocated to the yard blocks; thus, the total number of such containers being imported in all the blocks in a given period equals the number of importing containers in that period. It is important to note that it is assumed that the known delivery time of a container is within the planning horizon, $k \in \{0, ..., (|\mathcal{T}| - t)\}$, where $|\mathcal{T}|$ is the number of periods in the planning horizon. Constraint [5.3] calculates the total number of importing containers in a block in each period, whether they have a known delivery time in a future period, $\sum_{k=0}^{|\mathcal{T}|-t} X_{itkr}$ (up to the end of the planning horizon), or there is no information regarding their delivery times, $\tilde{d}_{itr}$. Constraint [5.4] calculates the number of containers being delivered to the customers during each period, which includes the containers that have already been imported to the yard block and should be delivered to the customer in the current period, $\sum_{k=0}^{t} X_{i(t-k)kr}$, plus the containers that were in the block at the beginning of the planning horizon and should also be delivered to the customers during the current period, z_{itr}^{0}. Constraint [5.5] calculates the number of the remaining containers at the end of each period (inventory level) for each block: the inventory level of the previous period plus the total number of importing containers minus the total number of delivered containers during the current period. Constraint [5.6] assures that the inventory level for each block, for all types of containers, is less than the allowed density level of that block, ηc_i. This is important to keep a specific portion of the capacity of each block free for the required shuffling operations within the block. Constraint [5.7] ensures that a special type of container is allocated to a specific block only if the allocation is allowed. Finally, constraint [5.8] defines the nature of the decision variables, which are non-negative integers.

5.1.2. GA for the SSAP

Because the SSAP is an NP-hard problem, exact methods are not suitable to solve it in large size and practical cases. A genetic algorithm [BAZ 09] with a complex representation of the solution for the SSAP is presented in this section. The same notations as the MIP model presented in section 5.1.1 are used for the GA in this section, and the objective function for the GA is presented in equation [5.1]. Since most of the constraints for the SSAP are as equality, it is very difficult to find feasible solutions for the problem. Thus, the GA spends much time and effort in finding these feasible solutions. As can be seen from the MIP model in section 5.1.1, the most important decision variable for the problem is X_{itkr}, and the other variables can be calculated using this variable. Thus, a four-dimensional matrix $(i \times t \times k \times r)$ represents a real-encoded chromosome for the GA, as shown in Figure 5.2. The chromosome represents the example of three types of containers being imported in three periods and stored temporarily in three yard blocks. For instance, the cell in the 2nd row of the 1st column in Figure 5.2 indicates that 30 containers of type 1, imported in the first period and delivered to the customer in the second period, should be stored in block 1. Obviously, knowing X_{itkr} and $\tilde{d}_{itr}$ (which is calculated through a heuristic method), it is possible to calculate the other decision variables for the problem (i.e. Y_{itr}, Z_{itr} and V_{itr}) and thus the objective value for the chromosome.

| | | $t = 1$ | | | $t = 2$ | | | $t = 3$ | | |
		$r = 1$	$r = 2$	$r = 3$	$r = 1$	$r = 2$	$r = 3$	$r = 1$	$r = 2$	$r = 3$
$i = 1$	$k = 0$	$r = 2$	$r = 3$	15	40	25	50	10	15	20
	$k = 1$	30	40	20	35	45	30	0	0	0
	$k = 2$	25	10	25	0	0	0	0	0	0
$i = 2$	$k = 0$	$X_{2101}=26$	0	30	25	0	15	35	0	40
	$k = 1$	30	0	15	15	0	35	0	0	0
	$k = 2$	40	0	10	0	0	0	0	0	0
$i = 3$	$k = 0$	$X_{3101}=15$	45	35	30	15	23	50	25	35
	$k = 1$	30	5	40	10	25	45	0	0	0
	$k = 2$	35	30	30	0	0	0	0	0	0

Figure 5.2. A sample chromosome for the GA in the SSAP

There are three main constraints that should be observed on a feasible chromosome. First, it is forbidden to have numbers other than zero in some cells. On the one hand, some specific types of containers are not allowed to be stored in a specific block (*i.e.* $S_{ir} = 0$), for example, containers of type 2 are not allowed to be stored in the 2nd block (shaded cells in Figure 5.2). On the other hand, it is obvious that containers being imported in a period cannot be delivered to the customers later than the end of the planning horizon (they are planned to be delivered to the customers in subsequent planning horizons). For example, the cell in the 6th row and 4th column has to get a zero value, because it represents containers that are being imported in the 2nd period, and will be delivered to the customer in the 4th period (which is beyond the end of current planning horizon). Second, constraint [5.2] should be observed, which means that the number of containers allocated to all the blocks should be equal to the total number of incoming containers in a specific period of time. For example, according to Figure 5.2, there are 76 containers of type 1 being imported during the 1st period that will be delivered to the customers during the same period and are distributed in blocks 1 to 3 ($X_{1101} + X_{2101} + X_{3101} \rightarrow 35+26+15=76$). Third, the level of remaining containers in each block, at the end of each period, should be less than its capacity. After creating the chromosomes, they are checked against the third constraint ($V_{itr} \leq \eta C_i$), and if the chromosome is not feasible, a penalty cost $w(V_{itr} - \eta C_i)$ is added to its objective value, leading to the elimination of the chromosome from the next generations. The first two constraints are observed during the process of creating an initial population and the next generations (as described in the following paragraphs).

The procedure of creating an initial chromosome is shown in Algorithm 5.1. This procedure guarantees that a feasible solution according to the first and second sets of constraints is created. If the procedure is repeated as the population size, then the initial random population is created. Here, it is described through an example. In the first step, the cells with $t + k > |T|$ are filled with zero (*e.g.* $X_{1221} = 0$). In the second step, a random integer number in $[0, S_{ir} \times d_{tkr}], \forall t, k, r$ is allocated to the upper cell of the columns (*i.e.* $i = 1$). We note that $S_{ir} = 0$ means that a specific type of container is not allowed to be stored in a specific block. For example, according to the data presented in Figure 5.2, X_{1101} should be an integer number in the interval $[0, 76]$. For the second cell in each column, the remaining number of containers is calculated (*i.e.* $d_{tkr} - X_{1tkr}$) and a random integer number in $[0, S_{ir} \times (d_{tkr} - X_{1tkr})]$, $\forall t, k, r$ is allocated to the cell. This process is repeated for all the cells in the column. Obviously, for the last cell in each column (other than the cells with zero value), all the remaining containers should be allocated to the cell.

To create the new generations, an arithmetic crossover operator (presented in equation [5.9]) mates any two selected parents. The parents are selected using the roulette wheel selection schema. The arithmetic crossover guarantees the production of feasible offspring if the parents are feasible. Because the numbers in the chromosome should be integers, only the integer part is allocated to the offspring. Obviously, selecting the integer parts for the offspring leads to some containers not being allocated to any block (*i.e.* $d_{tkr} - \sum_{i \in B} X_{itkr}^{offspring}$). Heuristically, these containers are allocated to the block with the minimum allocated number of containers (*i.e.* $\min_{i \in B} \{X_{itkr}^{offspring}\}$, $\forall t, k, r$).

$$X_{itkr}^{offspring} = \lfloor \lambda \times X_{itkr}^{Parent\ 1} + (1 - \lambda) \times X_{itkr}^{Parent\ 2} \rfloor \qquad 0 \leq \lambda \leq 1 \qquad [5.9]$$

For the mutation operator, the novel *stepping stone* mutation procedure is used, which is inspired by the stepping stone method of the classical transportation problem. The mutation operator guarantees the generation of feasible chromosomes if the originally selected chromosome is feasible. For a randomly selected chromosome (offspring or parent), the blocks with maximum and minimum allocated containers are identified (*i.e.* $X_{ptkr} = \max_{i \in B} \{X_{itkr}\}$, $\forall t, k, r$ and $X_{qtkr} = \min_{i \in B} \{X_{itkr}\}$, $\forall t, k, r$), and their differences are calculated ($\delta_{tkr} = X_{ptkr} - X_{qtkr}$). Then, the values of X_{ptkr} and X_{ptkr} are mutated according to equations [5.10] and [5.11]. Apparently, the mutation operator is repeated $t \times k \times r$ times for each selected chromosome.

$$X_{ptkr} = X_{ptkr} - \left\lceil \delta_{tkr} / 2 \right\rceil \qquad\qquad [5.10]$$

$$X_{qtkr} = X_{qtkr} + \delta_{tkr} - \left\lceil \delta_{tkr} / 2 \right\rceil \qquad\qquad [5.11]$$

$D = d_{tkr}$

For $r = 1: |\mathcal{R}|$

    For $t = 1: |\mathcal{T}|$

        For $k = 1: |\mathcal{T}|$

            For $i = 1: (|\mathcal{B}| - 1)$

                If $t + k > |\mathcal{T}|$

$$X_{itkr} = 0$$

                Else,

$$X_{itkr} = randbetween\ [0, D],$$

                End %If

$$D = D - X_{itkr}$$

            End %i

$$X_{|\mathcal{B}|tkr} = D$$

        End %k

    End %t

End %r

Algorithm 5.1. *Procedure to create a random initial chromosome for the GA in the SSAP*

Once the new offspring is created, only the members whose objective values are less than the average objective value of the parents are allowed to be in the next generation of the GA [BAZ 09]. The GA is run for a predetermined number of generations or until the standard deviation of the objective values of the current population is less than a predetermined level. The GA was evaluated in 22 numerical test cases of different sizes [BAZ 09], six of which have been solved using the MIP model presented in section 5.2. For these test cases, near-optimal solutions found by the GA were 5% worse than the optimal solutions on average. Because the problem is too difficult to solve, CPU time for the GA increases as the problem size increases.

5.2. Yard crane scheduling

As discussed in section 5.1, the storage yard is the temporary destination of every container in the CTs. For ease of readership, in this section, all types of cranes in the storage yard are called yard cranes or YCs (either the manned or the automated ones) unless the specific type of crane is emphasized. Typically, there are four types of operations in the storage yards, viz. storage, retrieval, reshuffling and housekeeping. In the storage operation (for the importing containers), a yard crane picks up a container from the L/U station (*i.e.* unloads a vehicle) and moves it to the specific storage slot predetermined in the SSAP. Similarly, in the retrieval operation (for the exporting containers), a YC picks up a container from its storage slot and moves it to the L/U station to load it on a vehicle. In the retrieval operation, some reshuffling may be required for the YC to reach the desired container, when this is stored beneath some other containers in the stack. In some occasions, the reshuffling operation is assumed independent of the retrieval operation, that is, it can be performed by another YC. The housekeeping operations consist of reshuffling operations that are predicted to be required for the future retrieval operations. Thus, the CT operators usually plan the housekeeping operations during the night or the periods with lower workloads. Moreover, the YCs are also used in the storage yard to receive and/or deliver the containers from and/or to the customers. A comprehensive review of the studies related to the planning of these four types of operations can be found in [CAR 14b].

Compared to QCs, yard cranes move in longer distances and need to perform additional operations (*i.e.* reshuffling and housekeeping operations as well as dealing with the customers in the land side). Moreover, YCs are bulky and operate slowly. Thus, in the CTs, the yard cranes are usually known as the bottleneck of a terminal, while the QCs are considered the most important equipment to deal with the ships. As adding more yard cranes is impractical, due to their high expenses, the higher productive operations of the existing yard cranes are of vital importance. Yard crane scheduling problem (YCSP) consists of finding a suitable sequence of storage and/or retrieval operations (including the required reshuffling operations) in the storage yard. Typically, the YC assignment (or dispatching) is decided in the YCSP as well. The typical objectives of the YCSP include, but are not limited to, minimizing the makespan, the total lateness and earliness as well as the deadhead moves of the YCs. The YC scheduling has a significant impact on the berthing time of the ships and thus has been studied widely. A comprehensive review on yard crane scheduling for manned and automated yard cranes can be found in [SPR 16] and [HUA 17]; moreover, Boysen *et al.* [BOY 17] reviewed and classified the general crane scheduling in industrial applications, including the container terminals. Evidently, the efficient scheduling of YCs greatly depends on the level of coordination with other equipment in the CTs (the vehicles and the QCs). Thus, many researchers focused on the integrated scheduling methods for this equipment, which is further reviewed in section 5.5.

In an early research, the YCSP was formulated by Ng and Mak [NG 05] with the aim of minimizing the sum of job waiting times. They proposed a branch and bound algorithm to solve the YCSP optimally and proved that yard crane scheduling is an NP-complete problem. The work was extended to multi-YC scheduling by Chen and Langevin [CHE 11] to include the interference constraint of cooperating multi-cranes in the storage yard (YCs cannot cross each other, and adjacent YCs must keep an operational safety distance). In general, multiple manned yard cranes are cooperating in several yard blocks, unlike AYCs, which work on rails, fixed to specific yard blocks. To solve the problem of multi-YCSP, Chen and Langevin [CHE 11] proposed a GA and a TS algorithm. Their work is further described in sections 5.2.1 and 5.2.2. For the multi-YCSP, a hybrid algorithm employing heuristic rules and parallel GA was proposed by He *et al.* [HE 10], with the aim of minimizing the total delayed workloads in addition to total time, when YCs move from one block to another. The heuristic algorithm allocates the YCs to the yard blocks to balance the workload between the blocks; the GA optimizes the sequence of storage and/or retrieval operations. The YCSP was solved by Liang *et al.* [LIA 13] with a multi-objective GA to minimize the total completion time of all the YCs and the variance of each yard crane completion time (*i.e.* to maximize balanced distribution of workload).

Scheduling of two cooperating AYCs (twin cranes) in each yard block was formulated as two MILP models and one nonlinear mathematical model by Hu *et al.* [HU 16], where both routing and sequencing of the storage and/or retrieval operations are optimized, considering the interference constraints. The two AYCs cooperate to serve both sides of the yard blocks (transferring area and landside). While each of the two cooperating AYCs in a yard block serve one side of the yard block and share the operations in the middle of the block, the idea of crossover AYCs allows the cranes to pass each other and serve both sides of the block. Crossover AYCs consist of one smaller and one larger AYC, working on the inner and outer rails, to allow their flexible movement. A graphical scheduling method for the scheduling of two crossover AYCs was proposed by Briskorn and Angeloudis [BRI 16]. Moreover, a branch and bound algorithm was developed by Speer [SPE 16] for the real-time scheduling of two crossover AYCs. They have extended the research to include two cooperating small AYCs and one large AYC, which can move on top of the two smaller ones (similar to the crossover AYCs). Recently, a simple but effective heuristic based on the "first come first serve" and "nearest neighbor" has been proposed by Gharehgozli et al. [GHA 17] for the scheduling of cooperative AYCs, which is tested through a simulation study.

In recent years, green transportation has gained more attention in the literature and in practice. For instance, [HE 15a] developed an MIP model for the YCSP, considering a trade-off between efficiency and energy consumption. They simplified the problem by converting the YCSP into a vehicle routing problem. Furthermore, a hybrid PSO–GA algorithm was developed to optimize the problem. The PSO is applied to search the local area, while the GA performs the global search.

5.2.1. *Mathematical formulation of the YCSP*

An MILP model for the YCSP was developed by Chen and Langevin [CHE 11], which is modified and described in this section. The yard crane scheduling problem is defined on a set of jobs, in which the storage and/or retrieval operations of containers in a scheduling horizon are considered. The storage yard is divided into yard blocks, in which containers are stored in rows (see Figure 5.1). It is assumed that the process time for the retrieval of a container is independent of the process sequence and the YC assigned to perform it. However, certain precedence relations (*e.g.* due to the process sequence by the QCs) were already defined between the containers.

A set of available YCs is present in the storage yard that can move among the blocks (*i.e.* they are not dedicated to the blocks). However, usually, the movement of a YC inside a yard block is much easier and less time-consuming than its movement between two yard blocks. Moreover, it is preferable to avoid such inter-block movements, due to possible traffic jams in the storage yard and the loss of crane capacity. Thus, it is assumed that a YC can move to another yard block only once in the scheduling horizon (typically, in practice, the CT operator predicts the workload of the next day and moves the YCs to the busiest yard blocks during the night or the periods with the lowest workload). Moreover, due to the limitations of block size and for safety reasons, only two YCs at most are allowed to serve each yard block in the scheduling horizon. Similarly, to avoid collisions between YCs, any two adjacent containers in the same block (*i.e.* the containers stored in the slots whose distance is less than five rows) cannot be processed by two YCs simultaneously. These relationships are known in advance. Furthermore, the MILP model observes the "crossing interference", that is, YCs cannot cross each other to process a container located on the other side of the YC. Sets and notations for the MILP model of the YCSP are reported as follows; the model is presented in equations [5.12]–[5.30].

Sets, indices and parameters:	
$\mathcal{J}$	Set of storage and/or retrieval jobs (containers) in the scheduling horizon,
$\mathcal{C}$	Set of yard cranes in the storage yard,
$\mathcal{B}$	Set of blocks in the storage yard,
i, j, k, m	Indices for the jobs (containers), $i, j, k, m \in \mathcal{J}$,
c	Index for the yard cranes, $c \in \mathcal{C}$,
$b, \textit{b}$	Indices for the yard blocks, $b, \textit{b} \in \mathcal{B}$,
$\mathcal{P}$	Set of pairs of containers (i, j), with precedence relationship. If $(i, j) \in \mathcal{P}$, then container $i \in \mathcal{J}$ must be processed before container $j \in \mathcal{J}$,
$\mathcal{U}$	Set of pairs of containers $(i, j \in \mathcal{J})$ that cannot be processed at the same time for safety reasons,
p_i	Processing time of container $i \in \mathcal{J}$,
l_i	Block number for container $i \in \mathcal{J}$,
r_i	Row number for container $i \in \mathcal{J}$,
$\{f, l\}$	First and last dummy jobs (containers) to be processed by each YC,
t_{ijc}	Time for YC $c \in \mathcal{C}$ to travel from container $i \in \mathcal{J}$ to container $j \in \mathcal{J}$ (including the first and last dummy jobs),
N_b^0	Number of YCs in block $b \in \mathcal{B}$ at the beginning of scheduling horizon,
M	A big positive number.
Decision Variables:	
X_{ijc}	=1, if container $j \in \mathcal{J}$ is immediately processed after container $i \in \mathcal{J}$, on YC $c \in \mathcal{C}$, and 0 otherwise,
Y_{ij}	=1, if process of container $j \in \mathcal{J}$ starts after completion of container $i \in \mathcal{J}$, and 0 otherwise,

$Z_{b\beta c}$	=1, if YC $c \in \mathcal{C}$ moves from block $b \in \mathcal{B}$ to block $\beta \in \mathcal{B}$ during the scheduling horizon, and 0 otherwise,
W_{ij}^{km}	An auxiliary binary variable to avoid crossing of YCs,
S_i	Starting time for the processing of container $i \in \mathcal{J}$,
C_{max}	Longest completion time for the jobs.

$$Min \ Z = C_{max}, \qquad\qquad [5.12]$$

Subject to

$$\sum_{j \in \mathcal{J} \cup \{l\}} X_{fjc} = 1 \qquad \forall c \in \mathcal{C}, \qquad [5.13]$$

$$\sum_{i \in \mathcal{J} \cup \{f\}} \sum_{c \in \mathcal{C}} X_{ijc} = 1 \qquad \forall j \in \mathcal{J}, \qquad [5.14]$$

$$\sum_{i \in \mathcal{J} \cup \{f\}} X_{ikc} - \sum_{j \in \mathcal{J} \cup \{l\}} X_{kjc} = 0 \qquad \forall k \in \mathcal{J}, \forall c \in \mathcal{C}, \qquad [5.15]$$

$$Z_{l_i l_j c} \geq X_{ijc} \qquad \forall i, j \in \mathcal{J} | l_i \neq l_j, \forall c \in \mathcal{C}, \qquad [5.16]$$

$$N_b^0 + \sum_{\beta \in \mathcal{B} | b \neq \beta} \sum_{c \in \mathcal{C}} Z_{\beta bc} \leq 2 \qquad \forall b \in \mathcal{B}, \qquad [5.17]$$

$$\sum_{\beta \in \mathcal{B} | b \neq \beta} Z_{b \beta c} \leq 1 \qquad \forall b \in \mathcal{B}, \forall c \in \mathcal{C}, \qquad [5.18]$$

$$C_{max} \geq S_i + p_i \qquad \forall i \in \mathcal{J} \qquad [5.19]$$

$$S_j \geq S_i + p_i + t_{ijc} + M\left(X_{ijc} - 1\right) \quad \forall i, j \in \mathcal{J}, \forall c \in \mathcal{C}, \qquad [5.20]$$

$$S_j \geq S_i + p_i \qquad \forall (i, j) \in \mathcal{P}, \qquad [5.21]$$

$$S_j - S_i - p_i \leq M \, Y_{ij} \qquad \forall i, j \in \mathcal{J}, \qquad [5.22]$$

$$S_i + p_i - S_j \leq M\left(1 - Y_{ij}\right) \forall i, j \in \mathcal{J}, \qquad [5.23]$$

$$Y_{ij} + Y_{ji} = 1 \qquad\qquad \forall (i,j) \in \mathcal{U}, \qquad\qquad [5.24]$$

$$\sum_{c \in \mathcal{C}} X_{ikc} \leq Y_{ij} + Y_{ji} \qquad\qquad \forall i,j,k \in \mathcal{J} | l_i = l_j = l_k, r_i < r_j < r_k, \quad [5.25]$$

$$\sum_{c \in \mathcal{C}} X_{jkc} \leq Y_{ij} + Y_{ji} \qquad\qquad \forall i,j,k \in \mathcal{J} | l_i = l_j = l_k, r_k < r_i < r_j, \quad [5.26]$$

$$\sum_{c \in \mathcal{C}} X_{imc} \leq Y_{ij} + Y_{ji} + M \left(1 - W_{ij}^{km}\right) \begin{array}{l} \forall i,j,k,m \in \mathcal{J} | l_i = l_k = l_m = l_j, \\ r_i < r_k < r_m < r_j, \end{array} \qquad [5.27]$$

$$\sum_{c \in \mathcal{C}} X_{jkc} \leq Y_{ij} + Y_{ji} + M \, W_{ij}^{km} \qquad \begin{array}{l} \forall i,j,k,m \in \mathcal{J} | l_i = l_k = l_m = l_j, \\ r_i < r_k < r_m < r_j, \end{array} \qquad [5.28]$$

$$X_{ijc}, Y_{ij}, Z_{b\&c} \in \{0,1\} \qquad \forall i,j \in \mathcal{J} \cup \{f,l\}, \forall b, \& \in \mathcal{B}, \forall c \in \mathcal{C}, \quad [5.29]$$

$$S_i, C_{max} \in \mathbb{R}^+ \qquad\qquad \forall i \in \mathcal{J}. \qquad\qquad [5.30]$$

The objective function (equation [5.12]) for the MILP model aims to minimize the makespan of the complete retrieval of a set of containers. Constraint [5.13] confirms that there is only one retrieval operation for each crane after its initial dummy starting operation. Constraint [5.14] assures that each container is processed by only one YC, and constraint [5.15] defines the sequence of operations for each YC. Constraint [5.16] defines that a YC has to move from a yard block to another if two of its immediately consequent operations are located in two different yard blocks (*i.e.* $l_i \neq l_j$). The number of YCs in each block (including its initially allocated YCs and the cranes that will move there during the scheduling horizon) should not exceed two, which is guaranteed in constraint [5.17]. For instance, if there are two YCs in a block at the beginning of the scheduling horizon (*i.e.* $N_b^0 = 2$), then no other YC can move there, even after one or both YCs leave that block during the scheduling horizon. This is to reduce traffic jams in the yard area, due to unnecessary movement of YCs between the blocks. Similarly, constraint [5.18] restricts YCs to move only once during the scheduling horizon from one block to another. The makespan is calculated in constraint [5.19], which is the longest completion time of all the retrieval operations in the scheduling horizon. Constraint [5.20] calculates the starting time of each operation, which is the completion time of the previous operation of the YC (*i.e.* $S_i + p_i$), plus its travel time to reach the location of the next operation, t_{ijc}. If container i is the precedent of container j, then the starting time of container j should be longer than the completion time of container i, which is guaranteed in constraint [5.21]. Constraints [5.22] and [5.23] define Y_{ij}, such that $Y_{ij} = 1$ if operations on container j start after completion of container i; for the containers that should not be processed at the same time (*i.e.* $(i, j) \in \mathcal{U}$), either Y_{ij} or Y_{ji} should be equal to one, which is guaranteed by constraint [5.24].

Suppose three containers i, j and k are located in the same block and $r_i < r_j < r_k$, if containers i and j are processed simultaneously by two YCs ($Y_{ij} + Y_{ji} = 0$), then the YC that processed container i cannot cross the other YC to reach container k, which is located after container j, as confirmed in constraint [5.25]; similarly, if container k is located before container i in the same block (*i.e.* $r_k < r_i < r_j$), the YC that processed container j cannot cross the other YC to reach container k, as confirmed in constraint [5.26]. In a similar case, suppose four containers i, j, k and m are located in the same block and $r_i < r_k < r_m < r_j$; if containers i and j are processed simultaneously by two YCs (*i.e.* $Y_{ij} + Y_{ji} = 0$), then the two YCs cannot cross each other to process containers located in between containers i and j (*i.e.* containers k and m). Thus, either $\sum_{c \in \mathcal{C}} X_{jkc}$ or $\sum_{c \in \mathcal{C}} X_{imc}$ can gain 1, while the other has to be 0. This is stated in constraints [5.27] and [5.28] using an auxiliary variable W_{ij}^{km}. Finally, constraints [5.29] and [5.30] determine the nature of the decision variables.

5.2.2. A hybrid TS algorithm for the YCSP

The multi-YC scheduling problem is a complex NP-hard problem, meaning that for large test cases or real practices, the MILP model fails to find optimum solutions for the problem. Thus, a Tabu search algorithm developed by Chen and Langevin [CHE 11] is presented in this section, which aims at finding good solutions within a reasonable CPU time, and its objective function is the one presented in equation [5.12]. In the storage yard, $|\mathcal{C}|$ yard cranes serve $|\mathcal{B}|$ yard blocks. The number of containers in the scheduling horizon is denoted by $|\mathcal{J}|$, and the storage location of each container is defined as $L_i \leftarrow (l_i, r_i)$, where l_i and r_i are the storage block and the storage row of the container, respectively. For instance, location of container 1 can be represented as $L_1 \leftarrow (01, 02)$. Similarly, for each YC, the initial position is defined as $L_c \leftarrow (l_c^1, r_c^1)$. Figure 5.3 illustrates a typical layout of the storage yard, in which three YCs serve four yard blocks for the retrieval operations of 12 containers.

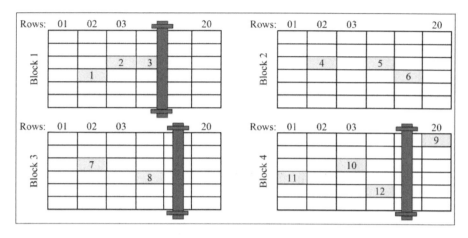

Figure 5.3. *A typical storage yard layout for the YCSP*

The TS algorithm starts with finding an initial random solution for the YCSP. The jobs (containers) are labeled with integer numbers from 1 to $|\mathcal{J}|$, the number of containers in the scheduling horizon. A solution is a string with $|\mathcal{J}|$ elements. For instance, as shown in Figure 5.3, suppose there are 12 containers in four yard blocks in the scheduling horizon. The scheduling string that corresponds to this example is shown in Figure 5.4. The solution string is created randomly, and any infeasibility due to violation of the precedence relations is repaired by swapping the infeasible genes. Suppose container i is a precedent to container j; if the position of container j in the scheduling string is before the position of container i, then these two elements are swapped.

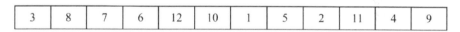

Figure 5.4. *Representation of solution string for the YCSP*

Although the sequence for the retrieval operations of the containers is determined in the solution string, the YC assignment and scheduling follows a greedy algorithm depicted in Algorithm 5.2. In this algorithm, the earliest available YC is assigned to process each container from left to right of the solution string. As mentioned earlier, the initial position of YC c is denoted by L_c. Travel time of YC c to reach location of container i from its current location is denoted by $t(L_c, L_i)$. Each time YC c is assigned to container i, and after it reaches the location of container i, its location is updated to L_i, *i.e.* $L_c = L_i$. Therefore, YC c is available to start processing container i at time $A_c = T_c + t(L_c, L_i)$, where T_c is the completion time of YC c. Evidently, T_c equals zero for all the YCs, in the beginning of the scheduling horizon, and is updated after completion of processing container i: $T_c = A_c + p_i$, where p_i is the process time of container i.

Initialize the parameters,

For $c = 1:|\mathcal{C}|$

$\qquad L_c \leftarrow (l_c^1, r_c^1),$

$\qquad T_c \leftarrow 0,$

End % c

For $i = 1:|\mathcal{J}|$

$\qquad$ For $c = 1:|\mathcal{C}|$

$\qquad\qquad A_c \leftarrow T_c + t(L_c, L_i),$

$\qquad$ End % c

$\qquad$ Sort set of containers, $\mathcal{C}$, according to A_c, in ascending mode,

$\qquad$ For $c = 1:|\mathcal{C}|$

$\qquad\qquad$ If YC c is available, and non-inference constraints are satisfied

$\qquad\qquad\qquad$ Assign YC c to process storage/retrieval operations of container i,

$\qquad\qquad\qquad T_c \leftarrow A_c + p_i,$

$\qquad\qquad\qquad L_c \leftarrow L_i,$

$\qquad\qquad\qquad$ Break,

$\qquad\qquad$ End

$\qquad$ End % c

End % i

$C_{max} \leftarrow \max_c\{T_c\},$

Algorithm 5.2. *Greedy heuristic algorithm to assign YCs in the YCSP*

As said before, the earliest available YC, that is, the YC with least A_c, is assigned to each container. However, assignment of YCs to the containers follows four main rules to identify the available YCs for a container:

– There should not be more than two YCs in each block;

– YCs that moved between blocks once earlier in the algorithm are not available for the containers stored in the other blocks;

– A YC cannot cross the location of another YC to reach its next assigned container;

– Two YCs cannot be assigned to process two near containers.

Once the YC assignment heuristic algorithm finishes, the makespan for the solution string is the longest completion time of the YCs (*i.e.* $\max_c \{T_c\}$).

The TS algorithm (shown in Algorithm 5.3) explores a possible reduction in the makespan by swapping two elements (α, β) of the solution string (denoted by π) and thus creating neighbor solutions (denoted by π'). A feasible swap operator does not violate the precedence relations between the containers, that is, if container i is a precedent to container j, after the swapping, the position of container i should be before container j in the neighbor solution string; otherwise, the swap operator is not feasible. The neighbors of a solution consist of all solutions created by a feasible swap operator. Obviously, the number of neighbors increases drastically by increasing the number of containers in the scheduling horizon. Therefore, Chen and Langevin [CHE 11] proposed to create $N(\pi') = |\mathcal{J}| / |\mathcal{B}|$ neighbor solutions by randomly swapping elements in the solution string. After creating the neighbor set for the current solution, the greedy heuristic algorithm is applied to calculate makespan for all the neighbor solutions (*i.e.* $C_{max}(\pi'_i), \forall i = \{1, ..., N(\pi')\}$). The neighbor solutions are sorted according to the makespan, in ascending mode.

After sorting the neighbor solutions, if the first neighbor solution has a lower makespan than the best solution, the best and current solutions (π^*, π) and their makespans $(C_{max}(\pi^*), C_{max}(\pi))$ are replaced by the first sorted neighbor solution (π'_1) and its makespan $(C_{max}(\pi'_1))$, respectively. Otherwise, the current solution and its makespan are replaced by π'_1, only if it is not listed in the Tabu list (E). If $\pi'_1 \in E$, then the algorithm searches for the next neighbor solution to replace it as the current solution of the problem, that is, the process continues to find a non-Tabu neighbor solution. Each time a neighbor solution is found for the current solution, the corresponding swapped jobs are appended to the current *Tabu list*. However, each Tabu element exits the *Tabu list* after a predetermined number of iterations (T^{max}).

Initialize the parameters,

$\pi \leftarrow$ Initial random feasible solution,

$\pi^* \leftarrow \pi, C^*_{max} \leftarrow C_{max}(\pi^*)$,

$E \leftarrow \emptyset$,

While $g \le g^{max}$ and $j \le g_n^{max}$

        Create random feasible neighbors to π, using swap operator ($\pi'_i, \forall i = \{1, ..., N(\pi')\}$),

        Calculate $C_{max}(\pi'_i), \forall i = \{1, ..., N(\pi')\}$,

        Sort the neighbors according to their $C_{max}(\pi')$, in ascending mode,

        For $i = 1: N(\pi')$ %*Find the neighbor*

            If $C_{max}(\pi'_i) < C^*_{max}$

                $\pi \leftarrow \pi'_i, C_{max} \leftarrow C_{max}(\pi)$,

                $\pi^* \leftarrow \pi'_i, C^*_{max} \leftarrow C_{max}(\pi^*)$,

                $j \leftarrow 0, (\alpha^*, \beta^*) \leftarrow (\alpha_i, \beta_i)$,

                Break,

            Else

                If $(\alpha_i, \beta_i) \notin E$

                    $\pi \leftarrow \pi'_i, C_{max} \leftarrow C_{max}(\pi)$,

                    $j \leftarrow j + 1, (\alpha^*, \beta^*) \leftarrow (\alpha_i, \beta_i)$,

                    Break,

                End

            End

        End % i

        For $t = 1: (T^{max} - 1)$ %*Update Tabu list*

            $E(t) \leftarrow E(t + 1)$,

        End % t

        $E(T^{max}) \leftarrow (\alpha^*, \beta^*)$

$g \leftarrow g + 1$,

End While % g, j

Return the best-known solution.

Algorithm 5.3. *Tabu search algorithm for the YCSP*

The Tabu search algorithm stops in two situations. First, if finding a neighbor solution without improvement in the best makespan continues for g_n^{max}, the TS algorithm stops and reports the best solution. Second, the algorithm stops after a predetermined number of iterations (g^{max}).

The Tabu search algorithm for the YCSP was evaluated by Chen and Langevin [CHE 11] in 60 small-size test cases. The maximum number of iterations was 1,000 (*i.e.* g^{max}=1,000) and the algorithm stopped after 100 non-improving replacement of neighbors (*i.e.* g_n^{max}=100). The Tabu elements exited the Tabu list after five iterations (T^{max}=5). In these test cases, the number of containers was kept between 10 and 20, stored in two yard blocks and served by one or two YCs. Results show that, while the CPU time for the MILP model reached longer than 2,000 s, it was only 1–4 s for the TS algorithm. The TS algorithm found the optimal solutions for these test cases. These test cases have also been solved using a GA proposed by Chen and Langevin [CHE 11], for which the CPU time was between 13 and 38 s; however, it could find the optimum solutions for 59 out of the 60 small-size test cases. For the larger test cases (50–500 containers in the scheduling horizon), the average gap between the solutions found by the TS algorithm and the lower bound solutions was 5.42%, while it was 10.77% for the solutions found by the GA. Similarly to the small-size test cases, the CPU time that the TS algorithm needed to solve the large-size test cases was lower than that for the GA (21–2,211 s vs. 83–3,864 s, respectively).

5.3. Intra-terminal transportation

In container terminals, vehicles are used to transfer containers between the ships and the storage yard. The management of CTs should make the most important strategic decisions on the type and number of vehicles connecting the quayside and the storage yard. On the contrary, various interacting elements affect the performance of vehicles. The primary functions in intra-terminal transportation are defined as follows:

– "Fleet management" is the process of selecting the most suitable type of vehicle (or a mix of various types of vehicles) and determining the number of required vehicles for a CT. As the problem is usually at the strategic level of the decision-making, the objective is to maximize the throughput of the CT in a long-term horizon at the minimum possible cost.

– "Dispatching" is the process of selecting and assigning tasks to vehicles. Objective functions in the dispatching problem usually minimize the makespan of all the loading/unloading tasks of a ship. As there are far more requests than vehicles, once a vehicle is available, it is assigned to a loading/unloading task.

– "Routing" is the process of selecting specific paths taken by the vehicles to reach their destinations. The vehicle routing problem focuses on the definition of paths and routes for the vehicles that eliminate deadlock occasions, congestions and/or ease of dispatching rules. While the number of vehicles used in the transferring area of the CTs is usually large (approximately 50–60), congestion and deadlock occasions are very common.

– "Scheduling" determines the delivery sequence as well as the arrival and departure times of the vehicles at each segment along their prescribed paths to ensure collision-free journeys. Since various types of vehicles are in service (refer to section 1.4), researchers have investigated several scheduling methods that take into account the limitations and constraints of the various types of vehicles.

Vehicle dispatching and scheduling are generally deemed more complicated due to strict pick-up and drop-off constraints, as well as the requirement for a near-perfect synchronization of container operations. The problem can be categorized as a sequence-dependent setup time (SDST) m-parallel machine scheduling, which is a well-known NP-hard problem. Inefficient vehicle schedules will cause a delay in container handling processes and thus affect the productivity of the CTs. A comprehensive literature review on dispatching, routing and scheduling methods for the vehicles in container terminals before 2012 can be found in [CAR 14a].

Due to the high uncertainty level in the transportation requests in container terminals, several researchers worked on simple but efficient heuristic rules for vehicle dispatching in a timely manner. The performance of these heuristic rules has been evaluated through simulation studies. For instance, Cheng et al. [CHE 05] developed a network flow formulation for optimal dispatching of a large number of AGVs. The objective of the algorithm is to minimize the total waiting time of the AGVs and it includes strategies to predict and avoid deadlock situations. The AGVs (and other non-lifting vehicles) are liable to deadlock because they need a crane to be loaded/unloaded. The simulation studies show an increase of 10% in throughput of the fleet of AGVs compared to the application of greedy dispatching rules (*i.e.* least waiting time for the vehicles). A similar study to detect and avoid deadlocks was proposed by Lehmann *et al.* [LEH 06], where two different methods detect the deadlock situation, and the transportation order for the AGVs are either reassigned or modified.

For the lifting vehicles (*e.g.* SCs and ALVs), the deadlock situation is less probable, because they can operate independently of the cranes. A dispatching and scheduling method for the SCs in container terminals was proposed by Das and Spasovic [DAS 03], aiming at the minimization of empty travels by the SCs. The proposed method was tested for Maher Terminals, which is the largest container terminal in the Port of New York, and in several simulation analyses. Results show that their algorithm outperforms two heuristic dispatching methods, viz. closest job assignment and greedy assignment procedure. Later, Hartmann [HAR 04] developed a general scheduling method that is applicable for straddle carriers, AGVs and stacking cranes to minimize the average lateness of the handling tasks. They proposed three dispatching methods, namely deterministic single-pass and multi-pass biased random sampling and a GA-based heuristic dispatching method. As the GA produced better results than the heuristic rules, in a reasonable CPU time, it was proposed for the real-time applications. Nguyen and Kim [NGU 09] proposed a dispatching method for the ALVs coordinated with the QCs. They proposed an MIP model for the problem aiming at minimizing the total travel time of the ALVs and total delays in tasks of QCs. A heuristic algorithm was developed to convert buffer constraints into time window constraints and dispatching of the ALVs based on the earliest available vehicle. It was shown that the buffer capacity highly influences the performance of this integrated scheduling method.

In recent years, the capacity of the vehicles has been increased to transfer 1 FEU or larger containers. Thus, they can carry two TEUs or even more of the smaller containers. In practice, it is not possible to have two fleets of vehicles to transfer larger containers individually in the CTs. Thus, multi-load traveling of the vehicles is considered as a new technique to increase the capacity of the vehicles in the transferring area and to decrease deadhead travels by the vehicles. However, although this is an efficient dispatching method, in practice, it is rarely used in the CTs [GRU 06]. A general description of the multi-load vehicles can be found in [CAR 14a]. An early discussion on multi-load AGVs can be found in [GRU 04]. The problem has been formulated as an MILP model, aiming at minimization of total lateness. They developed a flexible priority rule-based approach to control AGVs in an online logistic system. The total lateness of the AGVs under various scenarios is the objective function of their method. The dispatching rule solves the problem iteratively in low CPU time and thus can be applied to an online control system. The work was extended by Grunow *et al.* [GRU 06] to include all the transportation tasks in a scheduling horizon in an off-line dispatching method. They developed a simulation model to compare the off-line to the online approaches for twin-load dispatching of the AGVs. The mathematical model proposed by Grunow *et al.* [GRU 04] was simplified by Klerides and Hadjiconstantinou [KLE 11], yet it is efficient and useful. The new model chained a sequence of tasks for the vehicles, thus decreasing significantly the number of binary variables. The mathematical model developed by Klerides and Hadjiconstantinou [KLE 11] is reviewed later in section 5.3.1.

The fleet sizing and routing problem was the object of some research efforts, as found in the literature. As an instance, a two-stage method to calculate the minimum number of required vehicles in a planning horizon and the routing of the vehicles was proposed by Koo *et al.* [KOO 05]. In the first stage, a simple and quick mathematical model finds a lower bound for the number of vehicles, considering the overall transportation requirements in the planning horizon. In the second stage, a Tabu search algorithm constructs a vehicle routing and calculates the exact vehicle requirements on the horizon. The fleet sizing and routing problem is reviewed in section 5.3.2. A routing method for the AGV in container terminals was developed by Jeon *et al.* [JEO 10], where the waiting time for each vehicle, due to interferences among vehicles during the traveling, is estimated by a Q-learning technique. Then, shortest-time routes inclusive of the expected waiting times for each vehicle are constructed. A general overview of the vehicle routing problem can be further read in [PIL 13] and [LAB 16].

In offline scheduling methods, the sequence, routing and/or scheduling of a set of vehicles (*e.g.* yard trucks or AGVs) are assigned for the transportation of loading and/ or unloading tasks. For example, the vehicle scheduling problem (VSP) was formulated as an MIP model by Ng *et al.* [NG 07]. They proposed a GA using a greedy crossover operator for the problem, which showed a superior performance in the theoretical analysis. Their work will be reviewed in detail in sections 5.3.3 and 5.3.4. In a recent study, a dispatching and scheduling method for intelligent and autonomous vehicles (IAVs) was developed by Gelareh *et al.* [GEL 13], which is an extension to the study conducted by Ng *et al.* [NG 07] for the AGVs. Two IAVs can join to transport containers larger than 1 TEU (*e.g.* 1 FEU). They developed a solution method that decomposes the problem based on a Lagrangian relaxation and uses an efficient local search based on the principles of Tabu search to solve the problem. Vehicle scheduling in container terminals is highly related to the storage and QC operations. Therefore, most of the research related to vehicle scheduling focuses on the integrated scheduling methods. The integrated scheduling problems will be reviewed in sections 5.4 to 5.6.

5.3.1. *Formulation of the dispatching of multi-load vehicles*

In the twin-load dispatching of two loading containers, a vehicle travels to the storage location of the first container, then travels to the storage location of the second container and moves with the full load to the quayside to deliver the containers to the desired QCs. The twin-load of an unloading task is in reverse mode of the loading one. The twin-load vehicle dispatching problem is more complicated than the typical unit-load vehicle scheduling problem, especially when the two containers that are being transferred at the same time, on the same vehicle, follow two different routes. Thus, the expected cycle time might increase due to this increasing complexity. However, it can also decrease the deadhead travels by the vehicles and thus increase the throughput of the vehicle fleet in the CT.

The MILP model developed by Klerides and Hadjiconstantinou [KLE 11] is reproduced with minor modification and different notations in this section. There is a set of loading (pick-up) and a set of unloading (drop-off) tasks in the scheduling horizon. A loading task can be denoted by either 1, for one TEU, or 2, for one FEU container. Thus, in a pick-up task, either one TEU or one FEU container is added to the current load of the AGV (+1 or +2 containers); conversely, in drop-off tasks, either one TEU or one FEU container is subtracted from the current load of the AGV (−1 or −2 containers). The capacity of the AGVs is one FEU or two TEUs. Thus, if the current load of an AGV is one, it cannot transfer one more FEU container. Similarly, if the current load of the AGV is two TEU containers, it cannot transport any more containers, either one FEU or one TEU. If the previous sequence of tasks for an AGV is known, the current load of the AGV can be calculated by adding or subtracting the loads in the previous tasks. It is noted that an AGV can handle some loads at the beginning of the scheduling horizon. Notations for the MILP model of the twin-load AGV dispatching problem are as follows, and the model is presented in equations [5.31]–[5.48].

Sets, indices and parameters:	
$\mathcal{V}$	Set of all available vehicles on the horizon,
$\mathcal{J}^-$	Set of drop-off operations on the horizon,
$\mathcal{J}^+$	Set of pick-up operations on the horizon,
$\mathcal{F}$	Set of the first operation of the vehicles,
$\mathcal{L}$	Set of the last operation of the vehicles,
$\mathcal{J}$	Set of all the operations in the horizon, $\mathcal{J} = \mathcal{J}^- \cup \mathcal{J}^+ \cup \mathcal{F} \cup \mathcal{L}$,
i, j, k	Indices for operations, $i, j, k \in \mathcal{J}$,
v	Index for the vehicles, $v \in \mathcal{V}$,
f_v	Index for the first dummy operation of vehicle $v \in \mathcal{V}$,
l_v	Index for the last dummy operation of vehicle $v \in \mathcal{V}$,
h_{ij}	Handling time between any two operations $i \in \mathcal{J}$ and $j \in \mathcal{J}$,
q_v	Load of vehicle $v \in \mathcal{V}$ at its starting operation,
t_i	Target time to finish operation $i \in \mathcal{J}$,
q_i	Load of vehicle on operation $i \in \mathcal{J}$,
Q	Maximum allowed load of a vehicle.
Decision Variables:	
X_{ij}	=1 if operation $i \in \mathcal{J}$ preceeds operation $j \in \mathcal{J}$, and 0 otherwise,
Y_i	Load of vehicle on operation $i \in \mathcal{J}$,
D_i	Delays in completion time of operation $i \in \mathcal{J}$,
T_i^a	Arrival time of the vehicle to start operation $i \in \mathcal{J}$,
T_i^d	Departure time of the vehicle after finishing operation $i \in \mathcal{J}$.

$$Min\ Z = \sum_{i \in I^- \cup \mathcal{L}} D_i, \qquad [5.31]$$

Subject to

$$\sum_{i \in \mathcal{J}} X_{if_v} = 1 \qquad \forall v \in \mathcal{V}, \qquad [5.32]$$

$$\sum_{v \in \mathcal{V}} X_{f_v i} = 1 \qquad \forall i \in \mathcal{J} \backslash \mathcal{F}, \qquad [5.33]$$

$$X_{ii} = 0 \qquad \forall i \in \mathcal{J}, \qquad [5.34]$$

$$X_{f_v l_v} = 1 \qquad\qquad \forall v \in \mathcal{V}, \qquad\qquad [5.35]$$

$$X_{i^+ i^-} = 1 \qquad\qquad \forall (i^+, i^-) \in \mathcal{J}, \qquad\qquad [5.36]$$

$$X_{f_v i^+} = X_{f_v i^-} \qquad\qquad \forall v \in \mathcal{V}, \forall (i^+, i^-) \in \mathcal{J}, \qquad [5.37]$$

$$X_{ij} + X_{ji} \leq 1 \qquad\qquad \forall i, j \in \mathcal{J}, \qquad\qquad [5.38]$$

$$X_{f_v i} + X_{f_v j} \leq X_{ij} + X_{ji} \qquad \forall v \in \mathcal{V}, \forall i, j \in \mathcal{J}, \qquad [5.39]$$

$$X_{ij} + X_{jk} \leq X_{ik} \qquad\qquad \forall i, j, k \in \mathcal{J}, \qquad\qquad [5.40]$$

$$Y_j = q_j + \sum_{v \in \mathcal{V}} q_v X_{f_v j} + \sum_{i \in \mathcal{J} \backslash \mathcal{F}} q_i X_{ij} \quad \forall i, j \in \mathcal{J}, \qquad [5.41]$$

$$Y_j \leq Q \qquad\qquad \forall j \in \mathcal{J}, \qquad\qquad [5.42]$$

$$T_j^a - T_i^d \geq h_{ij} + M(1 - X_{ij}) \qquad \forall i, j \in \mathcal{J}, \qquad [5.43]$$

$$T_i^d \geq t_i \qquad\qquad \forall i \in \mathcal{J}, \qquad\qquad [5.44]$$

$$T_i^d \geq T_i^a \qquad\qquad \forall i \in \mathcal{J}, \qquad\qquad [5.45]$$

$$D_i \geq T_i^a - t_i \qquad\qquad \forall i \in \mathcal{J}^- \cup \mathcal{L}, \qquad\qquad [5.46]$$

$$X_{ij} \in \{0,1\} \qquad\qquad \forall i, j \in \mathcal{J}, \qquad\qquad [5.47]$$

$$T_i^a, T_i^d, D_i, Y_i \in \mathbb{R}^+ \qquad\qquad \forall i \in \mathcal{J}. \qquad\qquad [5.48]$$

The objective of the model is to minimize total delays in the drop-off operations (equation [5.31]). Constraint [5.32] states that there should be no operation preceding the first operation of any vehicle. Also, no operations can precede themselves, as stated by constraint [5.33]. Constraint [5.34] guarantees that any first dummy operation of a specific vehicle precedes only one of the operations on the horizon. Obviously, the last operation of an AGV should be after the first operation of the same vehicle, as stated in constraint [5.35]. For any job on the horizon, the pick-up operation should precede the drop-off operation, as ensured by constraint [5.36]. Constraint [5.37] assures that both pick-up and drop-off operations of a job are assigned to the same vehicle. Through constraint [5.38], it is guaranteed that only one of any two operations can precede the other one. Constraint [5.39] assures that two operations are assigned to the same vehicle only if one of them precedes the other. Constraint [5.40] guarantees the transitivity of the precedence decision variables. Constraint [5.41] calculates the load of the vehicle when it is assigned to a job. The calculation of the vehicle load depends on the load of the operation (q_j) and the balanced load of all precedent operations. The balanced load of the vehicle for any job should not exceed its capacity (*i.e.* 1 FEU or 2 TEUs), states constraint [5.42]. Constraint [5.43] calculates the arrival time of a vehicle, which depends on the arrival time of the vehicle to the precedent operation and the handling time of the vehicle between locations of two consecutive operations. The departure time of a vehicle for an operation should be longer than its target time and its arrival time, as stated by constraints [5.44] and [5.45], respectively. Constraint [5.46] calculates delays for the drop-off operations and the last operations of the vehicles. Finally, constraints [5.47] and [5.48] define the nature of the decision variables.

5.3.2. *A Tabu search for the vehicle routing*

The number of required vehicles in a scheduling horizon and the makespan of all the jobs on the horizon are the inter-related decisions. A lower number of vehicles yields a larger makespan. On the contrary, if one increases the number of vehicles to get a lower makespan, but the makespan becomes below the desired one (*i.e.* predetermined due dates, or a working shift), there would be a waste of resources (*i.e.* the vehicles). Therefore, a trade-off between the number of required vehicles and the makespan is quite necessary. Koo *et al.* [KOO 05] proposed a two-stage algorithm to determine the number of required vehicles and their routing to get the desired makespan. In the first stage, the lowest number of vehicles to get the desired makespan is roughly found. In the second stage, a Tabu search algorithm finds the optimal routing for the vehicles that minimizes the makespan. If the makespan is lower than the desired one, the problem has already been solved, or else the number of vehicles is increased by one and the Tabu search is applied to update the optimal vehicle routing and the makespan. The second stage is repeated until the desired makespan is reached.

Suppose there are $\mathcal{L}$ locations in the quayside and storage yard of a CT. A job (J_i) is defined for handling a container from location k to location l. The handling time includes loading the container in location k, transferring it from location k to location l, and unloading it in location l. For an identified job, the handling time is known in advance and is denoted by t_{kl}^H. The handling time is independent of the vehicle routing and can be denoted by T_i as well. However, the empty travel time from the dwell point of the vehicle in its previous job (*e.g.* J_j), in location m, to location k (the starting location of J_i), is dependent on the vehicle routing and is denoted by t_{mk}^U; it can also be denoted by t_{ji}.

According to the data provided at the beginning of the scheduling horizon, we can define c_{kl} as the number of jobs between locations k and l. Equivalently, it is the number of loaded travel between locations k and l. Therefore, $\sum_l c_{kl}$ is the number of outbound containers/jobs from location k, and $\sum_k c_{kl}$ is the number of inbound containers/jobs to location l. It is clear that we need $\sum_l c_{kl}$ empty vehicles at location k during the scheduling horizon and, similarly, we have $\sum_k c_{kl}$ empty vehicles at location l (which already delivered their containers to location l).

If some empty vehicles are in location k at the beginning of the scheduling horizon (denoted by S_k) and some empty vehicles are required at the same location at the end of the scheduling horizon (denoted by F_k), the net flow for location k during the scheduling horizon is the difference between its inbound and outbound jobs, which can be calculated as $v_k^{net} = (\sum_k c_{kl} + S_k) - (\sum_l c_{kl} + F_k)$. In this equation, $\sum_k c_{kl} + S_k$ indicates the number of required empty vehicles at location k and $\sum_l c_{kl} + F_k$ indicates the number of available empty vehicles at location k. Therefore, v_k^{net} empty vehicles are ready at location k to be assigned to other locations (if v_k^{net} is positive) or v_k^{net} empty vehicles are required at location k (if v_k^{net} is negative). X_{kl} is defined as the number of empty travels between locations k and l. The MILP model that calculates the minimum empty travel time is stated in equations [5.49]–[5.52]. According to the defined problem, if we minimize the total empty travels, with equation [5.49], between any two locations, the makespan to handle the jobs can be minimized as well. Constraint [5.50] guarantees that the total number of empty travels from any location equals the net number of empty vehicles if v_k^{net} is positive; constraint [5.51] ensures that the total number of empty travels to any location equals the net number of empty vehicles if v_k^{net} is negative. The number of empty travels X_{kl} is a non-negative integer, as stated in constraint [5.52].

$$Min\ Z = \sum_{k \in \mathcal{L}} \sum_{l \in \mathcal{L}} X_{kl} t_{kl}^U, \qquad\qquad [5.49]$$

Subject to

$$\sum_{l \in \mathcal{L}} X_{kl} = v_k^{net} \qquad \forall k \in \mathcal{L}\,|\, v_k^{net} \geq 0, \qquad [5.50]$$

$$\sum_{k \in \mathcal{L}} X_{kl} = -v_k^{net} \qquad \forall l \in \mathcal{L}\,|\, v_k^{net} < 0, \qquad [5.51]$$

$$X_{kl} \in \mathbb{W} \qquad \forall k, l \in \mathcal{L}. \qquad [5.52]$$

Next to finding the minimum empty travel time in the scheduling horizon, a lower bound to the minimum number of vehicles in the scheduling horizon can be defined by equation [5.53], where V^{min} is the immediate positive integer greater than the fraction and h is the total time of the desired makespan.

$$V^{min} = \left\lceil \frac{\sum_{k \in \mathcal{L}} \sum_{l \in \mathcal{L}} X_{kl}\, t_{kl}^U + \sum_{k \in \mathcal{L}} \sum_{l \in \mathcal{L}} C_{kl}\, t_{kl}^H}{h} \right\rceil \qquad [5.53]$$

In the second stage, a Tabu search finds the optimal vehicle routing for the problem and its corresponding makespan. The initial vehicle routing follows a greedy procedure (Algorithm 5.4), which is typical among the CT operators, that is, a vehicle that has completed its job is assigned to a job with the nearest starting location (least empty travel time for the vehicle). In the first step, n jobs are randomly selected and assigned to each vehicle in a random sequence. The completion time of a vehicle, $C(v_i)$, is the time to accomplish all its assigned jobs. In the second step, the vehicle with least $C(v_i)$ is selected, and the job among the unassigned jobs that adds least empty travel to that vehicle is appended as the last job of the vehicle. The second step is repeated until there are no more unassigned jobs.

Starting with the initial solution, two insertion operators (inertial and external) are applied to reduce the makespan. The TS algorithm is shown in Algorithm 5.5. In the inertial insertion, from the busiest vehicle (the vehicle with the longest $C(v_i)$, called v^*), a job is selected and inserted in a new route such that it reduces the $C(v^*)$ as much as possible. Suppose job j is currently routed between jobs p and q, and it is moved to route between jobs r and s. The reduction time in inertial insertion, if job j is inserted after job r, can be calculated as $\Delta_r^j = \left(t_{pj} + t_{jq} + t_{rs}\right) - \left(t_{pq} + t_{rj} + t_{js}\right)$, in which t_{ij} is the empty travel time between jobs i and j. It is clear that $\Delta_j^j = 0$. The process of inertial insertion is depicted in Figure 5.5. At the end of the inertial insertion operator, if there is at least one other vehicle with longer $C(v_i)$ than $C(v^*)$, the operator is repeated for a possible reduction in the new longest $C(v_i)$. It is noted that, to show that a job is the first job of a vehicle, a job denoted by 0 is added to the beginning of the routes for each vehicle. It is obvious that the job after job 0 is the first job of the vehicle.

Initialize the parameters (N is the number of jobs and V^{min} is the number of vehicles),

Select n random jobs for each vehicle ($n\ V^{min} \ll N$),

Assign the selected jobs in random sequence to each vehicle,

While there is an unassigned job

      Update $C(v_i)$ for all the vehicles,

      Select the vehicle with least $C(v_i)$; ($v^■ = \text{argmin}_i\ C(v_i)$),

      Assign the job that adds *least empty travel time* to $v^■$ as its last job in sequence,

            Tie break rule: select the job with largest handling time

End While

Algorithm 5.4. *Heuristic to create initial solution for TS algorithm in VSP*

Figure 5.5. *An example of the insertion operator*

The TS algorithm explores a possible reduction of the makespan through the external insertion operator. With this operator, a job from the vehicle with the longest completion time, $C(v^*)$, is selected and inserted in the route of the vehicle with the least completion time, $C(v^■)$. The job is selected such that it provides the longest reduction in the $C(v^*)$. Suppose job j is currently routed between jobs p and q and it is removed from the route. The reduction in empty travels of the $C(v^*)$ is $\delta_p^j = (t_{pj} + t_{jq} - t_{pq})$. We note that after any external insertion of a job, it is added to the *Tabu list*. Thus, if the selected job j is a member of the *Tabu list*, it should not be removed from its current route, as it has been already inserted in a previous external insertion operator. The TS algorithm is repeated for a predetermined number of iterations.

Initialize the parameters

$\quad\quad$ (V^{min} is the set of vehicles, and $C(v_i)$ is the completion time for the vehicles),

$Tabu\ list \leftarrow \emptyset$,

$C^*_{max} = 0$

For $g = 1: g^{max}$

$\quad\quad$ $z = 1$,

$\quad\quad$ While $z > 0$ %*Inertial insertion*

$\quad\quad\quad\quad$ $z = 0$,

$\quad\quad\quad\quad$ Select the vehicle with largest $C(v_i)$; $(v^* = \text{argmax}_i\ C(v_i))$,

$\quad\quad\quad\quad$ $N_{v^*} \leftarrow$ The number of jobs assigned to v^*,

$\quad\quad\quad\quad$ For $j = 1: N_{v^*}$

$\quad\quad\quad\quad\quad\quad$ For $r = 0: N_{v^*}$

$\quad\quad\quad\quad\quad\quad\quad\quad$ Calculate the Δ_r^j,

$\quad\quad\quad\quad\quad\quad$ End For % r

$\quad\quad\quad\quad$ End For % j

$\quad\quad\quad\quad$ If all the $\Delta_r^j \nleq 0$

$\quad\quad\quad\quad\quad\quad$ Insert job j^* after job r^*, with largest Δ_r^j, $((j^*, r^*) = \text{argmax}_{j,r}\ \Delta_r^j)$,

$\quad\quad\quad\quad\quad\quad$ $C(v^*) \leftarrow C(v^*) - \Delta_{r^*}^{j^*}$,

$\quad\quad\quad\quad\quad\quad$ For $i = 1: V^{min}$

$\quad\quad\quad\quad\quad\quad\quad\quad$ If $C(v_i) > C(v^*)$ then $z = z + 1$,

$\quad\quad\quad\quad\quad\quad$ End For % i

$\quad\quad\quad\quad$ End If

$\quad\quad$ End While % z

$\quad\quad$ %*External insertion*

$\quad\quad$ Select the vehicle with largest $C(v_i)$; $(v^* = \text{argmax}_i\ C(v_i))$,

$\quad\quad$ $N_{v^*} \leftarrow$ The number of jobs assigned to v^*,

$\quad\quad$ Select the vehicle with least $C(v_i)$; $(v^\blacksquare = \text{argmin}_i\ C(v_i))$,

$\quad\quad$ $N_{v^\blacksquare} \leftarrow$ The number of jobs assigned to $v^\blacksquare$,

$\quad\quad\quad\quad\quad\quad\quad\quad\quad\quad$ *%% to be Continued on next page*

%% Continued from previous page

For $j = 1: N_v$.

 For $r = 0: N_v$■

  Calculate the δ_r^j,

 End For % r

End For % j

Select job j^* and r^* $((j^*, r^*) \notin Tabu\ list)$ with largest δ_r^j, $((j^*, r^*) = argmax_{j,r}\ \delta_r^j)$

Insert job j^* after job r^*,

$Tabu\ list \leftarrow Tabu\ list \cup \{j^*, r^*\}$,

Update $C(v^*)$ and $C(v^■)$

%End of External insertion

$C_{max} \leftarrow largest\ C(v_i)$,

If $C_{max}^* \geq C_{max}$, then $C_{max}^* = C_{max}$

End For % g

Return the best-known solution.

Algorithm 5.5. *Tabu search algorithm for vehicle routing in CTs*

The two-stage algorithm has been applied to solve a fleet sizing and vehicle routing test problem in the Port of Busan to transport 162 containers in one working shift (480 min). In the first stage, the MILP model found 14 to be the minimum number of required vehicles. However, after running the Tabu search algorithm for 500 iterations, in the second stage, the makespan was 500 min. Therefore, the number of vehicles was increased to 15 and the Tabu search algorithm was run again. This time, the total traveling time of the vehicles and the makespan were calculated as 6,740 and 460 min, respectively, which is an acceptable makespan for a working shift.

5.3.3. Formulation of the vehicle scheduling problem

In the vehicle scheduling problem (VSP), a set of defined jobs, $\mathcal{J}$, in a typical container terminal is transported by a set of identical vehicles, $\mathcal{V}$. The jobs can be a mix of loading and unloading tasks, and these can even involve loading to or unloading from multiple ships. However, the pick-up ($P_i, i \in J$) and drop-off ($D_i, i \in J$) points for each job, as well as its ready time ($R_i, i \in J$), are known in advance. The ready time corresponds to the moment when the container can be delivered to the vehicle, in either the storage area (for loading tasks) or the quayside (for unloading tasks). The time for each vehicle to transfer a job from its pick-up to its drop-off points is denoted by T_i. The transfer time is constant and known in advance.

The dwell point of the vehicles ($D_v, v \in V$) in the beginning of the scheduling horizon is known and it is updated once the vehicle completes a job (to the drop-off point of the job). Similarly, the ready time of each vehicle ($R_v, v \in V$) at the beginning of the scheduling horizon is known, and it is updated after completing a job. There will be an empty journey for each vehicle, before starting a job, from its current dwell point to the pick-up point of its next assigned job, denoted by $t_{D_v}^{P_i}$. A simple, yet effective, MILP model for the VSP in CTs can be formulated through equations [5.54]–[5.67]. The model was developed by Ng et al. [NG 07]. Sets, notations and decision variables for the model are as follows:

Sets, indices and parameters:	
J	Set of loading and/or unloading jobs,
V	Set of vehicles,
i, j	Indices for the jobs, $i, j \in J$,
v	Index for the vehicles, $v \in V$,
$\{f, l\}$	Index for the first and last dummy jobs of the vehicles,
M	A relatively large positive number.
Decision Variables:	
C_i	Completion time of the job $i \in J$,
C_{max}	Longest completion time for the jobs,
X_{ij}^v	=1, if job $i \in J$ is immediately followed by job $j \in J$ on vehicle $v \in V$, and 0 otherwise,
Y_i^v	=1, if job $i \in J$ is transported by vehicle $v \in V$, and 0 otherwise.

$$Min \ Z = C_{max}, \hspace{3cm} [5.54]$$

Subject to

$$\sum_{v \in V} Y_i^v = 1 \qquad \forall i \in J, \qquad [5.55]$$

$$X_{fj}^v + \sum_{i \in J: i \neq j} X_{ij}^v = Y_j^v \qquad \forall j \in J, \forall v \in V, \qquad [5.56]$$

$$X_{il}^v + \sum_{j \in J: i \neq j} X_{ij}^v \leq Y_i^v \qquad \forall i \in J, \forall v \in V, \qquad [5.57]$$

$$\sum_{j \in J} X_{fj}^v = 1 \qquad \forall v \in V, \qquad [5.58]$$

$$\sum_{i \in J} X_{il}^v = 1 \qquad \forall v \in V, \qquad [5.59]$$

$$X_{ij}^v + X_{ji}^v \leq 1 \qquad \forall i, j \in J | i \neq j, \forall v \in V, \qquad [5.60]$$

$$C_i + t_{D_i}^{P_j} + T_j \leq M(X_{ij}^v - 1) + C_j \qquad \forall i, j \in J | i \neq j, \forall v \in V, \qquad [5.61]$$

$$R_i + T_i \leq C_i \qquad \forall i \in J, \qquad [5.62]$$

$$R_v + t_{D_v}^{P_i} + T_i \leq C_i \qquad \forall i \in J, \forall v \in V, \qquad [5.63]$$

$$C_i \geq C_{max} \qquad \forall i \in J, \qquad [5.64]$$

$$X_{ij}^v \in \{0,1\} \qquad \forall i, j \in J \cup \{f, l\} | i \neq j, \forall v \in V, \qquad [5.65]$$

$$Y_i^v \in \{0,1\} \qquad \forall i \in J \cup \{f, l\}, \forall v \in V, \qquad [5.66]$$

$$C_i, C_{max} \in \mathbb{R}^+ \qquad \forall i \in J. \qquad [5.67]$$

The objective function of the MILP model (equation [5.54]) minimizes the makespan of the jobs. Constraint [5.55] states that a specific job should be transported by one and only one vehicle. In constraints [5.56] and [5.57], it is clear that if two jobs (i and j) are transported by the same vehicle consecutively, then both Y_i^v and Y_j^v equal 1. Constraints [5.58] and [5.59] guarantee that there is only one start and one final dummy job for each vehicle. Constraint [5.60] ensures that if two jobs (i and j) are transported by the same vehicle, either job i can be transported before job j or job j can be transported before job i. Constraint [5.61] calculates completion time of the jobs according to their predecessor job on the same vehicle. Constraint [5.62] and [5.63] calculates the completion time of a job, if it is the first job of a vehicle; this corresponds to the longest between the ready time of the job, R_i, and the time that the vehicle reaches the pick-up point of the job from its initial dwell point, $R_v + t_{D_v}^{P_i}$, in addition to the transfer time of the job. Constraint [5.64] calculates the makespan, which is the longest completion of the jobs. Finally, constraints [5.65]–[5.67] determine the nature of the decision variables.

5.3.4. *GA for the vehicle scheduling problem*

As the vehicle scheduling problem is NP-hard, Ng *et al.* [NG 07] proposed a GA to solve it, with a reasonable CPU time. The objective function of the GA algorithm is to minimize the makespan of the jobs. In this algorithm, a chromosome is composed of two segments. The left segment is a string with $|\mathcal{J}|$ (the number of loading and/or unloading jobs) elements, called "*task scheduling*", which is filled with a permutation of integers from 1 to $|\mathcal{J}|$. The right segment is a string with $|\mathcal{V}|$ (the number of vehicles) elements, called "*vehicle assignment*", which is filled with $|\mathcal{V}|$ randomly generated non-negative integers, whose sum equals $|\mathcal{J}|$. As there are no precedence relations between the tasks, any random chromosome is feasible. Thus, the initial chromosome is constructed with random numbers. In fact, the numbers in the *vehicle assignment* show the number of tasks assigned to the corresponding vehicle, while the sequence of tasks is shown in the *task scheduling*. An example of a chromosome is illustrated in Figure 5.6, in which it is indicated that the first vehicle handles tasks 8, 1 and 6, while tasks 10 and 3 are handled by the second vehicle; tasks 5, 4, 12 and 11 are handled by the third vehicle and tasks 7, 9 and 2 are handled by the fourth vehicle. The corresponding cells in *task scheduling* and *vehicle assignment* are painted with the same colors.

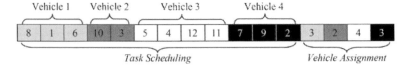

Figure 5.6. *An example of the chromosome for the GA in the vehicle scheduling problem*

To create the population for the next generation, parents are selected by roulette wheel operator for the current population. Then, a greedy crossover operator (GCO) creates two offspring by mating the parents. In GCO, the jobs are scheduled for a vehicle that maintains the minimum earliest possible completion time for the jobs. The procedure for the GCO to create the first offspring is shown in Algorithm 5.6. The earliest possible time (E_i^v) to complete the ith job by the vth vehicle can be calculated through equation [5.68]. To create the second offspring, the same algorithm is applied, except that the jobs are sorted in descending mode. A simple swap mutation operator, applied to the population except the elites, maintains the exploitation abilities of the GA. An example for the offspring generated by GCO is illustrated in Figure 5.7, in which the bold numbers in offspring are the common jobs for vehicles 1, 2 and 3. There is no common job for vehicle 4 in the parents. It is noted that the sequence of jobs in the offspring is based on the assumed E_i^v calculated for each vehicle. The calculations and the required data are not reported here in this text.

$$E_i^v = max\left(R_v + t_{D_v}^{P_i}, R_i\right) + T_i \quad \forall i \in J, \forall v \in V \qquad [5.68]$$

Input two parents;

Sort the job set (J) according to the ready time in ascending mode ($J' \leftarrow$ sorted job set),

Find the jobs that are common for each vehicle in both parents,

Schedule the common jobs for each vehicle according to their rank in J',

Delete the common jobs from the J', ($J'' \leftarrow J'$ without common jobs)

$|J''| \leftarrow Number\ of\ jobs\ in\ J''$

For $i = 1: |J''|$

    Schedule the job for the vth vehicle with smallest E_i^v,

End For % i

Insert the scheduled jobs for vehicles 1 to $|V|$ from left to right in *task scheduling*,

Insert number of jobs for each vehicle in the corresponding cell in *vehicle assignment.*

Algorithm 5.6. *Greedy crossover operator to create the first offspring*

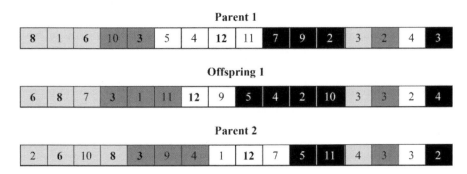

Figure 5.7. *An example of the parents and offspring of GCO*

The GA with GCO (GA-GCO) for the vehicle scheduling problem was examined by Ng *et al.* [NG 07] in a set of 800 random test problems, with 8 to 300 jobs in the scheduling horizon being transported by 3 to 50 vehicles. They evaluated the performance of the GA-GCO with six other GAs with the same structure but different crossover operators, viz. PMX, OX, position-based, order-based, union and enhanced edge crossover operators, which are the common crossover operators in the literature for similar scheduling problems with permutation encoding. For all the GAs, the following control parameters have been used: population size, 80; number of generations, 100; crossover rate, 0.8 and mutation rate, 0.05.

The results show that GA-GCO can find good results for the small-size test cases (*i.e.* 200 test cases with 8 jobs and 3 vehicles; 15 jobs and 5 vehicles). The mean deviation for the GA-GCO is 0.7%, and the minimum and maximum deviations for the other six GAs are 1.1 and 2.8%, respectively, compared to the optimal solutions found by the MILP model. Moreover, GA-GCO outperforms the other six GAs in terms of the quality of the solutions, in all 800 test cases. The average deviation of the solutions found by the six GAs, compared to the ones found by GA-GCO, is 4.97% (*i.e.* their solutions are generally worse than the ones of GA-GCO), with minimum and maximum deviations of 0.0 and 19.3%, respectively. However, the GA-GCO needs slightly more CPU time to solve the test problems, especially when these are relatively large.

5.4. Integrated storage space allocation problem

As reviewed in section 5.1, the storage yard is a place to store containers temporarily before loading them on a ship or delivering them to the customers or to another mode of transportation. Although the SSAP has been studied as an individual problem, in the literature, researchers state that decisions related to the SSAP have a significant impact on the overall performance of the CTs. Wrong or non-integrated solutions for the SSAP might lead to congestion of the vehicles in some yard blocks and idle times in others. Eventually, they will lead to longer berthing time of the ships. An extensive review on the integrated scheduling of vehicles and allocation problems in CTs can be found in [CAR 14b], and a comprehensive review on BAP and SSAP can be found in [BIE 15].

The integrated BAP and SSAP have been the focus of recent research works, particularly the BAP for the bulk seaports, as compared to the one for the CTs in the context of SSAP. The BAP and stock level conditions of bulk commodities were investigated by Barros et al. [BAR 11], in a tidal bulk port, where the draft conditions depend on high-tide conditions. For instance, keeping the stock level of mineral grains higher than the safety stock levels is very important for in-land producers; thus, giving higher priority to the ships related to the most critical mineral stock levels is common in bulk seaports. Barros et al. [BAR 11] developed an SA to solve the problem of minimizing the demurrage costs in the planning horizon. An exact method based on a branch and price framework and a meta-heuristic based on critical-shaking neighborhood search were proposed by Robenek et al. [ROB 14] aiming at minimizing the berthing time of the ships. The integrated BAP and SSAP in a bulk seaport, where belt conveyors transport the bulks between quayside and the storage yard, was studied by Tang et al. [TAN 14]. They developed an MILP model, followed by a Benders decomposition algorithm, to solve the problem.

For the liquid bulks, there is much less research considering the BAP and SSAP. A novel PSO for the resource allocation in liquid bulk seaports (e.g. crude oil terminal) was proposed by Martins et al. [MAR 13], with the objective function of maximizing the profit of the terminal. The unloaders and tanks are allocated to the incoming crude oil tanker ships. They considered decision-making for a multi-commodity problem because the tankers might transport different types of oil with different qualities. The objective function is calculated through a simulation model to cover the uncertainties of tankers arrival times (*e.g.* due to the bad weather conditions).

The BAP and SSAP are highly interdependent in the hub CTs, where a large portion of workload is dedicated to the transshipment containers (*i.e.* the containers that are imported and stored in the CT temporarily to be exported to another containership). Salido *et al.* [SAL 11] worked on a two-stage integrated SSAP–BAP, in which the optimal sequence of berthing containerships and the optimal storage space for the container, to minimize the number of reshuffling operations, are determined simultaneously. Later, Tao and Lee [TAO 15] formulated the SSAP–BAP as a quadratic mathematical model to minimize the total traveling distance of the containers and the imbalances among the yard blocks. They proposed a multi-cluster stacking strategy to split each transshipment flow into a number of container clusters and store each cluster in different yard blocks. Recently, Zeng *et al.* [ZEN 17] have considered the SSAP–BAP to minimize the operational cost of vehicles and YCs, as well as the demurrage costs of containerships. They developed a two-stage nearest searching heuristic algorithm based on GA to solve the problem: in the first stage, a heuristic rule is designed to find feasible berthing positions and a transshipment plan; in the second stage, the storage space allocation plan is optimized according to the outcome of the first stage.

Research on the integrated decision on storage allocation and vehicle scheduling was introduced by Kozan and Preston [KOZ 06], who proposed a mathematical model for the integrated container transfers and storage strategy, aiming at minimizing the berthing time of the ships. They presented a GA, a TS and a hybrid TS/GA for the problem. Cao *et al.* [CAO 08] stated that the travel time and queuing time of each container in the storage yard for unloaded containers should be balanced in the SSAP. They proposed an MIP model to minimize the congestion and waiting time of YTs. A parallel objective was to decrease the makespan of unloading containers. Moreover, they proposed a GA and a greedy heuristic algorithm to solve the problem. Later, Lee *et al.* [LEE 09b] studied the same problem, with the aim of minimizing the weighted sum of the total delay of jobs and the total travel time of YTs. This problem has been formulated as an MIP model and a heuristic scheme, namely a hybrid insertion algorithm has been developed to obtain effective solutions. A two-stage algorithm for the integrated SSAP–VSP was developed by Xue *et al.* [XUE 13], where an ACO allocates storage locations for importing containers and, in the second stage, a greedy heuristic algorithm and a local search algorithm find the integrated scheduling of YTs and QCs.

Recently, Niu *et al.* [NIU 16] have proposed two swarm intelligence algorithms, viz. PSO and bacterial colony optimization (BCO) for the integrated SSAP–VSP, and compared their performance with a real-coded GA. In section 5.4.1, their work is reviewed in more detail. An extended version of the problem to include the YCSP was proposed by Luo *et al.* [LUO 16], where a GA finds the sequence of operations of the YCs and AGVs for the importing containers and allocates them to the storage location simultaneously. Their work is reviewed in detail in section 5.4.2.

5.4.1. *A PSO for integrated SSAP–VSP*

As both SSAP and VSP are NP-hard problems, the integrated SSAP–VSP is an NP-hard problem as well. In this section, a PSO algorithm by Niu *et al.* [NIU 16] to solve the integrated SSAP–VSP is presented. Suppose there are J jobs (containers) in the scheduling horizon, of which J^- are the importing containers (*i.e.* $(J - J^-)$ are the exporting jobs), and V vehicles are in service in the transferring area. The problem defined by Niu *et al.* [NIU 16] follows the double cycling methodology. The output of the VSP is to assign the vehicles to transfer the jobs between the quayside and the storage yard, while the output of the SSAP is to assign the storage location for the importing containers. The objective of the SSAP–VSP is to minimize total delays in the transference of containers by the vehicles.

Similar to other planning and scheduling problems reviewed in this book, the solution for the SSAP–VSP is a permutation of integer numbers. Therefore, the SPV rule [TAS 06] is applied to convert continuous numbers in the permutation integer numbers. A solution for the SSAP–VSP is a string (particle) with $(J + J^- + V)$ elements filled with uniform random numbers $[0, 1]$. Particle i in the swarm $(i = \{1, ..., S^{max}\})$ is denoted by $X_i = [x_{i1}, x_{i2}, ..., x_{ij}, ..., x_{i(J+J^-+V)}]$. The last V elements (*i.e.* $j = \{(J + J^- + 1), ..., (J + J^- + V)\}$) indicate the number of transferring jobs for each vehicle; the sequence of the jobs to be transferred by each vehicle is presented by the first J elements. Similarly, the storage location for the importing containers is represented in elements $(J + 1)$ to $(J + J^-)$. The solution string needs to be converted to a feasible solution. Feasible solution i $(i = \{1, ..., S^{max}\})$ is denoted by $\Pi_i = [\pi_{i1}, \pi_{i2}, ..., \pi_{ij}, ..., \pi_{i(J+J^-+V)}]$.

Similar to the PSO algorithm for the B&CAP (section 4.4.1), the random numbers in the VSP segment of the particle are ranked in ascending mode, and the ranked numbers present the sequence of the jobs for the vehicles. Similarly, the random numbers in the SSAP segment are ranked in ascending mode and they present the allocated storage slot for the importing containers. Later in this section, we describe a heuristic algorithm to assign the jobs to the vehicles. For example, suppose there are eight defined jobs in the scheduling horizon, of which four are the importing containers (*e.g.* containers 1, 2, 3 and 4). As depicted in Figure 5.8, the 1st vehicle transfers container 7; the 2nd vehicle transfers containers 5, 2 and 4 and the 3rd vehicle transfers containers 8, 6, 3 and 1. In the SSAP segment, it is evident that container 1 (first importing container) is stored in the 2nd storage location, while containers 2, 3 and 4 are stored in the 3rd, 1st and 4th storage locations, respectively.

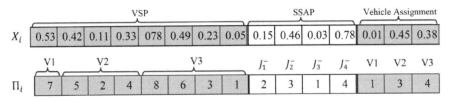

Figure 5.8. *Representation of solutions in the PSO for the SSAP–VSP*

In order to convert the vehicle assignment segment of the particle, a heuristic algorithm is implemented, as shown in Algorithm 5.7. In the first two steps, the number of jobs for the vehicles is calculated, which is the immediate integer larger than $\frac{x_{ij}}{Sum}J$, where $Sum = \sum_{j=(J+J^-+1)}^{(J+J^-+V)} x_{ij}$. We note that the summation of the number of jobs for all the vehicles $(\sum_{j=(J+J^-+1)}^{(J+J^-+V)} \pi_{ij})$ should equal J in a feasible solution. Thus, if the total number of assigned jobs is more than J, the vehicle with the maximum number of assigned jobs is identified, and this number will be decreased by 1; otherwise (*i.e.* the summation is lower than J), the vehicle with the minimum number of assigned jobs will have it increased by 1. For tie breaks (*i.e.* two or more vehicles with the maximum or minimum number of assigned jobs), the first vehicle from left to right is selected. With reference to the example in Figure 5.8, the algorithm follows these steps: $(0.01, 0.45, 0.38) \rightarrow (1,4,5) \rightarrow (1,4,4) \rightarrow (1,3,4)$ to find a feasible vehicle assignment.

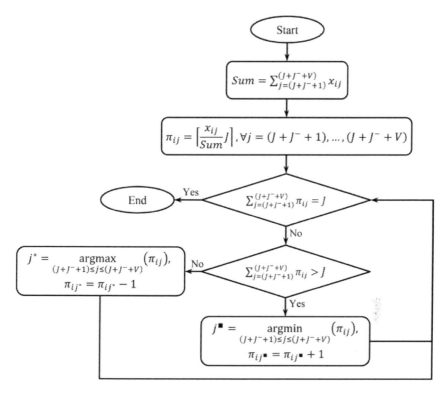

Algorithm 5.7. *Algorithm for the vehicle assignment of particle i in the SSAP–VSP*

The PSO for the SSAP–VSP follows the general procedure of the PSO described in section 2.5. Each feasible solution (Π_i) is evaluated through the calculation of total delays in the assigned jobs. For the next iteration, the velocity and the particles (X_i) are updated using equations [3.41] and [3.42], respectively.

The performance of the PSO in the SSAP–VSP has been compared to GA and bacterial colony optimization (BCO), through eight test cases with 9 to 500 jobs in the scheduling horizon, transferred by 3 to 40 vehicles [NIU 16]. The results show that both PSO and GA found the best solutions in two test cases, while the BCO found the best solutions in four test cases. Moreover, the convergence to the optimal solution is much faster for the BCO algorithm.

5.4.2. *GA for the integrated SSAP–VSP and dispatching of YCs*

As a pioneer research for the integrated planning and scheduling methods in CTs, Luo *et al.* [LUO 16] proposed a GA for the integrated SSAP and the dispatching of YCs and AGVs, in what seems to be the first research study to consider the problem. The method has been developed for the set of unloading tasks of a containership, but it can be extended to the loading tasks as well. It is clear that selecting the best storage location for a container affects the traveling times of the YCs and AGVs. Moreover, the storage location determines YC schedules, which, in turn, influence the time at which the container can be received from the AGVs. Similarly, the traveling time of an AGV influences the delivery time of containers to the YCs. Obviously, delivery time and schedules for the AGVs affect the unloading process of a containership (*i.e.* it affects berthing time of containerships). Thus, the objective of the problem is to minimize total traveling times and, consequently, berth time of the containership.

Suppose N imported containers are to be transferred and stored in the storage yard. The storage yard is divided into several blocks, each of which consists of several stacks (see Figure 5.1), where up to six containers can be stored on top of each other. A number of AGVs (v) and YCs (c) are there to serve the containership. It is assumed that AGVs are not dedicated to the QCs and, thus, can be randomly assigned to transfer the containers. Similarly, the YCs are randomly assigned to handle containers in the storage yard. The stacks are numbered sequentially throughout the storage yard. It is necessary to determine the number of empty tiers in each stack. This way, if a stack is allocated to an imported container, its storage location (block, stack and tier) can be found.

The GA developed by Luo *et al.* [LUO 16] is interesting because of the novel design of the chromosomes. This innovation can be used for further integration of the handling equipment in CTs to include QCSP as well. The chromosome is a three-row matrix, in which the first and second rows assign an AGV and a YC for the transportation of the corresponding container in the transferring and storage areas, respectively. The third row dedicates a stack to store the container. The algorithm follows the general steps of the GA presented in section 2.4.

Suppose there are three AGVs and three YCs for unloading 15 containers. In the storage yard, there are five available stacks with four available tiers in the 1st stack, two tiers in the 3rd stack and three tiers in each remaining stack. As an example, Parent 1 in Figure 5.9 shows that the 1st container of the 1st QC should be handled by the 3rd AGV and the 1st YC, and be stored in the 5th storage stack. The sequence of operations for the AGVs and YCs can be obtained from the chromosome. For example, for Parent 1 in Figure 5.9, the 1st AGV will transfer the 1st and 2nd containers of the 1st QC, the 2nd container of the 2nd QC and the 3rd container of the 3rd QC. However, it is obvious that the solution found by the GA dispatches AGVs and YCs, but does not provide the optimal scheduling for them.

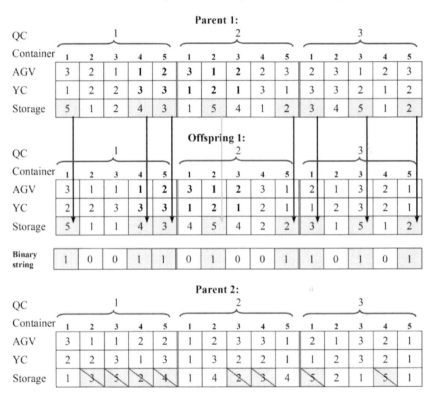

Parent 1:

QC		1					2					3			
Container	1	2	3	4	5	1	2	3	4	5	1	2	3	4	5
AGV	3	2	1	1	2	3	1	2	2	3	2	3	1	2	3
YC	1	2	2	3	3	1	2	1	3	1	3	3	2	1	2
Storage	5	1	2	4	3	1	5	4	1	2	3	4	5	1	2

Offspring 1:

QC		1					2					3			
Container	1	2	3	4	5	1	2	3	4	5	1	2	3	4	5
AGV	3	1	1	1	2	3	1	2	3	1	2	1	3	2	1
YC	2	2	3	3	3	1	2	1	2	1	1	2	3	2	1
Storage	5	1	1	4	3	4	5	4	2	2	3	1	5	1	2

Binary string	1	0	0	1	1	0	1	0	0	1	1	0	1	0	1

Parent 2:

QC		1					2					3			
Container	1	2	3	4	5	1	2	3	4	5	1	2	3	4	5
AGV	3	1	1	2	2	1	2	3	3	1	2	1	3	2	1
YC	2	2	3	1	3	1	3	2	2	1	1	2	3	2	1
Storage	1	3	5	2	4	1	4	2	3	4	5	2	1	5	1

Figure 5.9. *Illustration of the crossover operator for the GA*

To create the initial population for the GA, the first and second rows of the chromosomes are filled with randomly generated numbers from 1 to v and from 1 to c, respectively. For the storage space allocation, a greedy heuristic algorithm is applied. From left to right of the chromosome, the total travel time of a container to all the available storage locations is calculated, which consists of the travel time of the AGV from the QC to the L/U station of the block, where the storage space is located, and the travel time by the YC from the L/U station to the stack, where the storage space is located. The storage location with the least travel time is allocated to that container. Obviously, the allocated storage locations will not be considered for further allocations to containers. The greedy heuristic is repeated for all the containers. Then, the corresponding stack number of the storage locations is inserted as the third row of the chromosome. The greedy heuristic algorithm for the storage space allocation respects the limited number of empty tiers in each stack, which means that the constructed chromosomes are feasible. The chromosomes can be evaluated by calculating the makespan of completing the transfer of all containers.

To create next generations from the current population, a number of parents are selected for the crossover operator. Figure 5.9 shows an example of an offspring generated by the crossover operator. For the first and second rows of the chromosome, a two-point crossover operator is applied, because each container can be handled by any AGV and YC. Two points along the length of the chromosome are selected randomly, and the corresponding cells of the first and second rows of Parent 1 are copied directly to the corresponding cells of Offspring 1. The rest of the cells in the first and second rows of Offspring 1 are filled with the corresponding cells of Parent 2.

Due to the limited empty tiers in each storage stack, a simple two-point crossover for the third row of the chromosomes might result in infeasible solutions. Thus, a uniform order-based crossover is performed to generate the third row of the offspring, in which a "binary string" is generated randomly. Then, the cells that have the same positions as "1"s from Parent 1 are directly copied into the same cells of Offspring 1. In the second step, the storage racks that have already been allocated to a container in Offspring 1 (*i.e.* cells with the same positions as 1s in binary string) are eliminated from Parent 2, from left to right. In Figure 5.9, the storage racks 5, 4, 3, 5, 2, 3, 5 and 2 are eliminated from Parent 2 (scratched cells). Then, the remaining cells from Parent 2 are copied to the cells that have the same position as "0"s in Offspring 1. Offspring 2 can be generated by a similar method. Obviously, if the parents are feasible solutions (by the greedy heuristic algorithm, a feasible population is generated), the generated offspring are also feasible. For the mutation operator, a simple swap operator is performed, in which two randomly selected columns of a chromosome are swapped. The algorithm is repeated for a predetermined number of generations to find a (near)optimal solution for the problem.

The GA for the integrated SSAP and scheduling of YCs and AGVs has been evaluated in 10 small size (5–20 containers in the scheduling horizon) and 32 large size (21–200 containers in the scheduling horizon) test cases by Luo *et al.* [LUO 16]. The number of available AGVs was considered between 3 and 10, the YCs between 2 and 5 and the yard blocks between 2 and 8. They set the crossover and mutation rates as 0.8 and 0.02, and the population size and the maximum number of generations as 100 and 50, respectively. Their proposed MIP model has solved eight of the small-size test cases. The average gap between the best solutions found by the GA and the optimal solutions was 1.72%, with a maximum gap of 3.38%. The two larger test cases (with more than 15 containers in the scheduling horizon) among the small size cases had no optimal solutions. The GA was able to solve the large-size test cases within minutes; it was shown that increasing the number of cranes (QCs or YCs) had more impact than the number of AGVs on increasing the objective values.

5.5. Integrated scheduling of handling equipment

Although the integrated scheduling methods have shown a superior performance in increasing the throughput of the seaports, few research studies take into account all the handling equipment in the container terminals. In most cases, even in practice, it is assumed that the vehicles are always available to transfer a container to/from a QC or a YC (e.g. see [HOM 13]). For the non-lifting vehicles, the problem is more complicated, because they need a crane to load or unload them. The integrated scheduling of QCs, vehicles and storage tasks will be designated as 3D scheduling problem in this section. According to the literature, Meersmans and Wagelmans [MEE 01a, MEE 01b] were the first researchers to investigate the 3D scheduling in CTs. Meersmans and Wagelmans [MEE 01a] considered this problem in a dynamic environment, which means that the travel and handling times are not known exactly in advance. Moreover, the sequence of the tasks for the various types of equipment is not specified earlier. As the main conclusion, they state that the longer the integrated scheduling period, the better the performance of the CT. On the contrary, Meersmans and Wagelmans [MEE 01b] proved that the integrated scheduling of handling equipment is an NP-hard problem. They formulated an MIP for this problem and solved it using the B&B method. Moreover, they proposed a beam search algorithm to solve very large instances. Later, the problem was formulated as a hybrid flow shop scheduling problem with precedence and blocking constraints by Chen *et al.* [CHE 07], aiming at minimizing makespan or service time of loading or unloading a ship. They assumed that a ship is unloaded before any loading task. However, for several ships being served at the same time, the loading and unloading tasks could be scheduled simultaneously. This means that the yard vehicles are shared between two or more ships being loaded or unloaded at the same time, thus reducing the deadhead traveling of the vehicles. A Tabu search algorithm has been developed for the problem, where the initial solution is found by two greedy heuristic algorithms: first, to add minimum extra time to the makespan (by adding a container to the sequence of tasks), and second, to avoid idle time for the QCs in the scheduling sequence.

A mathematical formulation of the 3D scheduling problem was developed by Lau and Zhao [LAU 08], aiming at combinatorial minimization of delays in the tasks of QCs and total travel time of both AGVs and AYCs. Moreover, they developed two meta-heuristic algorithms to solve the problem, namely the multi-layer genetic algorithm (MLGA) and the genetic algorithm plus maximum matching (GAPM). The MLGA decomposes the problem into QC scheduling and vehicle scheduling layers. The upper layer restricts the solutions found in the lower level. On the contrary, the GAPM method solves the whole problem at once, which means that, in large instances, it would be too time-consuming. However, for a regular number of containers, the GAPM outperforms MLGA. They stated that when the number of AGVs is small, MLGA shows a significant improvement.

A hybrid simulation–optimization method for the 3D scheduling of the loading or unloading tasks of a ship was developed by Zeng and Yang [ZEN 09]. The sequence of tasks for the QCs is proposed by a GA, which is evaluated through a simulation model. The required simulation time can be decreased with a neural network algorithm, in which the objective function of the proposed sequences is predicted and potentially bad solutions are filtered out. Recently, the energy consumption of the handling equipment has been considered by He *et al.* [HE 15b]. They have developed an MIP model for the integrated scheduling of QCs, vehicles and yard cranes, aiming at minimizing the total delays of all ships and the total transportation energy consumption of all tasks. They have developed a simulation-based hybrid

PSO–GA algorithm to solve the problem. The PSO searches for local solutions, while the GA explores the whole solution space of the problem. The simulation model was used to calculate the fitness value of the solutions.

The integrated scheduling of QCs, vehicles and storage operations in the SP–AS/RS was formulated for the first time by Homayouni *et al.* [HOM 12] (the work was further studied by Homayouni and Tang [HOM 16]). They formulated the problem of constructing four sets of chained tasks for the QCs, the AGVs and the vertical and horizontal platforms of the SP–AS/RS. Moreover, they developed an SA algorithm for the 3D scheduling problem, including a novel solution representation, and a neighborhood search algorithm to observe the precedence relationships between the tasks of the QCs. Their work is further reviewed in sections 5.5.1 and 5.5.2. Later, a GA was developed by Homayouni *et al.* [HOM 14], where a novel crossover operator was applied to create the next population. The numerical analysis shows that the SA algorithm can solve the problem when the number of QCs in the scheduling problem is less than three. However, for a higher number of QCs and a higher number of tasks per QC, the GA performs better than the SA algorithm. The GA is further reviewed in section 5.5.3.

5.5.1. *Mathematical formulation of the 3D scheduling*

In this section, the integrated scheduling of QCs, vehicles and storage tasks is presented, for which an MILP model was developed by Homayouni *et al.* [HOM 12] and Homayouni and Tang [HOM 16]. In a container terminal with the advanced layout, the split-platform automated storage/retrieval system is in service to store the importing and exporting containers (refer section 1.4.3 for further description). The storage yard consists of several storage racks, and a set of QCs operate in the seaside. QCs unload importing containers from the containership and deliver them to the AGVs in the pick-up/delivery (P/D) point; in a reverse mode, QCs receive the exporting containers from the AGVs in the P/D point to load them on the containership. We note that the AGVs cannot pick-up or deliver the containers independently.

For each storage rack, there is a load/unload (L/U) station, where the AGV delivers its load to the storage rack (for importing containers) or receives its load to transfer it to the P/D point (for exporting containers). Each storage rack consists of two storage bays, each of which is served by a vertical platform (VP), that is, there are two VPs for each storage rack. Each row of the storage racks is served by a horizontal platform (HP), that is, there are as many HPs as the number of rows in each storage rack. The containers are transferred from the HPs to the VPs in a handover (H/O) station. Although the containers must be transferred to the storage cell by an HP serving the specific row (where the storage cell is located), it is indifferent which VP handles them from/to the L/U station.

In the 3D scheduling problem, for all the handling equipment, a double cycling technique is applied (described in section 4.3.4), that is, the loading and unloading operations are mixed to decrease deadhead travels of the equipment. The AGVs are not dedicated to a specific QC, and they can perform any task without a predetermined sequence. Moreover, it is assumed that the QCs are assigned to a containership, in QCAP, and the sequence of loading and/or unloading tasks for each QC is decided in the QCSP. However, the timing of operations is determined in the 3D scheduling problem. Tasks assigned to each QC are numbered in ascending mode according to their precedence relationships, that is, task 1 should be performed before task 2 for a specific QC. For easier development of the model, the tasks are denoted by T_{ij} for the jth task of QC number i (QC_i). Similarly, the storage operations are denoted by O_{mn} for the nth operation on the storage rack number m. A binary parameter $\Psi_{ij}^{mn} = 1$ shows that T_{ij} and O_{mn} are the handling operations of one container; otherwise, it equals 0. The storage location of a container (unloading from there or loading to there) is shown by three numbers (rack-row-cell). The container is (or will be) stored in the storage rack number m (denoted by $SR_{ij} = m$); the exact storage location of the container is in a storage cell (C_{mn}), which is located in a row (R_{mn}). Examples of the notations for the task of the QCs and their corresponding storage operations are shown in Table 5.1.

Task No.	QC	T_{ij}	Storage cell (rack-row-cell)	O_{mn}	Task type	Ψ_{ij}^{mn}	R_{mn}	C_{mn}
1	1	T_{11}	5-2-20	O_{51}	Loading	$\Psi_{11}^{51} = 1$	$R_{51} = 2$	$C_{51} = 20$
2	1	T_{12}	4-4-17	O_{41}	Unloading	$\Psi_{41}^{12} = 1$	$R_{41} = 4$	$C_{41} = 17$
3	2	T_{21}	3-4-36	O_{31}	Unloading	$\Psi_{31}^{21} = 1$	$R_{31} = 4$	$C_{31} = 36$
4	3	T_{31}	5-1-6	O_{52}	Loading	$\Psi_{52}^{31} = 1$	$R_{52} = 1$	$C_{52} = 6$
....								

Table 5.1. *A sample list of loading/unloading tasks*

For any of the handling equipment (QCs, AGVs, VPs or HPs), the travels have two parts, viz. initial and final. The initial part of a travel, from the dwell point of the equipment to the starting point of its next assigned task, is a deadhead travel. See Figure 5.10 for illustration, where the deadhead travels are shown as dashed lines and the loaded travels are shown as solid lines.

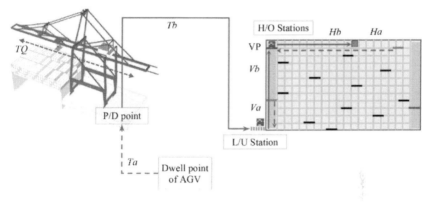

Figure 5.10. *Illustration of traveling of handling equipment in the 3D scheduling problem*

In the double cycling technique, the traveling time of the equipment depends on the sequence of tasks assigned to it. Suppose that the previous task of a QC is a loading one, followed by another loading task. Thus, the spreader of the QC is now on top of the containership. It has a deadhead travel to the P/D point (taking Q_a seconds), picks-up the container (it might wait for the AGV to reach the P/D point), travels back to the containership (taking Q_a seconds) and stores the container in the hold (taking Q_b seconds). Similarly, the AGV that performs a loading task, followed by another loading task, needs to move from the QC (where it has finished the previous task) to the storage rack (where it needs to load the next task), denoted by $QC_i \rightarrow SR_{kl}$ (the deadhead travel). The AGV receives the container (it might wait for the container to reach L/U station by the VP) and moves back to the QC (where the container is loaded to the containership), denoted by $SR_{kl} \rightarrow QC_k$ (the loaded travel). The travel time for the horizontal platform in two consecutive loading tasks is composed of traveling from the H/O station (where HP delivered the previous container to the VP) to the storage cell of the next task, denoted by $H/O \rightarrow C_{mp}$ (the deadhead travel), and moving back to the H/O station after picking-up the container, denoted by

$C_{mp} \to H/O$ (the loaded travel). The vertical platform travels from the L/U station (where it delivered the previous container) to the row where the next task is located, denoted by $L/U \to R_{mp}$ (the deadhead travel). The VP receives the container (it might wait for the HP to reach the H/O station) and travels back to the L/U station, denoted by $R_{mp} \to L/U$ (the loaded travel). Details for the initial and final travel times of the handling equipment are shown in Table 5.2.

T_{ij}/O_{mn}	T_{kl}/O_{mp}	Ta_{ij}^{kl}	Tb_{ij}^{kl}	Ha_{mn}^{mp}	Hb_{mn}^{mp}	Va_{mn}^{mp}	Vb_{mn}^{mp}
$\in \mathcal{L}$	$\in \mathcal{L}$	$QC_i \to SR_{kl}$	$SR_{kl} \to QC_k$	$H/O \to C_{mp}$	$C_{mp} \to H/O$	$L/U \to R_{mp}$	$R_{mp} \to L/U$
$\in \mathcal{L}$	$\in \mathcal{U}$	$QC_i \to QC_k$	$QC_k \to SR_{kl}$	$H/O \to H/O$	$H/O \to C_{mp}$	$L/U \to L/U$	$L/U \to R_{mp}$
$\in \mathcal{U}$	$\in \mathcal{L}$	$SR_{ij} \to SR_{kl}$	$SR_{kl} \to QC_k$	$C_{mn} \to C_{mp}$	$C_{mp} \to H/O$	$R_{mn} \to R_{mp}$	$R_{mp} \to L/U$
$\in \mathcal{U}$	$\in \mathcal{U}$	$SR_{ij} \to QC_k$	$QC_k \to SR_{kl}$	$C_{mn} \to H/O$	$H/O \to C_{mp}$	$R_{mn} \to L/U$	$L/U \to R_{mp}$

Table 5.2. *Illustration of travel times for AGVs,*
HPs and VPs in the 3D scheduling problem

For the mathematical formulation of the 3D scheduling problem, two dummy tasks are defined for the initial and final journeys of each AGV, VP and HP. For example, Y_{mV}^{mn} and Y_{mW}^{mn} show the initial journey for the first and second VPs of the storage rack number m, respectively. The earliest possible time for the completion of the cranes' tasks is calculated with the assumption that there are no delays in QC operations due to the vehicles. Therefore, S_{ij} is the cumulative pure time for the container being transferred and loaded/unloaded by the QC. The MILP model for the 3D scheduling problem is presented in equations [5.69]–[5.102]; the following sets, notations and decision variables are defined for the problem.

Sets, indices and parameters:	
$\mathcal{L}$	Set of loading tasks,
$\mathcal{U}$	Set of unloading tasks,
$\mathcal{K}$	Set of QCs to load and/or unload the ships,
$\mathcal{R}$	Set of storage racks in the storage yard,
$\mathcal{A}$	Set of active AGVs,
Q_i	Set of tasks for the ith QC,
$\mathcal{N}_m$	Set of storage operations in the mth storage rack,
$\mathcal{F}$	Set of first and last dummy tasks for the vehicles,
$\mathcal{V}$	Set of first and last dummy tasks for the first VPs in storage racks,
$\mathcal{W}$	Set of first and last dummy tasks for the second VPs in storage racks,

$\mathcal{T}_m$	Set of first and last dummy tasks for the HPs in m^{th} storage rack,
i, k	Indices for the QCs, $i, k \in \mathcal{K}$,
j, l	Indices for the tasks of QCs, $j, l \in Q_i, i \in \mathcal{K}$,
m	Index of the storage racks, $m \in \mathcal{R}$,
n, p	Indices for the operations in a storage rack, $n, p \in \mathcal{N}_m, m \in \mathcal{R}$,
Ψ_{ij}^{mn}	=1, if O_{mn} is the storage operation of the T_{ij} task, and 0 otherwise,
S_{ij}	Earliest possible completion time of T_{ij},
M	A relatively big positive number.
Decision Variables:	
TQ_{ij}	Completion time of the QC in operations of T_{ij},
TL_{ij}	Completion time of the L/U station in operations of T_{ij},
H'_{mn}	Time that HP finishes its initial operation on O_{mn},
H_{mn}	Completion time of HP operations on O_{mn},
V'_{mn}	Time that VP finishes its initial operation on O_{mn},
V_{mn}	Completion time of VP operations on O_{mn},
X_{ij}^{kl}	=1, if T_{ij} is immediately followed by T_{kl} by the same vehicle, and 0 otherwise,
Y_{mn}^{mp}	=1, if O_{mn} is immediately followed by O_{mp} on the same VP of SR_m, and 0 otherwise,
Z_{mn}^{mp}	=1, if O_{mn} is immediately followed by O_{mp} on the same HP of SR_m, and 0 otherwise.

$$Min\ Z = \alpha \left(\sum_{i \in \mathcal{K} \cup \mathcal{F}} \sum_{j \in Q_i} \sum_{k \in \mathcal{K} \cup \mathcal{F}} \sum_{l \in Q_k} (Ta_{ij}^{kl} + Tb_{ij}^{kl}) X_{ij}^{kl} \right)$$

$$+ \beta \left(\sum_{i \in \mathcal{K}} TQ_{iQ_i} - S_{iQ_i} \right)$$

$$+ \gamma \left(\sum_{m \in \mathcal{R}} \sum_{n \in \mathcal{N}_m \cup \{V,W\}} \sum_{n \in \mathcal{N}_m \cup \{V,W\}} (Va_{mn}^{mp} + Vb_{mn}^{mp}) Y_{mn}^{mp} \right) \qquad [5.69]$$

$$+ \gamma \left(\sum_{m \in \mathcal{R}} \sum_{n \in \mathcal{N}_m \cup \mathcal{T}_m} \sum_{n \in \mathcal{N}_m \cup \mathcal{T}_m} (Ha_{mn}^{mp} + Hb_{mn}^{mp}) Z_{mn}^{mp} \right),$$

Subject to

$$\sum_{k \in \mathcal{F}} \sum_{l \in \mathcal{A}} X_{ij}^{kl} + \sum_{k \in \mathcal{K}} \sum_{l \in Q_k} X_{ij}^{kl} = 1 \quad \forall i \in \mathcal{K}, \forall j \in Q_i \ \& \ \forall i \in \mathcal{F}, \forall j \in \mathcal{A}, \qquad [5.70]$$

$$\sum_{i \in \mathcal{F}} \sum_{j \in \mathcal{A}} X_{ij}^{kl} + \sum_{i \in \mathcal{K}} \sum_{j \in Q_i} X_{ij}^{kl} = 1 \quad \forall k \in \mathcal{K}, \forall l \in Q_k \ \& \ \forall k \in \mathcal{F}, \forall l \in \mathcal{A}, \qquad [5.71]$$

$$\sum_{n \in \mathcal{N}_m \cup \{\mathcal{V}, \mathcal{W}\}} Y_{mn}^{mp} = 1 \qquad \forall m \in \mathcal{R}, \forall p \in \mathcal{N}_m \cup \{\mathcal{V}, \mathcal{W}\} | \ p \neq n, \qquad [5.72]$$

$$\sum_{p \in \mathcal{N}_m \cup \{\mathcal{V}, \mathcal{W}\}} Y_{mn}^{mp} = 1 \qquad \forall m \in \mathcal{R}, \forall n \in \mathcal{N}_m \cup \{\mathcal{V}, \mathcal{W}\} | \ p \neq n, \qquad [5.73]$$

$$\sum_{n \in \mathcal{N}_m \cup \mathcal{T}_m} Z_{mn}^{mp} = 1 \qquad \forall m \in \mathcal{R}, \forall p \in \mathcal{N}_m \cup \mathcal{T}_m | \ R_{mn} = R_{mp} \ \& \ p \neq n, \qquad [5.74]$$

$$\sum_{p \in \mathcal{N}_m \cup \mathcal{T}_m} Z_{mn}^{mp} = 1 \qquad \forall m \in \mathcal{R}, \forall p \in \mathcal{N}_m \cup \mathcal{T}_m | \ R_{mn} = R_{mp} \ \& \ p \neq n, \qquad [5.75]$$

$$V_{mp}' - \left(V_{mn} + Va_{mn}^{mp} + Vb_{mn}^{mp}\right) \geq M\left(Y_{mn}^{mp} - 1\right)$$

$$\forall m \in \mathcal{R}, \forall n, p \in \mathcal{N}_m \cup \{\mathcal{V}, \mathcal{W}\} | O_{mp} \in \mathcal{U}, \qquad [5.76]$$

$$V_{mp}' - \left(TQ_{kl} + Tb_{ij}^{kl} + Vb_{mn}^{mp}\right) \geq M\left(Y_{mn}^{mp} + X_{ij}^{kl} - 2\right)$$

$$\forall m \in \mathcal{R}, \forall n, p \in \mathcal{N}_m \cup \{\mathcal{V}, \mathcal{W}\}, \forall \ i, k \in \mathcal{K}, \forall j \in Q_i, \forall l \in Q_k | \qquad [5.77]$$
$$\Psi_{kl}^{mn} = 1 \ \& \ T_{kl} \in \mathcal{U},$$

$$H_{mp}' - \left(H_{mn} + Ha_{mn}^{mp}\right) \geq M\left(Z_{mn}^{mp} - 1\right)$$

$$\forall m \in \mathcal{R}, \forall n, p \in \mathcal{N}_m \cup \mathcal{T}_m | O_{mp} \in \mathcal{U}, \qquad [5.78]$$

$$V_{mn} - V_{mp}' \geq 0 \qquad \forall m \in \mathcal{R}, \forall n \in \mathcal{N}_m \cup \{\mathcal{V}, \mathcal{W}\} | O_{mn} \in \mathcal{U}, \qquad [5.79]$$

$$V_{mn} - H_{mp}' \geq 0 \qquad \forall m \in \mathcal{R}, \forall n \in \mathcal{N}_m \cup \{\mathcal{V}, \mathcal{W}\} | O_{mn} \in \mathcal{U}, \qquad [5.80]$$

$$H_{mn} - \left(V_{mn} + Hb_{mn}^{mp}\right) \geq M\left(Z_{mn}^{mp} - 1\right)$$

$$\forall m \in \mathcal{R}, \forall n, p \in \mathcal{N}_m \cup \mathcal{T}_m | O_{mp} \in \mathcal{U}, \qquad [5.81]$$

$$V_{mp}' - \left(V_{mn} + Va_{mn}^{mp}\right) \geq M\left(Y_{mn}^{mp} - 1\right)$$

$$\forall m \in \mathcal{R}, \forall n, p \in \mathcal{N}_m \cup \{\mathcal{V}, \mathcal{W}\} | O_{mp} \in \mathcal{L}, \qquad [5.82]$$

$$V_{mp} - \left(H_{mp} + Vb_{mn}^{mp}\right) \geq M\left(Y_{mn}^{mp} - 1\right)$$

$$\forall m \in \mathcal{R}, \forall n, p \in \mathcal{N}_m \cup \{\mathcal{V}, \mathcal{W}\} | O_{mp} \in \mathcal{L}, \qquad [5.83]$$

$$V_{mp} - \left(TQ_{ij} - Qa - Qb + Ta_{ij}^{kl}\right) \geq M\left(X_{ij}^{kl} - 1\right)$$

$\forall m \in \mathcal{R}, \forall p \in \mathcal{N}_m \cup \{V, W\}, \forall\, i, k \in \mathcal{K}; \forall j \in \mathcal{Q}_i, \forall l \in \mathcal{Q}_k|$
$\Psi_{kl}^{mp} = 1 \,\&\, T_{ij} \in \mathcal{L}, O_{mp} \in \mathcal{L},$ \hfill [5.84]

$$V_{mp} - \left(TL_{ij} + Ta_{ij}^{kl}\right) \geq M\left(X_{ij}^{kl} - 1\right)$$

$\forall m \in \mathcal{R}, \forall p \in \mathcal{N}_m \cup \{V, W\}, \forall\, i, k \in \mathcal{K}, \forall j \in \mathcal{Q}_i, \forall l \in \mathcal{Q}_k|$
$\Psi_{kl}^{mp} = 1 \,\&\, T_{ij} \in \mathcal{U}, O_{mp} \in \mathcal{L},$ \hfill [5.85]

$$H'_{mp} - \left(H_{mn} + Ha_{mn}^{mp} + Hb_{mn}^{mp}\right) \geq M\left(Z_{mn}^{mp} - 1\right)$$

$\hspace{4cm}\forall m \in \mathcal{R}, \forall n, p \in \mathcal{N}_m \cup \mathcal{T}_m| \, O_{mp} \in \mathcal{L},$ \hfill [5.86]

$$H_{mn} - H'_{mn} \geq 0 \hspace{2cm} \forall m \in \mathcal{R}, \forall n \in \mathcal{N}_m \cup \mathcal{T}_m| \, O_{mn} \in \mathcal{L},$$ \hfill [5.87]

$$H_{mn} - V'_{mn} \geq 0 \hspace{2cm} \forall m \in \mathcal{R}, \forall n \in \mathcal{N}_m \cup \mathcal{T}_m| \, O_{mn} \in \mathcal{L},$$ \hfill [5.88]

$$TL_{ij} = V_{mn}$$

$\forall\, i \in \mathcal{K}, \forall j \in \mathcal{Q}_i, \forall m \in \mathcal{R}, \forall n \in \mathcal{N}_m| \, \Psi_{ij}^{mn} = 1 \,\&\, T_{ij} \in \mathcal{L},$ \hfill [5.89]

$$TL_{ij} - \left(V'_{mp} - Vb_{mn}^{mp}\right) \geq M\left(Y_{mn}^{mp} - 1\right)$$

$\forall\, i \in \mathcal{K}; \forall j \in \mathcal{Q}_i, \forall m \in \mathcal{R}, \forall n, p \in \mathcal{N}_m| \, \Psi_{ij}^{mp} = 1 \,\&\, T_{ij} \in \mathcal{U},$ \hfill [5.90]

$$TQ_{ij} - \left(TQ_{i(j-1)} + 2Qa + Qb\right) \geq 0$$

$\forall\, i \in \mathcal{K} \cup \mathcal{F}, \forall j \in$
$\mathcal{Q}_i \backslash \{1\}| \left(T_{ij} \& T_{i(j-1)} \in \mathcal{U}\right) \, or \, \left(T_{ij} \& T_{i(j-1)} \in \mathcal{L}\right),$ \hfill [5.91]

$$TQ_{ij} - \left(TQ_{i(j-1)} + Qa + Qb\right) \geq 0$$

$\forall\, i \in \mathcal{K} \cup \mathcal{F}, \forall j \in \mathcal{Q}_i \backslash \{1\} \,|\left(T_{ij} \in \mathcal{L} \,\&\, T_{i(j-1)} \in \mathcal{U}\right) \, or$
$\left(T_{ij} \in \mathcal{U} \,\&\, T_{i(j-1)} \in \mathcal{L}\right),$ \hfill [5.92]

$$TQ_{kl} - \left(TL_{kl} + Tb_{ij}^{kl} + Qa + Qb\right) \geq M\left(X_{ij}^{kl} - 1\right)$$

$\forall\, i, k \in \mathcal{K} \cup \mathcal{F}, \forall j \in \mathcal{Q}_i, \forall l \in \mathcal{Q}_k| T_{kl} \in \mathcal{L},$ \hfill [5.93]

$$TQ_{kl} - \left(TL_{ij} + Ta_{ij}^{kl}\right) \geq M\left(X_{ij}^{kl} - 1\right)$$

$$\forall\, i, k \in \mathcal{K} \cup \mathcal{F}, \forall j \in Q_i, \forall l \in Q_k | T_{ij} \& T_{kl} \in \mathcal{U}, \qquad [5.94]$$

$$TQ_{kl} - \left(TQ_{ij} - Qa - Qb + Ta_{ij}^{kl}\right) \geq M\left(X_{ij}^{kl} - 1\right)$$

$$\forall\, i, k \in \mathcal{K} \cup \mathcal{F}, \forall j \in Q_i, \forall l \in Q_k | T_{ij} \in \mathcal{L} \,\&\, T_{kl} \in \mathcal{U}, \qquad [5.95]$$

$$TQ_{ij} \geq S_{ij} \qquad\qquad\qquad \forall\, i \in \mathcal{K}, \forall j \in Q_i, \qquad [5.96]$$

$$TQ_{ij} - TQ_{i(j-1)} \geq S_{ij} - S_{i(j-1)} \quad \forall\, i \in \mathcal{K}, \forall j \in Q_i \backslash \{1\}, \qquad [5.97]$$

$$X_{ki}^{lj} \in \{0,1\} \qquad\qquad \forall\, i, k \in \mathcal{K} \cup \mathcal{F}, \forall j \in Q_i, \forall l \in Q_k, \qquad [5.98]$$

$$Y_{mn}^{mp} \in \{0,1\} \qquad\qquad \forall m \in \mathcal{R}, \forall n, p \in \mathcal{N}_m \cup \{\mathcal{V}, \mathcal{W}\}, \qquad [5.99]$$

$$Z_{mn}^{mp} \in \{0,1\} \qquad\qquad \forall m \in \mathcal{R}, \forall n, p \in \mathcal{N}_m \cup \mathcal{T}_m, \qquad [5.100]$$

$$TQ_{ij}, TL_{ij} \in \mathbb{R}^+ \qquad\qquad \forall\, i \in \mathcal{K}, \forall j \in Q_i, \qquad [5.101]$$

$$V_{mn}', V_{mn}, H_{mn}', H_{mn} \in \mathbb{R}^+ \qquad \forall m \in \mathcal{R}, \forall n \in \mathcal{N}_m. \qquad [5.102]$$

The objective function of the model [5.69] includes minimizing total travel time for the AGVs, VPs and HPs and the delays in loading and unloading tasks. The first set of constraints ([5.70]–[5.75]) construct chains of tasks for the vehicles, and the vertical and horizontal platforms. Constraints [5.70] and [5.71] guarantee that any task assigned to an AGV is immediately preceded or followed by one and only one other task performed by the same vehicle. Operations of the VPs immediately start from either $\mathcal{V}$ or $\mathcal{W}$ initial dummy tasks, which is preceded or followed by one and only one other task by the same VP, as stated in constraints [5.72] and [5.73]. Similarly, a chain of operations is scheduled for each HP in constraints [5.74] and [5.75].

Constraints [5.76]–[5.97] calculate the completion time for the tasks of the QCs, the vehicles and the vertical and horizontal platforms. Any unloading or loading tasks by either HP or VP consist of two parts (initial and final). The time to finish the initial part of the travel by the VPs in unloading tasks depends on the time it takes for the VP or the AGV to reach the L/U station ($V_{mn} + Va_{mn}^{mp}$ and $TQ_{kl} + Tb_{ij}^{kl}$, respectively), as stated by constraints [5.76] and [5.77]. The time to finish the initial part of the travel by the HPs in unloading tasks equals the travel time from its current dwell point to the H/O station, as expressed in constraint [5.78]. Then, the completion time of the VPs is the time taken to finish the initial part of the travel by either the HP or the VP, as stated in constraints [5.79] and [5.80]. Similarly, the HP travels to the storage cell to complete its unloading task (constraint [5.81]).

Constraint [5.82] calculates the time to finish the initial part of the travel by the VPs in loading tasks, which consists of traveling from its current dwell point to the H/O station. Once the VP receives the container from the HP, it can travel to the L/U station (constraint [5.83]). However, the VP may have to wait for the vehicle where it will load the container. The AGV comes from either a ship, if its previous task was a loading one (constraint [5.84]), or an L/U station, if its previous task was an unloading one (constraint [5.85]). The time of the initial part of the travel by the HPs is the time at which the HP reaches the H/O station in loading tasks (constraint [5.86]). The completion time of the HP in loading tasks depends on the time taken for the initial part of the travels of the HP and the VP, as expressed in constraints [5.87] and [5.88].

The completion time of the L/U station (*TL*) is the time at which the VP delivers (in loading tasks, constraint [5.89]) or receives (in unloading tasks, constraint [5.90]) the container to or from the vehicle. The precedence relationship between tasks of the QCs is expressed in constraints [5.91]–[5.95]. Constraint [5.96] states that the completion time of QCs tasks should be greater than its earliest possible completion time; the difference between the completion times of two consecutive tasks of the same QC should be greater than the difference between their earliest possible completion times, as expressed in constraint [5.97]. Finally, constraints [5.98]–[5.102] define the nature of the decision variables.

5.5.2. *SA for the 3D scheduling*

As the 3D scheduling is an NP-hard problem, an SA algorithm was developed by Homayouni and Tang [HOM 16] to solve it in a reasonable CPU time, where the objective function is the same as the one for the MILP model in section 5.5.1. A solution string for the problem is represented by an N-element string ($N = \sum_{i \in K} Q_i$), filled by random integer numbers from 1 to N. Encoding of the tasks is illustrated in Figure 5.11. Obviously, a random string might be infeasible, due to violation of the precedence relationships between QCs tasks. Thus, a repair algorithm is applied to the randomly generated string, to convert it into a string observing the precedence relations (shown in Algorithm 5.8). In the first section, the algorithm gets the initial random string, finds the integers that correspond to each QC and sets them to the integer number that represents the first task of the QCs. For instance, as shown in Figure 5.12, tasks 1, 2, 3, 4 and 5 are converted to 1 and the resulting string has as many 1s as the number of tasks of the 1st QC; the same is valid for the other QCs. In the second section, these integer numbers are converted to the corresponding tasks of each QC, but in a correct sequence (see Figure 5.12).

The string represents the sequence of loading and/or unloading tasks in the quayside and in the storage area. Thus, the QCs and HPs are dedicated to the tasks according to the location of the containers, in either the containership or the storage racks. However, in each storage rack, there are two VPs to perform the task. The scheduling algorithm selects the VP with the earliest available starting time to perform the task. Moreover, any of the following three heuristic rules are applied to assign AGVs to transport the containers:

– Random assignment (RA): this rule emphasizes the random scheduling of vehicles, regardless of the influence of this assignment on the objective function of the problem.

– Nearest vehicle (NV): the nearest vehicle (by distance) to the starting point of the current task (the P/D point for unloading task and the L/U station for loading tasks) is selected.

– Earliest available vehicle (EAV): this rule selects the vehicle that arrives at the starting point of the task earliest, that is, the AGV that finishes its previous task and travels to the starting point of the next task.

Initialize the parameters (N, K, Q_i as numbers of tasks, QCs and tasks for i^{th} QC),

Create an N-element string of random integers 1 to N,

$i = 1, c = 1$,

For $j = 1: N$

    For $k = 1: N$

        If $Cell_k = j$, then $Cell_k = c$,

    End For % k

    If $j \geq c + Q_i - 1$,

        $c = c + Q_i$,

        $i = i + 1$,

End If

End For % j

$i = 1, c = 1$,

For $j = 1: K$

    For $k = 1: N$

        If $Cell_k = i$,

            $Cell_k = c$,

            $c = c + 1$,

        End If

    End For % k

    $i = i + Q_j$

End for % j

Algorithm 5.8. *Algorithm to create a random feasible solution for the integrated scheduling of handling equipment*

T_{11}	T_{12}	T_{13}	T_{14}	T_{15}	T_{21}	T_{22}	T_{23}	T_{24}	T_{25}	T_{31}	T_{32}	T_{33}	T_{34}	T_{35}	T_{41}	T_{42}	T_{43}	T_{44}	T_{45}
1	2	3	4	5	6	7	8	9	10	11	12	13	14	15	16	17	18	19	20

Figure 5.11. *An example solution string for the SA in the 3D scheduling problem*

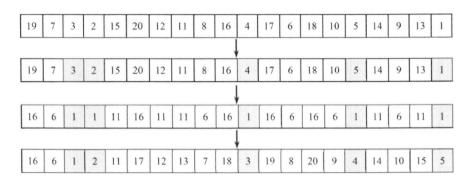

Figure 5.12. *An example of the creation of an initial feasible solution*

After performing the most appropriate VP and AGV assignments, the fitness function of the solution string can be calculated, which is the same as equation [5.69].

To create a neighbor solution, Homayouni and Tang [HOM 16] developed an operator to select and swap two random cells, so that the precedence relationships are observed, that is, the neighbor solution is feasible and it does not need to be repaired. Suppose i^{th} and k^{th} cells ($i < k$) are selected. If the task in the ith cell is the last task of a QC, it can be swapped to the kth cell. Otherwise, if the subsequent task of the ith cell is positioned in any of the cells after the kth cell, it can be swapped to the kth cell. On the contrary, if the task in the kth cell is the first task of a QC, it can be swapped to the ith cell. Otherwise, if the precedent task of the kth cell is positioned in any of the cells before the ith cell, then it can be swapped to the ith cell. Obviously, the previous rules should be observed for both selected cells, or else another two cells should be selected for the swap operator. The procedure to find a feasible neighbor solution is depicted in Figure 5.13. An example of creating a neighbor solution is represented in Figure 5.16: task 20 is the last task of the 4th QC and can be swapped to the 2nd cell; the precedent of task 14 (*i.e.* task 13) is located before the 1st cell; thus, the tasks can be swapped to create a feasible neighbor solution.

The algorithm continues the search at the current temperature level, before decreasing it to a lower level with a geometric cooling process. By decreasing the temperature, the probability of selecting a poor solution is decreased as well. At temperatures near the final temperature, the SA algorithm converges to a good solution for the problem.

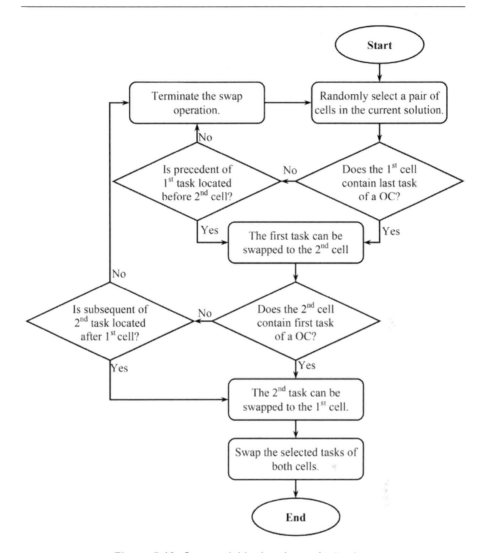

Figure 5.13. *Swap neighborhood search structure*

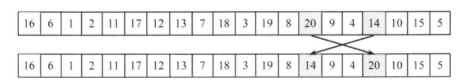

Figure 5.14. *A neighbor solution by swapping two tasks*

5.5.3. *A GA for the 3D scheduling*

A hybrid GA for the 3D scheduling was developed by Homayouni *et al.* [HOM 14], in which a novel crossover operator is applied to explore the search space. The objective function of the GA is the same as the MILP model in section 5.5.1; the chromosome structure and the heuristic rules to allocate AGVs and VPs to the tasks are the same as the ones described for the SA algorithm (see Figure 5.11 for the chromosome representation). To create the next population, two parents produce two offspring, based on the following steps of the crossover operator. The crossover operator observes the precedence relationships between the tasks. An example of the crossover is illustrated in Figure 5.15.

– Randomly select a $QC_i, i \in \mathcal{K}$;

– In the parents, highlight the tasks of the selected QC;

– Copy the tasks of the selected QC in Parent 2 onto the matching positions of Offspring 1;

– Copy the tasks of the selected crane in Parent 1 onto the matching positions of Offspring 2;

– Fill the unfilled cells in Offspring 1 with the tasks of unselected cranes according to their order of appearance in Parent 1 from left to right;

– Fill the unfilled positions of Offspring 2 with the tasks of unselected cranes according to their order of appearance in Parent 2 from left to right.

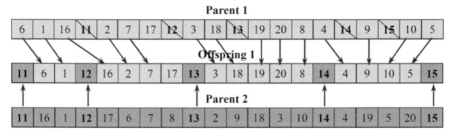

Figure 5.15. *An illustrative example of the crossover operator for the 3D scheduling*

To exploit the search space, some of the chromosomes in the current population are randomly selected and for each one the swap operator, described in section 5.2.2 for the SA algorithm, is applied. The algorithm is repeated for several iterations to find the optimal solution of the problem.

To evaluate the performance of the SA algorithm and the GA in the 3D scheduling problem, 30 test cases were designed by Homayouni and Tang [HOM 16]. The small-size test cases (designated S1–S10) include 8 to 18 loading and/or unloading tasks on two to four QCs, while two to six AGVs serve the transferring area. The medium-size test cases (designated M1–M10) include 30 to 60 tasks on three to four QCs, with three to six vehicles in the transferring area. The large-size test cases (L1–L10) include 64 to 100 tasks on four to six cranes, with four to six vehicles. In all test cases, the storage yard includes two to six storage racks.

In the first test, the performance of the heuristic rules in the 3D scheduling problem was evaluated. The GA solved five of the medium-size test cases for all 10 replications; the mean objectives of the 10 replications are shown in Figure 5.16. Obviously, the "earliest available vehicle" shows the best performance in these test cases.

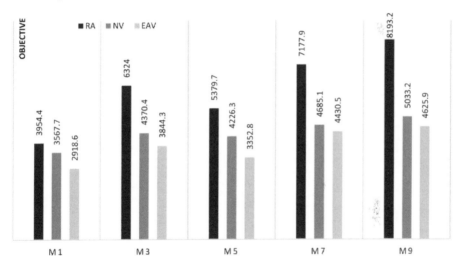

Figure 5.16. *Comparison of heuristic rules in medium-size test cases of the 3D scheduling*

The performances of the SA algorithm, the GA and the optimal solutions in the small-size test cases are reported in Table 5.3. Both the SA algorithm and GA use the EAV heuristic rule to allocate AGVs and VPs to the tasks. Specifications of the test cases, including number of tasks, QCs, storage racks and AGVs, are shown as T-Q-L-A in the result tables. It is noted that, in cases S7, S9 and S10, the MILP model was not able to find the optimal solution at a reasonable CPU time (*i.e.* 9 h for this test). Therefore, the best available solutions in the limited computational time were recorded. The GA could not find a near-optimal solution for test cases S1 to S4, perhaps due to the structure of its crossover operator. Evidently, the crossover operator needs more than two QCs in the scheduling problem to substitute their sequence of tasks. In these test cases, the SA algorithm showed a great performance (the average optimality gap for the SA algorithm was 2.75%). However, the overall performance of the GA and the SA algorithm is acceptable for the 3D scheduling problem; the average optimality gaps for the six small-size test cases, S5 to S10, were 6.4% and 3.7%, respectively. As a rule of thumb, it can be concluded that, for a lower number of QCs in the scheduling problem, the SA algorithm can search the solution space more efficiently. However, in medium- and large-size test cases, Homayouni *et al.* [HOM 14] stated that the GA outperforms the SA algorithm, because it found solutions for the 3D scheduling problem 13.5% better than the ones found by the SA algorithm.

		MILP		SAA				GA			
No.	T-Q-L-A	Optimal	CPU Time	Best	Mean	CPU Time	Opt. Gap%	Best	Mean	CPU Time	Opt. Gap%
S1	8-2-2-3	873.3	22	890.3	938.15	7	1.9	983.3	994.54	8	12.6
S2	9-3-3-2	951.2	235	1,024.4	1,024.4	6	7.7	1,183.1	1,183.1	6	24.4
S3	10-2-2-5	729.5	26	735.5	742.42	9	0.8	936.2	936.2	9	28.3
S4	12-2-2-6	948	185	954.2	990.84	10	0.6	1,218.3	1,311.82	14	28.5
S5	12-3-3-4	1,296.4	1,143	1,303.8	1,305.76	8	0.6	1,342.9	1,360.85	10	3.6
S6	12-3-4-4	1,198.9	499	1,254	1,278.78	7	4.6	1,288.1	1,298.36	10	7.4
S7	12-4-2-3	2,568.3*	32,400	2,688.2	2,774.53	10	4.7	2,739.3	2,756.48	8	6.7
S8	15-3-3-5	1,175.6	3,100	1,192.8	1,217.4	10	1.5	1,267.8	1,267.8	13	7.8
S9	16-4-4-4	2,388.5*	32,400	2,400.7	2,501.25	10	5.1	2,485.6	2,520.06	12	4.1
S10	18-3-3-6	1,624.4*	32,400	1,721	1,788.38	12	5.9	1,767.2	1,834.06	16	8.7

Table 5.3. *Comparison of the SA algorithm and the GA with optimal solutions in small-size test cases*

In the last test, the performance of the integrated scheduling was compared to the non-integrated scheduling method. In the non-integrated scheduling method, all the tasks are scheduled based on a typical heuristic rule, first come first serve. From the results (shown in Figure 5.17), solutions found by the GA for the integrated scheduling method are 29.8% better than the solutions found in the non-integrated scheduling method.

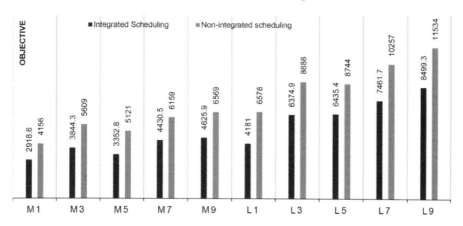

Figure 5.17. *Non-integrated against integrated scheduling method in medium- and large-sized test cases*

5.6. Conclusions

We started this chapter with a review of stand-alone planning and scheduling problems in the seaports. The most important daily decisions, particularly regarding the container terminals, are too complicated, as shown by the mathematical formulations. Although several researchers focused on the improvements of the metaheuristic algorithms for stand-alone problems, in recent years the need for integrated scheduling methods has been more pressing. These problems are even more complicated than the stand-alone ones; however, they have a greater impact on improving the performance of the seaports. The mathematical model presented for the 3D scheduling problem shows the level of complexity of the daily scheduling in container terminals. The resolution of this problem needs more effort, as well as more sophisticated and better metaheuristics. Nonetheless, it seems that even the preliminary methods for the integrated scheduling problem can give more benefits to the port authorities than the development of more efficient algorithms for the stand-alone problems.

Conclusion

Metaheuristic methods have been successfully applied to solve real-world optimization problems in a wide variety of application areas (e.g. cryptography, manufacturing scheduling, molecular modeling, inventory allocation, project scheduling, real options valuation). Maritime operations are not an exception. This book presented and examined several metaheuristic applications in maritime operations related to ship routing, berth allocation, quay crane assignment and scheduling, storage space allocation, yard crane scheduling, and vehicle scheduling.

Maritime operation problems have also been approached by some traditional optimization methods, such as branch-and-bound and dynamic programming. These methods are capable of obtaining optimal solutions and guaranteeing their optimality. However, maritime operation problems have a complex problem structure and are combinatorial in nature. Furthermore, real-world applications involve large-sized instances; which together with the aforementioned issues cause traditional optimization methods to fail to deliver an optimal solution in a reasonable amount of time; sometimes even a feasible one. Nevertheless, for a widely accepted and basic version of the problems discussed, we also present a mathematical programming model.

Another advantage of using metaheuristics is that they are not problem specific, and they can be easily adapted to incorporate additional problem features, whenever required. In addition, nowadays many real-world applications involve multiple objectives. Metaheuristics are particularly interesting to address this type of problem as they work with a set of solutions, rather than just one. Furthermore, operational problems need to be solved quickly, sometimes online, and thus, we do have the luxury of waiting hours or days, sometimes even more, for a solution. Finally, metaheuristic algorithms can find near-optimal solutions and can do so quickly; however, solution quality and/or efficiency are not easy to prove theoretically; usually only empirical evidence can be given.

The specific works discussed in this book were chosen such that a wider variety of approaches and problem specificities were achieved. Thus, although this does not mean that they are the most recent ones or the ones that reported the best values, they generally achieve a good compromise regarding the range of problems presented and the range of approaches discussed; while ensuring it is relatively recent publication from a reputable journal. Regarding solutions quality, it is not easy to analyze or infer since, typically, no comparisons are provided. It is worth noticing that there are no benchmark problem instances. Researchers, typically, generated their own instances for parameter tuning and other computational purposes and then finally tested the proposed approach using a specific version of the problem considered, many times a real-world application, related to or based on real-world application in other cases.

Although a diverse range of problems is covered by this book, it is not exhaustive. On the one hand, some problems do not have presence enough in the literature and, on the other hand, some problems are a particular case of problems addressed. For example, the integrated quay crane and vehicle scheduling problem is not addressed on its own; however, it is a specific case of the integrated quay crane, vehicle and storage scheduling problem, discussed in Chapter 5. Finally, every work must, at some point, be finished.

Since most of the problems related to the maritime operations are interconnected, they ideally should be solved in an integrated approach, which would make maritime operations even harder to solve. Although integrated planning and scheduling problems are much more complex and have larger computational requirements, they must be addressed in order to respond to the higher productivity requirements in seaports. From a practical point of view, focusing on integrated scheduling and planning problems has the potential of providing a larger impact on the ports' throughput and thus the ports' profitability, than further developing and improving algorithms for the problems stand-alone version. Although we reviewed several metaheuristics for integrated problems (e.g. berth allocation and quay crane assignment, storage space allocation and vehicle scheduling, and yard crane scheduling and vehicle scheduling), there are many more that need and are worthwhile to research further. More specifically, integrated scheduling methods to cover more parts of the decision-making process (from the seaside to the yard operations) would have a very large impact on the performance of the seaports and ship operators. Another immediate research opportunity is to integrate ship routing/scheduling with port operations (e.g. berth allocation). We believe that a large and significant impact can be attained by developing metaheuristics for progressively more integrated problems. Nevertheless, developing fast (meta)heuristics for the online decision-making problems (e.g. ship speed adjustment, tramp ship routing and/or dispatching, vehicle dispatching, and storage space allocation) is also a very important area for future research.

As a response to the ever-increasing demand for maritime transportation, new technologies and operation procedures are introduced continuously by manufacturing technology companies and/or port operators. Examples include the double cycling strategy (to perform a mix of loading and unloading tasks), discussed in Chapters 4 and 5, multi-load vehicles (that can transfer either one FEU container, two TEUs, etc.), discussed in Chapter 5, and automated storage/retrieval systems for the container terminals, discussed in Chapter 5. However, there are many other issues that are relevant and worth discussing that were left out of this book; dual-spreader crane operations both in the quayside and in storage yards, integrated operations in new berth layouts (e.g. indented berths) and integrated scheduling methods for the newly launched automated guided vehicle (that can pick up/drop off containers independently), to name but a few.

Bibliography

[AAR 05] AARTS E., KORST J., KICHIELS W., "Simulated annealing", in BURKE E.K., KENDALL G. (eds), *Search Methodologies*, Springer, Boston, 2005.

[AGR 15] AGRA A., CHRISTIANSEN M., DELGADO A. *et al.*, "A maritime inventory routing problem with stochastic sailing and port times", *Computers & Operations Research*, vol. 61, pp. 18–30, 2015.

[AGR 18] AGRA A., OLIVEIRA M., "MIP approaches for the integrated berth allocation and quay crane assignment and scheduling problem", *European Journal of Operational Research*, vol. 264, no. 1, pp. 138–148, 2018.

[ALD 15] AL-DHAHERI N., DIABAT A., "The quay crane scheduling problem", *Journal of Manufacturing Systems*, vol. 36, pp. 87–94, 2015.

[ALD 16] AL-DHAHERI N., JEBALI A., DIABAT A., "A simulation-based genetic algorithm approach for the quay crane scheduling under uncertainty", *Simulation Modelling Practice and Theory*, vol. 66, pp. 122–138, 2016.

[AND 15] ANDERSSON H., FAGERHOLT K., HOBBESLAND K., "Integrated maritime fleet deployment and speed optimization: Case study from RoRo shipping", *Computers & Operations Research*, vol. 55, pp. 233–240, 2015.

[ANG 98] ANGELINE P.J., "Evolutionary optimization versus particle swarm optimization: Philosophy and performance differences", *Lecture Notes in Computer Science: Evolutionary Programming VII*, vol. 1447, pp. 601–610, 1998.

[AYD 17] AYDIN N., LEE H., MANSOURI S.A., "Speed optimization and bunkering in liner shipping in the presence of uncertain service times and time windows at ports", *European Journal of Operational Research*, vol. 259, no. 1, pp. 143–154, 2017.

[BAE 11] BAE H., CHOE R., PARK T. *et al*, "Comparison of operations of AGVs and ALVs in an automated container terminal", *Journal of Intelligent Manufacturing*, vol. 22, no. 3, pp. 413–426, 2011.

[BAR 11] BARROS V.H., COSTA T.S., OLIVEIRA A.C.M. *et al.*, "Model and heuristic for berth allocation in tidal bulk ports with stock level constraints", *Computers & Industrial Engineering*, vol. 60, no. 4, pp. 606–613, 2011.

[BAR 13] BARTOŠEK A., MAREK O., "Quay cranes in container terminals", *Transactions on Transport Sciences*, vol. 6, no. 1, pp. 9–18, 2013.

[BAS 17] BASU S., SHARMA M., GHOSH P.S., "Efficient preprocessing methods for tabu search: an application on asymmetric travelling salesman problem", *Information Systems and Operational Research*, vol. 55, no. 2, pp. 134–158, 2017.

[BAT 94] BATTITI R., TECCHIOLLI G., "The Reactive Tabu Search", *ORSA Journal of Computing*, vol. 6, no. 2, pp. 126–140, 1994.

[BAZ 09] BAZZAZI M., SAFAEI N., JAVADIAN N., "A genetic algorithm to solve the storage space allocation problem in a container terminal", *Computers & Industrial Engineering*, vol. 56, no. 1, pp. 44–52, 2009.

[BIE 09] BIERWIRTH C., MEISEL F., "A fast heuristic for quay crane scheduling with interference constraints", *Journal of Scheduling*, vol. 12, no. 4, pp. 345–360, 2009.

[BIE 10] BIERWIRTH C., MEISEL F., "A survey of berth allocation and quay crane scheduling problems in container terminals", *European Journal of Operational Research*, vol. 202, no. 3, pp. 615–627, 2010.

[BIE 15] BIERWIRTH C., MEISEL F., "A follow-up survey of berth allocation and quay crane scheduling problems in container terminals", *European Journal of Operational Research*, vol. 244, no. 3, pp. 675–689, 2015.

[BIR 01] BIRATTARI M., PAQUETE L., STUTZLE T. *et al.*, "Classification of metaheuristics and design of experiments for the analysis of components", report, Darmstadt University of Technology, Germany, 2001.

[BLU 03] BLUM C., ROLI A., "Metaheuristics in combinatorial optimization: Overview and conceptual comparison", *ACM Computing Surveys*, vol. 35, no. 3, pp. 268–308, 2003.

[BON 17] BONYADI M.R., MICHALEWICZ Z., "Particle swarm optimization for single objective continuous space problems: a review", *Evolutionary Computation*, vol. 25, no. 1, pp. 1–54, 2017.

[BOY 17] BOYSEN N., BRISKORN D., MEISEL F., "A generalized classification scheme for crane scheduling with interference", *European Journal of Operational Research*, vol. 258, no. 1, pp. 343–357, 2017.

[BRA 15] BRANCHINI R.M., ARMENTANO V.A., MORABITO R., "Routing and fleet deployment in liner shipping with spot voyages", *Transportation Research Part C: Emerging Technologies*, vol. 57, pp. 188–205, 2015.

[BRI 16] BRISKORN D., ANGELOUDIS P., "Scheduling co-operating stacking cranes with predetermined container sequences", *Discrete Applied Mathematics*, vol. 201, pp. 70–85, 2016.

[BRO 14] BROUER B.D., DESAULNIERS G., PISINGER D., "A metaheuristic for the liner shipping network design problem", *Transportation Research Part E: Logistics and Transportation Review*, vol. 72, pp. 42–59, 2014.

[BUH 11] BUHRKAL K., ZUGLIAN S., ROPKE S. *et al.*, "Models for the discrete berth allocation problem: a computational comparison", *Transportation Research Part E: Logistics and Transportation Review*, vol. 47, no. 4, pp. 461–473, 2011.

[BUL 97] BULLNHEIMER B., HARTL R.F., STRAUSS C., "A new rank based version of the ant system - a computational study", *Central European Journal for Operations Research and Economics*, vol. 7, pp. 25–38, 1997.

[CAO 08] CAO J.X., SHI Q., LEE D.-H., "A decision support method for truck scheduling and storage allocation problem at container", *Tsinghua Science & Technology*, vol. 13, suppl 1, pp. 211–216, 2008.

[CAR 14a] CARLO H.J., VIS I.F.A., ROODBERGEN K.J., "Transport operations in container terminals: literature overview, trends, research directions and classification scheme", *European Journal of Operational Research*, vol. 236, no. 1, pp. 1–13, 2014.

[CAR 14b] CARLO H.J., VIS I.F.A., ROODBERGEN K.J., "Storage yard operations in container terminals: literature overview, trends, and research directions", *European Journal of Operational Research*, vol. 235, no. 2, pp. 412–430, 2014.

[CAR 18] CARNARIUS J., "Modes of Transportation Explained. Which is the Best?", *Freight Hub*, available at: https://freighthub.com/en/blog/modes-transportation-explained-best/, 2018.

[CAS 09] CASERTA M., VOß S., "Metaheuristics: intelligent problem solving", in MANIEZZO V., STÜTZLE T., VOß S. (eds), *Metaheuristics: Annals of Information Systems*, vol. 10, Springer, Boston, 2009.

[CHA 08] CHANG D., ZUHUA W.Y., CHEN C.-H. *et al.*, "A berth allocation strategy using heuristics algorithm and simulation optimisation", *International Journal of Computer Applications in Technology*, vol. 32, no. 4, pp. 272–281, 2008.

[CHA 10] CHANG D., JIANG Z., YAN W. *et al.*, "Integrating berth allocation and quay crane assignments", *Transportation Research Part E: Logistics and Transportation Review*, vol. 46, no. 6, pp. 975–990, 2010.

[CHA 11] CHAO S.-L., LIN Y.-J., "Evaluating advanced quay cranes in container terminals", *Transportation Research Part E: Logistics and Transportation Review*, vol. 47, no. 4, pp. 432–445, 2011.

[CHA 17] CHAUDHRY I.A., USMAN M., "Integrated process planning and scheduling using genetic algorithms", *Tehnički Vjesnik - Technical Gazette*, vol. 24, no. 5, pp. 1401–1409, 2017.

[CHE 00] CHELOUAH R., SIARRY P., "Tabu search applied to global optimization", *European Journal of Industrial Engineering*, vol. 123, no. 2, pp. 256–270, 2000.

[CHE 03] CHEN C., HUANG S.Y., HSU W.J. *et al.*, "Platform-based AS/RS for container storage", *IEEE International Conference on Robotics and Automation (ICRA'03)*, Taipei, Taiwan, pp. 181–187, 2003.

[CHE 05] CHENG Y.-L., SEN H.-C., NATARAJAN K. *et al.*, "Dispatching automated guided vehicles in a container terminal", *Supply Chain Optimization*, vol. 98, pp. 355–389, 2005.

[CHE 07] CHEN L., BOSTEL N., DEJAX P. *et al.*, "A tabu search algorithm for the integrated scheduling problem of container handling systems in a maritime terminal", *European Journal of Operational Research*, vol. 181, no. 1, pp. 40–58, 2007.

[CHE 11] CHEN L., LANGEVIN A., "Multiple yard cranes scheduling for loading operations in a container terminal", *Engineering Optimization*, vol. 43, no. 11, pp. 1205–1221, 2011.

[CHR 08] CHRISTENSEN C.G., HOLST C.T., "Berth allocation in container terminal", PhD thesis, Technical University of Denmark, 2008.

[CHR 13] CHRISTIANSEN M., FAGERHOLT K., NYGREEN B. *et al.*, "Ship routing and scheduling in the new millennium", *European Journal of Operational Research*, vol. 228, no. 3, pp. 467–483, 2013.

[CHU 05] CHU C.Y., HUANG W.C., "Determining container terminal capacity on the basis of an adopted yard handling system", *Transport Reviews*, vol. 25, no. 2, pp. 181–199, 2005.

[CHU 12] CHUNG S.H., CHOY K.L., "A modified genetic algorithm for quay crane scheduling operations", *Expert Systems with Applications*, vol. 39, no. 4, pp. 4213–4221, 2012.

[CHU 13] CHUNG S.H., CHAN F.T.S., "A workload balancing genetic algorithm for the quay crane scheduling problem", *International Journal of Production Research*, vol. 51, no. 16, pp. 4820–4834, 2013.

[COL 88] COLLINS N.E., EGLESE R.W., GOLDEN B.L., "Simulated annealing - an annotated bibliography", *American Journal of Mathematical and Management Sciences*, vol. 8, nos 3–4, pp. 209–307, 1988.

[COR 05] CORDEAU J.F., LAPORTE G., LEGATO P. *et al.*, "Models and tabu search heuristics for the berth allocation problem", *Transportation Science*, vol. 39, no. 4, pp. 526–538, 2005.

[COR 17] CORRECHER J.F., ALVAREZ-VALDES R., "A biased random-Key genetic algorithm for the time-invariant berth allocation and quay crane assignment problem", *Expert Systems with Applications*, vol. 89, pp. 112–128, 2017.

[CRE 83] CREUTZ M., "Microcanonical Monte Carlo simulation", *Physical Review Letters*, vol. 50, no. 19, pp. 1411–1414, 1983.

[ČRE 13] ČREPINŠEK M., LIU S.-H., MERNIK M., "Exploration and exploitation in evolutionary algorithms", *ACM Computing Surveys*, vol. 45, no. 3, pp. 1–33, 2013.

[CVI 95] CVIJOVICACUTE D., KLINOWSKI J., "Taboo search: an approach to the multiple minima problem", *Science*, vol. 267, no. 5198, pp. 664–666, 1995.

[DAB 17] DABAH A., BENDJOUDI A., AITZAI A., "An efficient tabu search neighborhood based on reconstruction strategy to solve the blocking job shop scheduling problem", *Journal of Industrial and Management Optimization*, vol. 13, no. 4, pp. 29–29, 2017.

[DAG 89] DAGANZO C.F., "The crane scheduling problem", *Transportation Research Part B*, vol. 23, no. 3, pp. 159–175, 1989.

[DAS 03] DAS S.K., SPASOVIC L., "Scheduling material handling vehicles in a container terminal", *Production Planning and Control*, vol. 14, no. 7, pp. 623–633, 2003.

[DE 16] DE A., MAMANDURU V.K.R., GUNASEKARAN A. *et al.*, "Composite particle algorithm for sustainable integrated dynamic ship routing and scheduling optimization", *Computers & Industrial Engineering*, vol. 96, pp. 201–215, 2016.

[DE 17] DE A., KUMAR S.K., GUNASEKARAN A. *et al.*, "Sustainable maritime inventory routing problem with time window constraints", *Engineering Applications of Artificial Intelligence*, vol. 61, pp. 77–95, 2017.

[DEN 90] DENEUBOURG J.L., ARON S., GOSS S. *et al.*, "The self-organizing exploratory pattern of the argentine ant", *Journal of Insect Behavior*, vol. 3, no. 2, pp. 159–168, 1990.

[DOR 91] DORIGO M., MANIEZZO V., COLORNI A., Positive feedback as a search strategy, Technical Report no. 91-016, Politecnico di Milano, Italy, 1991.

[DOR 92] DORIGO M., Optimization, learning and natural algorithms, PhD thesis, Politecnico di Milano, Italy, 1992.

[DOR 96] DORIGO M., MANIEZZO V., COLORNI A., "Ant system: Optimization by a colony of cooperating agents", *IEEE Transactions on Systems, Man, and Cybernetics, Part B: Cybernetics*, vol. 26, no. 1, pp. 29–41, 1996.

[DOR 97] DORIGO M., GAMBARDELLA L.M., "Ant colony system: A cooperative learning approach to the traveling salesman problem", *IEEE Transactions on Evolutionary Computation*, vol. 1, no. 1, pp. 53–66, 1997.

[DOR 99a] DORIGO M., DI CARO G., "The ant colony optimization meta-heuristic", *New Ideas in Optimization*, vol. 2, pp. 11–32, 1999.

[DOR 99b] DORIGO M., DI CARO G., GAMBARDELLA L.M., "Ant algorithms for discrete optimization", *Artificial Life*, vol. 5, no. 2, pp. 137–172, 1999.

[DOR 04] DORIGO M., STUTZLE T., *Ant Colony Optimization*, MIT Press, 2004.

[DUE 90] DUECK G., SCHEUER T., "Threshold accepting: A general purpose optimization algorithm appearing superior to simulated annealing", *Journal of Computational Physics*, vol. 90, no. 1, pp. 161–175, 1990.

[DUL 17] DULEBENETS M.A., "Green vessel scheduling in liner shipping: Modeling carbon dioxide emission costs in sea and at ports of call", *International Journal of Transportation Science and Technology*, available online: https://www.sciencedirect.com/science/article/pii/S204604301730045X, 2017.

[EBE 95] EBERHART R., KENNEDY J., "A new optimizer using particle swarm theory", *Proceedings of the Sixth International Symposium on Micro Machine and Human Science*, pp. 39–43, 1995.

[EBE 96] EBERHART R., SIMPSON P.K., DOBBINS R.W., *Computational Intelligence PC Tools*, AP Professional, San Diego, 1996.

[ELM 17] ELMI A., TOPALOGLU S., "Cyclic job shop robotic cell scheduling problem: Ant colony optimization", *Computers & Industrial Engineering*, vol. 111, pp. 417–432, 2017.

[ENG 16] ENGELBRECHT A.P., "Particle swarm optimization with crossover: a review and empirical analysis", *Artificial Intelligence Review*, vol. 45, no. 2, pp. 131–165, 2016.

[ERN 17] ERNST A.T., OGUZ C., SINGH G. *et al.*, "Mathematical models for the berth allocation problem in dry bulk terminals", *Journal of Scheduling*, vol. 20, no. 5, pp. 1–15, 2017.

[EUR 15] EUROPEAN COMMISSION, Study on the analysis and evolution of international and EU shipping, report, University of Antwerp, Belgium, 2015.

[FAG 15] FAGERHOLT K., GAUSEL N.T., RAKKE J.G. *et al.*, "Maritime routing and speed optimization with emission control areas", *Transportation Research Part C: Emerging Technologies*, vol. 52, pp. 57–73, 2015.

[FAT 16] FATHI M., RODRÍGUEZ V., FONTES D.B.M.M. *et al.*, "A modified particle swarm optimisation algorithm to solve the part feeding problem at assembly lines", *International Journal of Production Research*, vol. 54, no. 3, pp. 878–893, 2016.

[FIT 15] FITZGERALD J.M., RYAN C., MEDERNACH D., "An integrated approach to stage 1 breast cancer detection", *Proceedings of the 2015 Annual Conference on Genetic and Evolutionary Computation - GECCO'15*, pp. 1199–1206, 2015.

[FON 07] FONTES D.B.M.M., GONÇALVES J.F., "Heuristic solutions for general concave minimum cost network flow problems", *Networks*, vol. 50, no. 1, pp. 67–76, 2007.

[FON 13] FONTES D.B.M.M., GONÇALVES J.F., "A multi-population hybrid biased random key genetic algorithm for hop-constrained trees in nonlinear cost flow networks", *Optimization Letters*, vol. 7, no. 6, pp. 1303–1324, 2013.

[FON 15] FONTES D.B.M.M., GONÇALVES J.F., "A genetic algorithm for scheduling alternative tasks subject to technical failure", *Proceedings in Mathematics and Statistics*, Springer, Cham, Switzerland, pp. 139–152, 2015.

[GAN 10] GANJI S.R.S., BABAZADEH A., ARABSHAHI N., "Analysis of the continuous berth allocation problem in container ports using a genetic algorithm", *Journal of Marine Science and Technology*, vol. 15, no. 4, pp. 408–416, 2010.

[GEL 13] GELAREH S., MERZOUKI R., MCGINLEY K. *et al.*, "Scheduling of intelligent and atonomous vehicles under pairing/unpairing collaboration strategy in container terminals", *Transportation Research Part C: Emerging Technologies*, vol. 33, pp. 1–21, 2013.

[GEM 84] GEMAN S., GEMAN D., "Stochastic relaxation, Gibbs distributions, and the bayesian restoration of images", *IEEE Transactions on Pattern Analysis and Machine Intelligence*, vol. 6, no. 6, pp. 721–741, 1984.

[GEN 03] GENDREAU M., "An introduction to tabu search", *Handbook of Metaheuristics*, vol. 57, pp. 37–54, July 2003.

[GEN 14] GENDREAU M., POTVIN J.-Y., "Tabu search", *Search Methodologies*, Springer, Boston, pp. 243–263, 2014.

[GHA 17] GHAREHGOZLI A.H., VERNOOIJ F.G., ZAERPOUR N., "A simulation study of the performance of twin automated stacking cranes at a seaport container terminal", *European Journal of Operational Research*, vol. 261, no. 1, pp. 108–128, 2017.

[GIL 02] GILBERT R., IRWIN N., HOLLINGWORTH B. *et al.*, "Sustainable transportation performance indicators", *Sustainable Development*, pp. 1–20, 2002.

[GLO 86] GLOVER F., "Future paths for integer programming and links to artificial intelligence", *Computers & Operations Research*, vol. 13, no. 5, pp. 533–549, 1986.

[GLO 89] GLOVER F., "Tabu Search – Part I", *ORSA Journal on Computing*, vol. 21, no. 3, pp. 4–32, 1989.

[GLO 90] GLOVER F., "Tabu Search – Part II", *ORSA Journal on Computing*, vol. 2, no. 1, pp. 4–32, 1990.

[GLO 93] GLOVER F., LAGUNA M., *Modern Heuristic Techniques for Combinatorial Problems*, Halsted Press, 1993.

[GLO 94] GLOVER F., "Tabu search for nonlinear and parametric optimization (with links to genetic algorithms)", *Discrete Applied Mathematics*, vol. 49, nos 1–3, pp. 231–255, 1994.

[GLO 97] GLOVER F., LAGUNA M., *Tabu Search*, Springer, 1997.

[GLO 98] GLOVER F., "Tabu search wellsprings and challenges", *European Journal of Operational Research*, vol. 106, no. 5, pp. 221–222, 1998.

[GLO 07] GLOVER F., "Tabu search – Uncharted domains", *Annals of Operations Research*, vol. 149, no. 1, pp. 89–98, 2007.

[GOO 07] GOODCHILD A., DAGANZO C.F., "Crane double cycling in container ports: Planning methods and evaluation", *Transportation Research Part B: Methodological*, vol. 41, no. 8, pp. 875–891, 2007.

[GOS 89] GOSS S., DENEUBORG J.L., PASTEELS J.M., "Self-organized shortcuts in the Argentine ant", *Naturwissenschaften*, vol. 76, no. 1959, pp. 579–581, 1989.

[GRU 04] GRUNOW M., GÜNTHER H.-O., LEHMANN M., "Dispatching multi-load AGVs in highly automated seaport container terminals", *OR Spectrum*, vol. 26, no. 2, pp. 211–235, 2004.

[GRU 06] GRUNOW M., GÜNTHER H.-O., LEHMANN M., "Strategies for dispatching AGVs at automated seaport container terminals", *OR Spectrum*, vol. 28, no. 4, pp. 587–610, 2006.

[GUA 05] GUAN Y., CHEUNG R.K., "The berth allocation problem: models and solution methods", in GÜNTHER H.-O., KIM K.H. (eds), *Container Terminals and Automated Transport Systems*, Springer, pp. 141–158, 2005.

[GUA 10] GUAN Y., YANG K.H., "Analysis of berth allocation and inspection operations in a container terminal", *Maritime Economics and Logistics*, vol. 12, no. 4, pp. 347–369, 2010.

[GUL 11] GULDOGAN E., "Simulation-based analysis for hierarchical storage assignment policies in a container terminal", *Simulation*, vol. 87, no. 6, pp. 523–537, 2011.

[HAJ 88] HAJEK B., "Cooling schedules for optimal annealing", *Mathematics of Operations Research*, vol. 13, no. 2, pp. 311–329, 1988.

[HAR 04] HARTMANN S., "A general framework for scheduling equipment and manpower at container terminals", *OR Spectrum*, vol. 26, no. 1, pp. 51–74, 2004.

[HE 10] HE J., CHANG D., MI W. *et al.*, "A hybrid parallel genetic algorithm for yard crane scheduling", *Transportation Research Part E: Logistics and Transportation Review*, vol. 46, no. 1, pp. 136–155, 2010.

[HE 15a] HE J., HUANG Y., YAN W., "Yard crane scheduling in a container terminal for the trade-off between efficiency and energy consumption", *Advanced Engineering Informatics*, vol. 29, no. 1, pp. 59–75, 2015.

[HE 15b] HE J., HUANG Y., YAN W. *et al.*, "Integrated internal truck, yard crane and quay crane scheduling in a container terminal considering energy consumption", *Expert Systems with Applications*, vol. 42, no. 5, pp. 2464–2487, 2015.

[HE 16] HE J., "Berth allocation and quay crane assignment in a container terminal for the trade-off between time-saving and energy-saving", *Advanced Engineering Informatics*, vol. 30, no. 3, pp. 390–405, 2016.

[HE 17] HE R., MA C., JIA X. *et al.*, "Optimisation of dangerous goods transport based on the improved ant colony algorithm", *International Journal of Computing Science and Mathematics*, vol. 8, no. 3, pp. 210–217, 2017.

[HER 90] HERTZ A., DE WERRA D., "The tabu search metaheuristic: How we used it", *Annals of Mathematics and Artificial Intelligence*, vol. 1, nos 1–4, pp. 111–121, 1990.

[HIL 18] HILLEBRAND J.F., "Carbon Emissions Calculator: User Guide", available at: https://www.jfhillebrand.com/SitePages/en/Carbon_calculator_readme.aspx, 2018.

[HOL 92] HOLLAND. J.H., *Adaptation in Natural and Artificial Systems*, MIT Press, 1992.

[HOM 09] HOMAYOUNI S.M., TANG S.H., ISMAIL N., "Development of genetic fuzzy logic controllers for complex production systems", *Computers & Industrial Engineering*, vol. 57, no. 4, pp. 1247–1257, 2009.

[HOM 12] HOMAYOUNI S.M., VASILI M.R., KAZEMI S.M. *et al.*, "Integrated scheduling of SP-AS/RS and handling equipment in automated container terminals", *Proceedings of the International Conference on Computers & Industrial Engineering*, 2012.

[HOM 13] HOMAYOUNI S.M., TANG S.H., "Multi objective optimization of coordinated scheduling of cranes and vehicles at container terminals", *Mathematical Problems in Engineering*, Article ID 746781, p. 9, 2013.

[HOM 14] HOMAYOUNI S.M., TANG S.H., MOTLAGH O., "A genetic algorithm for optimization of integrated scheduling of cranes, vehicles, and storage platforms at automated container terminals", *Journal of Computational and Applied Mathematics*, vol. 270, pp. 545–556, 2014.

[HOM 16] HOMAYOUNI S.M., TANG S.H., "Optimization of integrated scheduling of handling and storage operations at automated container terminals", *WMU Journal of Maritime Affairs*, vol. 15, no. 1, pp. 17–39, 2016.

[HSU 16] HSU H.P., "A HPSO for solving dynamic and discrete berth allocation problem and dynamic quay crane assignment problem simultaneously", *Swarm and Evolutionary Computation*, vol. 27, pp. 156–168, 2016.

[HU 14] HU Q.M., HU Z.H., DU Y., "Berth and quay-crane allocation problem considering fuel consumption and emissions from vessels", *Computers & Industrial Engineering*, vol. 70, no. 1, pp. 1–10, 2014.

[HU 05] HU Y.H., HUANG S.Y., CHEN C. *et al.*, "Travel time analysis of a new automated storage and retrieval system", *Computers & Operations Research*, vol. 32, no. 6, pp. 1515–1544, 2005.

[HU 08] HU Y.H., ZHU Z., HSU W., "AS/RS based yard and yard planning", *Journal of Zhejiang University - Science A*, vol. 9, no. 8, pp. 1083–1089, 2008.

[HU 15] HU Z.H., "Multi-objective genetic algorithm for berth allocation problem considering daytime preference", *Computers & Industrial Engineering*, vol. 89, pp. 2–14, 2015.

[HU 16] HU Z.H., SHEU J.B., LUO J.X., "Sequencing twin automated stacking cranes in a block at automated container terminal", *Transportation Research Part C: Emerging Technologies*, vol. 69, pp. 208–227, 2016.

[HUA 17] HUANG S.Y., LI Y., "Yard crane scheduling to minimize total weighted vessel loading time in container terminals", *Flexible Services and Manufacturing Journal*, vol. 29, pp. 689–720, 2017.

[IMA 07] IMAI A., NISHIMURA E., HATTORI M. *et al.*, "Berth allocation at indented berths for mega-containerships", *European Journal of Operational Research*, vol. 179, no. 2, pp. 579–593, 2007.

[IMA 08] IMAI A., CHEN H.C., NISHIMURA E. *et al.*, "The simultaneous berth and quay crane allocation problem", *Transportation Research Part E: Logistics and Transportation Review*, vol. 44, no. 5, pp. 900–920, 2008.

[IMO 18] IMO, "International Convention for the Prevention of Pollution from Ships (MARPOL)", available at: http://www.imo.org/en/about/conventions/ listofconventions/pages/international-convention-for-the-prevention-of-pollution-from-ships-(marpol). aspx, 2018.

[JEO 10] JEON S.M., KIM K.H., KOPFER H., "Routing automated guided vehicles in container terminals through the Q-learning technique", *Logistic Research*, vol. 3, no. 1, pp. 19–27, 2010.

[JER 06] JERALD J., ASOKAN P., SARAVANAN R. *et al.*, "Simultaneous scheduling of parts and automated guided vehicles in an FMS environment using adaptive genetic algorithm", *The International Journal of Advanced Manufacturing Technology*, vol. 29, no. 5, pp. 584–589, 2006.

[KAD 17] KADDOURI Z., OMARY F., "Application of the tabusearch algorithm to cryptography", *International Journal of Advanced Computer Science and Applications*, vol. 8, no. 7, pp. 82–87, 2017.

[KAD 18] KADRI R.L., BOCTOR F.F., "An efficient genetic algorithm to solve the resource-constrained project scheduling problem with transfer times: The single mode case", *European Journal of Operational Research*, vol. 265, no. 2, pp. 454–462, 2018.

[KEM 13] KEMME N., *Design and Operation of Automated Container Storage Systems*, Springer-Verlag, Berlin Heidelberg, 2013.

[KEN 01] KENNEDY J., EBERHART R.C., *Swarm intelligence*, Morgan Kaufmann Publishers, San Francisco, California, 2001.

[KEN 02] KENNEDY J., MENDES R., "Population structure and particle swarm performance", *Proceedings of the 2002 Congress on Evolutionary Computation*, pp. 1671–1676, 2002.

[KIM 03] KIM K.H., PARK K.T., "A note on a dynamic space-allocation method for outbound containers", *European Journal of Operational Research*, vol. 148, no. 1, pp. 92–101, 2003.

[KIM 04] KIM K.H., PARK Y.-M., "A crane scheduling method for port container terminals", *European Journal of Operational Research*, vol. 156, no. 3, pp. 752–768, 2004.

[KIR 83] KIRKPATRICK S., GELATT C.D., VECCHI M.P. *et al.*, "Optimization by simulated annealing", *Science*, vol. 220, no. 4598, pp. 671–680, 1983.

[KJE 11] KJELDSEN K.H., "Classification of ship routing and scheduling problems in liner shipping", *INFOR: Information Systems and Operational Research*, vol. 49, no. 2, pp. 139–152, 2011.

[KLE 11] KLERIDES E., HADJICONSTANTINOU E., "Modelling and solution approaches to the multi-load AGV dispatching problem in container terminals", *Maritime Economics & Logistics*, vol. 13, no. 4, pp. 371–386, 2011.

[KON 11] KONTOVAS C.A., PSARAFTIS A.H.N., "Reduction of emissions along the maritime intermodal container chain: Operational models and policies", *Maritime Policy and Management*, vol. 38, no. 4, pp. 451–469, 2011.

[KON 14] KONTOVAS C.A., "The green ship routing and scheduling problem (GSRSP): a conceptual approach", *Transportation Research Part D: Transport and Environment*, vol. 31, pp. 61–69, 2014.

[KOO 05] KOO P.H., LEE W.S., JANG D.W., "Fleet sizing and vehicle routing for container transportation in a static environment", in GÜNTHER H.-O., KIM K.H. (eds), *Container Terminals and Automated Transport Systems*, Springer-Verlag, Berlin, Heidelberg, pp. 123–139, 2005.

[KOS 12] KOSMAS O.T., VLACHOS D.S., "Simulated annealing for optimal ship routing", *Computers & Operations Research*, vol. 39, no. 3, pp. 576–581, 2012.

[KOZ 06] KOZAN E., PRESTON P., "Mathematical modelling of container transfers and storage locations at seaport terminals", *OR Spectrum*, vol. 28, no. 4, pp. 519–537, 2006.

[LAB 16] LABADIE N., PRINS C., PRODHON C. *et al.*, *Metaheuristics for Vehicle Routing Problems*, ISTE Ltd and John Wiley & Sons, Inc., 2016.

[LAL 12] LALLA-RUIZ E., MELIÁN-BATISTA B., MARCOS MORENO-VEGA J.M., "Artificial intelligence hybrid heuristic based on tabu search for the dynamic berth allocation problem", *Engineering Applications of Artificial Intelligence*, vol. 25, no. 6, pp. 1132–1141, 2012.

[LAL 14] LALLA-RUIZ E., GONZÁLEZ-VELARDE J.L., MELIÁN-BATISTA B. *et al.*, "Biased random key genetic algorithm for the tactical berth allocation problem", *Applied Soft Computing Journal*, vol. 22, pp. 60–76, 2014.

[LAL 16] LALLA-RUIZ E., VOß S., "POPMUSIC as a metaheuristic for the berth allocation problem", *Annals of Mathematics and Artificial Intelligence*, vol. 76, no. 1, pp. 173–189, 2016.

[LAU 08] LAU H.Y.K., ZHAO Y., "Integrated scheduling of handling equipment at automated container terminals", *International Journal of Production Economics*, vol. 112, no. 2, pp. 665–682, 2008.

[LEE 08] LEE D.-H., WANG H.Q., MIAO L., "Quay crane scheduling with non-interference constraints in port container terminals", *Transportation Research Part E: Logistics and Transportation Review*, vol. 44, no. 1, pp. 124–135, 2008.

[LEE 09a] LEE Y., CHEN C.-Y., "An optimization heuristic for the berth scheduling problem", *European Journal of Operational Research*, vol. 196, no. 2, pp. 500–508, 2009.

[LEE 09b] LEE D.-H., CAO J.X., SHI Q.X. *et al.*, "A heuristic algorithm for yard truck scheduling and storage allocation problems", *Transportation Research Part E: Logistics and Transportation Review*, vol. 45, no. 5, pp. 810–820, 2009.

[LEE 10] LEE D.-H., WANG H.Q., "Integrated discrete berth allocation and quay crane scheduling in port container terminals", *Engineering Optimization*, vol. 42, no. 8, pp. 747–761, 2010.

[LEE 15] LEE J., KIM B.I., "Industrial ship routing problem with split delivery and two types of vessels", *Expert Systems with Applications*, vol. 42, no. 22, pp. 9012–9023, 2015.

[LEH 06] LEHMANN M., GRUNOW M., GÜNTHER H.O., "Deadlock handling for real-time control of AGVs at automated container terminals", *OR Spectrum*, vol. 28, no. 4, pp. 631–657, 2006.

[LI 17] LI J., KE L., YE G. *et al.*, "Ant colony optimisation for the routing problem in the constellation network with node satellite constraint", *International Journal of Bio-Inspired Computation*, vol. 10, no. 4, p. 267, 2017.

[LIA 13] LIANG C.-J., CHEN M., GEN M. *et al.*, "A multi-objective genetic algorithm for yard crane scheduling problem with multiple work lines", *Journal of Intelligent Manufacturing*, vol. 25, no. 5, pp. 1–12, 2013.

[LIN 11] LIN D.-Y., LIU H.-Y., "Combined ship allocation, routing and freight assignment in tramp shipping", *Transportation Research Part E: Logistics and Transportation Review*, vol. 47, no. 4, pp. 414–431, 2011.

[LIN 14a] LIN D.-Y., TSAI Y.-Y., "The ship routing and freight assignment problem for daily frequency operation of maritime liner shipping", *Transportation Research Part E: Logistics and Transportation Review*, vol. 67, pp. 52–70, 2014.

[LIN 14b] LIN S.-W., TING C.-J., "Solving the dynamic berth allocation problem by simulated annealing", *Engineering Optimization*, vol. 46, no. 3, pp. 308–327, 2014.

[LIN 17a] LIN D.-Y., CHIANG C.-W., "The storage space allocation problem at a container terminal", *Maritime Policy & Management*, vol. 44, no. 6, pp. 685–704, 2017.

[LIN 17b] LIN S.W., TING C.J., WU K.C., "Simulated annealing with different vessel assignment strategies for the continuous berth allocation problem", *Flexible Services and Manufacturing Journal*, pp. 1–24, 2017.

[LIU 09] LIU S.-H., MERNIK M., BRYANT B.R., *To explore or to exploit: An entropy-driven approach for evolutionary algorithms*, IOS Press, 2009.

[LIU 15] LIU M., CHU F., ZHANG Z. *et al.*, "A polynomial-time heuristic for the quay crane double-cycling problem with internal-reshuffling operations", *Transportation Research Part E: Logistics and Transportation Review*, vol. 81, pp. 52–74, 2015.

[LIU 17] LIU S., YANG B., "Optimal placement of water-lubricated rubber bearings for vibration reduction of flexible multistage rotor systems", *Journal of Sound and Vibration*, vol. 407, pp. 332–349, 2017.

[LUO 16] LUO J., WU Y., MENDES A.B., "Modelling of integrated vehicle scheduling and container storage problems in unloading process at an automated container terminal", *Computers & Industrial Engineering*, vol. 94, pp. 32–44, 2016.

[MAE 18] MAERSK LINE, "AE1 Eastbound time table", available at: https://www.maerskline.com/routes/search-routes, 2018.

[MAN 15] MANSOURI S.A., LEE H., ALUKO O., "Multi-objective decision support to enhance environmental sustainability in maritime shipping: A review and future directions", *Transportation Research Part E: Logistics and Transportation Review*, vol. 78, pp. 3–18, 2015.

[MAR 13] MARTINS M.S.R., FUCHS S.C., PANDO L.U. *et al.*, "PSO with path relinking for resource allocation using simulation optimization", *Computers & Industrial Engineering*, vol. 65, no. 2, pp. 322–330, 2013.

[MEE 01a] MEERSMANS P.J.M., WAGELMANS A.P.M., *Dynamic scheduling of handling equipment at automated container terminals*, Erasmus University Rotterdam, The Netherlands, 2001.

[MEE 01b] MEERSMANS P.J.M., WAGELMANS A.P.M., *Effective algorithms for integrated scheduling of handling equipment at automated container terminals*, Erasmus University Rotterdam, The Netherlands, 2001.

[MEN 14] MENG Q., WANG S., ANDERSSON H. *et al.*, "Containership routing and scheduling in liner shipping: overview and future research directions", *Transportation Science*, vol. 48, no. 2, pp. 265–280, 2014.

[MET 53] METROPOLIS N., ROSENBLUTH A.W., ROSENBLUTH M.N. *et al.*, "Equation of state calculations by fast computing machines", *Journal Chemical Physics*, vol. 21, no. 6, pp. 1087–1092, 1953.

[MOC 06] MOCCIA L., CORDEAU J.F., GAUDIOSO M. *et al.*, "A branch-and-cut algorithm for the quay crane scheduling problem in a container terminal", *Naval Research Logistics*, vol. 53, no. 1, pp. 45–59, 2006.

[MOK 15] MOKHTARI H., DADGAR M., "Scheduling optimization of a stochastic flexible job-shop system with time-varying machine failure rate", *Computers & Operations Research*, vol. 61, pp. 31–45, 2015.

[MON 13] MONTEIRO M.S.R., FONTES D.B.M.M., FONTES F.A.C.C., "Concave minimum cost network flow problems solved with a colony of ants", *Journal of Heuristics*, vol. 19, no.1, pp. 1–33, 2013.

[MON 15] MONTEIRO M.S.R., FONTES D.B.M.M., FONTES F.A.C.C., "The hop-constrained minimum cost flow spanning tree problem with nonlinear costs: an ant colony optimization approach", *Optimization Letters*, vol. 9, no. 3, pp. 451–464, 2015.

[MOS 17] MOSES S.A., SANGPLUNG W., "Resource planning for just-in-time make-to-order environments: A scalable methodology using tabu search", *Cogent Engineering*, vol. 4, no. 1, pp. 1–19, 2017.

[NAN 17] NANDI S., MCANANAMA-BRERETON S.R., WALLER M.P. *et al.*, "A tabu-search based strategy for modeling molecular aggregates and binary reactions", *Computational and Theoretical Chemistry*, vol. 1111, pp. 69–81, 2017.

[NG 05] NG W.C., MAK K.L., "Yard crane scheduling in port container terminals", *Applied Mathematical Modelling*, vol. 29, no. 3, pp. 263–276, 2005.

[NG 07] NG W.C., MAK K.L., ZHANG Y.X., "Scheduling trucks in container terminals using a genetic algorithm", *Engineering Optimization*, vol. 39, no. 1, pp. 33–47, 2007.

[NGU 09] NGUYEN V.D., KIM K.H., "A dispatching method for automated lifting vehicles in automated port container terminals", *Computers & Industrial Engineering*, vol. 56, no. 3, pp. 1002–1020, 2009.

[NGU 13] NGUYEN S., ZHANG M., JOHNSTON M. *et al.*, "Hybrid evolutionary computation methods for quay crane scheduling problems", *Computers & Operations Research*, vol. 40, no. 8, pp. 2083–2093, 2013.

[NIS 01] NISHIMURA E., IMAI A., PAPADIMITRIOU S., "Berth allocation planning in the public berth system by genetic algorithms", *European Journal of Operational Research*, vol. 131, no. 2, pp. 282–292, 2001.

[NIU 16] NIU B., XIE T., TAN L. *et al.*, "Swarm intelligence algorithms for yard truck scheduling and storage allocation problems", *Neurocomputing*, vol. 188, pp. 284–293, 2016.

[NOR 11] NORSTAD I., FAGERHOLT K., LAPORTE G., "Tramp ship routing and scheduling with speed optimization", *Transportation Research Part C: Emerging Technologies*, vol. 19, no. 5, pp. 853–865, 2011.

[PAR 11] PARK T., CHOE R., HUN KIM Y. *et al.*, "Dynamic adjustment of container stacking policy in an automated container terminal", *International Journal of Production Economics*, vol. 133, no. 1, pp. 385–392, 2011.

[PIL 13] PILLAC V., GENDREAU M., GUÉRET C. *et al.*, "A review of dynamic vehicle routing problems", *European Journal of Operational Research*, vol. 225, no. 1, pp. 1–11, 2013.

[PSA 13] PSARAFTIS H.N., KONTOVAS C.A., "Speed models for energy-efficient maritime transportation: A taxonomy and survey", *Transportation Research Part C: Emerging Technologies*, vol. 26, pp. 331–351, 2013.

[PSA 14] PSARAFTIS A.H.N., KONTOVAS C.A., "Ship speed optimization: Concepts, models and combined speed-routing scenarios", *Transportation Research Part C: Emerging Technologies*, vol. 44, pp. 52–69, 2014.

[RAN 98] RANGASWAMY B., GLOVER F., "Tabu search candidate list strategies in scheduling", in WOODRUFF D.L. (ed.), *Advances in Computational and Stochastic Optimization, Logic Programming, and Heuristic Search*, Boston, Massachusetts, Springer, pp. 215–233, 1998.

[ROB 14] ROBENEK T., UMANG N., BIERLAIRE M. *et al.*, "A branch-and-price algorithm to solve the integrated berth allocation and yard assignment problem in bulk ports", *European Journal of Operational Research*, vol. 235, no. 2, pp. 399–411, 2014.

[RON 82] RONEN D., "The effect of oil price on the optimal speed of ships", *Journal of the Operational Research Society*, vol. 33, no. 11, pp. 1035–1040, 1982.

[RON 11] RONEN D., "The effect of oil price on containership speed and fleet size", *Journal of the Operational Research Society*, vol. 62, no. 1, pp. 211–216, 2011.

[ROQ 14] ROQUE L.A.C., FONTES D.B.M.M., FONTES F.A.C.C., "A biased random key genetic algorithm approach for unit commitment problem", *Journal of Combinatorial Optimization*, vol. 28, no. 1, pp. 140–166, 2014.

[ROQ 17] ROQUE L.A.C., FONTES D.B.M.M., FONTES F.A.C.C., "A multi-objective unit commitment problem combining economic and environmental criteria in a metaheuristic approach", *Energy Procedia*, vol. 136, pp. 362–368, 2017.

[SAL 11] SALIDO M.A., RODRIGUEZ-MOLINS M., BARBER F., "Integrated intelligent techniques for remarshaling and berthing in maritime terminals", *Advanced Engineering Informatics*, vol. 25, no. 3, pp. 435–451, 2011.

[SAM 07] SAMMARRA M., CORDEAU J.F., LAPORTE G. *et al.*, "A tabu search heuristic for the quay crane scheduling problem", *Journal of Scheduling*, vol. 10, nos 4–5, pp. 327–336, 2007.

[SEA 18] SEARATES, "Transit time, distance calculator & port to port distances", available at: https://www.searates.com/reference/portdistance/?, 2018.

[SHA 13] SHARIF O., HUYNH N., "Storage space allocation at marine container terminals using ant-based control", *Expert Systems with Applications*, vol. 40, no. 6, pp. 2323–2330, 2013.

[SHA 17] SHANG Y., LU S., GONG J. *et al.*, "Improved genetic algorithm for economic load dispatch in hydropower plants and comprehensive performance comparison with dynamic programming method", *Journal of Hydrology*, vol. 554, pp. 306–316, 2017.

[SHI 98] SHI Y., EBERHART R., "A modified particle swarm optimizer", *Proceedings of the IEEE International Conference on Evolutionary Computation*, pp. 69–73, 1998.

[SHI 08] SHI W., STAPERSMA D., GRIMMELIUS H.T., "Comparison study on moving and transportation performance of transportation modes", *International Journal of the Energy and Environment*, vol. 2, no. 4, pp. 179–190, 2008.

[SIV 08] SIVANANDAM S.N., DEEPA S.N., *Introduction to genetic algorithms*, Springer Verlag, Berlin, 2008.

[SON 12] SONG L., CHERRETT T., GUAN W., "Study on berth planning problem in a container seaport: Using an integrated programming approach", *Computers & Industrial Engineering*, vol. 62, no. 1, pp. 119–128, 2012.

[SPE 16] SPEER U., "Scheduling of different automated yard crane systems at container terminals", *Transportation Science*, vol. 51, no. 1, pp. 305–324, 2016.

[STA 08] STAHLBOCK R., VOß S., "Operations research at container terminals: a literature update", *OR Spectrum*, vol. 30, no. 1, pp. 1–52, 2008.

[STU 97] STUTZLE T., HOOS H., "MAX-MIN ant system and local search for the traveling salesman problem", *Proceedings of the 1997 IEEE International Conference on Evolutionary Computation (ICEC'97)*, pp. 309–314, 1997.

[SUM 06] SUMAN B., KUMAR P., "A survey of simulated annealing as a tool for single and multiobjective optimization", *Journal of the Operational Research Society*, vol. 57, no. 10, pp. 1143–1160, 2006.

[TAL 02] TALBI E.G., "A taxonomy of hybrid metaheuristics", *Journal of Heuristics*, vol. 8, no. 5, pp. 541–564, 2002.

[TAN 08] TAN C.M., *Simulated Annealing*, InTech, 2008.

[TAN 14] TANG L., ZHAO J., LIU J., "Modeling and solution of the joint quay crane and truck scheduling problem", *European Journal of Operational Research*, vol. 236, no. 3, pp. 978–990, 2014.

[TAO 15] TAO Y., LEE C.Y., "Joint planning of berth and yard allocation in transshipment terminals using multi-cluster stacking strategy", *Transportation Research Part E: Logistics and Transportation Review*, vol. 83, pp. 34–50, 2015.

[TAS 06] TASGETIREN F.M., LIANG Y.-C., SEVKLI M. *et al.*, "Particle swarm optimization and differential evolution for the single machine total weighted tardiness problem", *International Journal of Production Research*, vol. 44, no. 22, pp. 4737–4754, 2006.

[TIN 14] TING C.-J., WU K.-C., CHOU H., "Particle swarm optimization algorithm for the berth allocation problem", *Expert Systems with Applications*, vol. 41, no. 4, pp. 1543–1550, 2014.

[TOT 03] TOTH P., VIGO D., "The granular tabu search and its application to the vehicle-routing problem", *INFORMS Journal on Computing*, vol. 15, no. 4, pp. 333–346, 2003.

[TSO 13] TSOU M.-C., CHENG H.-C., "An ant colony algorithm for efficient ship routing", *Polish Maritime Research*, vol. 20, no. 79, pp. 28–38, 2013.

[TÜR 14] TÜRKOĞULLARI Y.B., TAŞKIN Z.C., ARAS N. *et al.*, "Optimal berth allocation and time-invariant quay crane assignment in container terminals", *European Journal of Operational Research*, vol. 235, no. 1, pp. 88–101, 2014.

[TÜR 16] TÜRKOĞULLARI Y.B., TAŞKIN Z.C., ARAS N. *et al.*, "Optimal berth allocation, time-variant quay crane assignment and scheduling with crane setups in container terminals", *European Journal of Operational Research*, vol. 254, no. 3, pp. 985–1001, 2016.

[UMA 11] UMANG N., BIERLAIRE M., VACCA I., "The berth allocation problem in bulk ports", *Swiss Transport Research Conference*, 2011.

[UMA 13] UMANG N., BIERLAIRE M., VACCA I., "Exact and heuristic methods to solve the berth allocation problem in bulk ports", *Transportation Research Part E: Logistics and Transportation Review*, vol. 54, pp. 14–31, 2013.

[UMA 14] UMANG N., From container terminals to bulk ports: models and algorithms for integrated planning and robust scheduling, PhD Thesis, École Polytechnique Fédérale de Lausanne, 2014.

[UNC 17] UNCTAD, Review of maritime transport, United Nations, New York and Geneva, 2017.

[UNI 18] UNITED NATIONS, "2030 Agenda for sustainable developments", available at: http://www.un.org/sustainabledevelopment/development-agenda/, 2018.

[VAC 07] VACCA I., BIERLAIRE M., SALANI M. *et al.*, "Optimization at container terminals: status, trends and perspectives", *7th Swiss Transport Research Conference*, p. 21, 2007.

[VAS 06] VASILI M.R., TANG S.H., HOMAYOUNI S.M. *et al.*, "Comparison of different dwell point policies for split-platform automated storage and retrieval system", *International Journal of Engineering and Technology*, vol. 3, no. 1, pp. 91–106, 2006.

[VAS 08] VASILI M.R., TANG S.H., HOMAYOUNI S.M. *et al.*, "A statistical model for expected cycle time of SP-AS/RS: An application of Monte Carlo simulation", *Applied Artificial Intelligence: An International Journal*, vol. 22, nos 7–8, pp. 824–840, 2008.

[VIL 15] VILHELMSEN C., LARSEN J., LUSBY R.M., Tramp ship routing and scheduling - models, methods and opportunities, PhD Thesis, Technical University of Denmark, 2015.

[VIL 17] VILHELMSEN C., LUSBY R.M., LARSEN J., "Tramp ship routing and scheduling with voyage separation requirements", *OR Spectrum*, vol. 39, no. 4, pp. 913–943, 2017.

[VIS 04] VIS I.F.A., HARIKA I., "Comparison of vehicle types at an automated container terminal", *OR Spectrum*, vol. 26, no. 1, pp. 117–143, 2004.

[VIS 06] VIS I.F.A., "A comparative analysis of storage and retrieval equipment at a container terminal", *International Journal of Production Economics*, vol. 103, no. 2, pp. 680–693, 2006.

[VOß 96] VOß S., "Observing logical interdependencies in tabu search: Methods and results", in RAYWARD-SMITH V.J., OSMAN I.H., REEVES C.R. *et al.* (eds), *Modern Heuristic Search Methods*, pp. 41–59, 1996.

[WAN 15] WANG Y., LU J., "Optimization of China crude oil transportation network with genetic ant colony algorithm", *Information*, vol. 6, no. 3, p. 467, 2015.

[WAN 16] WANG K., YAN X., YUAN Y. *et al.*, "Optimizing ship energy efficiency: Application of particle swarm optimization algorithm", *Journal of Engineering for the Maritime Environment*, 2016.

[WEN 16] WEN M., ROPKE S., PETERSEN H.L. *et al.*, "Full-shipload tramp ship routing and scheduling with variable speeds", *Computers & Operations Research*, vol. 70, pp. 1–8, 2016.

[WER 89] DE WERRA D., HERTZ A., "Tabu search techniques: A tutorial and an application to neural networks", *OR Spectrum*, vol. 11, no. 3, pp. 131–141, 1989.

[XU 12] XU D., LI C.L., LEUNG J.Y.T., "Berth allocation with time-dependent physical limitations on vessels", *European Journal of Operational Research*, vol. 216, no. 1, pp. 47–56, 2012.

[XUE 13] XUE Z., ZHANG C., MIAO L. *et al.*, "An ant colony algorithm for yard truck scheduling and yard location assignment problems with precedence constraints", *Journal of Systems Science and Systems Engineering*, vol. 22, no. 1, pp. 21–37, 2013.

[YAN 04] YANG C.H., CHOI Y.S., HA T.Y., "Simulation-based performance evaluation of transport vehicles at automated container terminals", *OR Spectrum*, vol. 26, no. 2, pp. 149–170, 2004.

[YU 13] YU M., QI X., "Storage space allocation models for inbound containers in an automatic container terminal", *European Journal of Operational Research*, vol. 226, no. 1, pp. 32–45, 2013.

[YUA 16] YUAN Z., "A brief literature review on ship management in maritime transportation", *IRIDIA*, TR/IRIDA/2016-001, 2016.

[ZEN 09] ZENG Q., YANG Z., "Integrating simulation and optimization to schedule loading operations in container terminals", *Computers & Operations Research*, vol. 36, no. 6, pp. 1935–1944, 2009.

[ZEN 11] ZENG Q., YANG Z., HU X., "Disruption recovery model for berth and quay crane scheduling in container terminals", *Engineering Optimization*, vol. 43, no. 9, pp. 967–983, 2011.

[ZEN 15] ZENG Q., DIABAT A., ZHANG Q., "A simulation optimization approach for solving the dual-cycling problem in container terminals", *Maritime Policy & Management*, vol. 42, no. 8, pp. 806–826, 2015.

[ZEN 17] ZENG Q., FENG Y., CHEN Z., "Optimizing berth allocation and storage space in direct transshipment operations at container terminals", *Maritime Economics & Logistics*, vol. 19, no. 3, pp. 474–475, 2017.

[ZHA 03] ZHANG C., LIU J., WAN Y.-W. *et al.*, "Storage space allocation in container terminals", *Transportation Research Part B: Methodological*, vol. 37, no. 10, pp. 883–903, 2003.

[ZHA 09] ZHANG H., KIM K.H., "Maximizing the number of dual-cycle operations of quay cranes in container terminals", *Computers & Industrial Engineering*, vol. 56, no. 3, pp. 979–992, 2009.

[ZHA 12] ZHANG S.X., BABOVIC V., "A real options approach to the design and architecture of water supply systems using innovative water technologies under uncertainty", *Journal of Hydroinformatics*, vol. 14, no. 1, p. 13, 2012.

[ZHA 16] ZHANG X., ZENG Q., YANG Z., "Modeling the mixed storage strategy for quay crane double cycling in container terminals", *Transportation Research Part E: Logistics and Transportation Review*, vol. 94, pp. 171–187, 2016.

[ZHA 17] ZHANG A., ZHANG W., CHEN Y. *et al.*, "Approximate the scheduling of quay cranes with non-crossing constraints", *European Journal of Operational Research*, vol. 258, no. 3, pp. 820–828, 2017.

Index

Other titles from

in

Computer Engineering

2018

ARNALDI Bruno, PASCAL Guitton, GUILLAUME Moreau
Virtual Reality and Augmented Reality
(Digital Tools and Uses Set – Volume 5)

2017

BENMAMMAR Badr
Concurrent, Real-Time and Distributed Programming in Java

HÉLIODORE Frédéric, NAKIB Amir, ISMAIL Boussaad, OUCHRAA Salma,
SCHMITT Laurent
Metaheuristics for Intelligent Electrical Networks
(Metaheuristics Set – Volume 10)

MA Haiping, SIMON Dan
Evolutionary Computation with Biogeography-based Optimization
(Metaheuristics Set – Volume 8)

PÉTROWSKI Alain, BEN-HAMIDA Sana
Evolutionary Algorithms
(Metaheuristics Set – Volume 9)

PAI G A Vijayalakshmi
Metaheuristics for Portfolio Optimization
(Metaheuristics Set – Volume 11)

2016

BLUM Christian, FESTA Paola
Metaheuristics for String Problems in Bio-informatics
(Metaheuristics Set – Volume 6)

DEROUSSI Laurent
Metaheuristics for Logistics
(Metaheuristics Set – Volume 4)

DHAENENS Clarisse and JOURDAN Laetitia
Metaheuristics for Big Data
(Metaheuristics Set – Volume 5)

LABADIE Nacima, PRINS Christian, PRODHON Caroline
Metaheuristics for Vehicle Routing Problems
(Metaheuristics Set – Volume 3)

LEROY Laure
Eyestrain Reduction in Stereoscopy

LUTTON Evelyne, PERROT Nathalie, TONDA Albert
Evolutionary Algorithms for Food Science and Technology
(Metaheuristics Set – Volume 7)

MAGOULÈS Frédéric, ZHAO Hai-Xiang
Data Mining and Machine Learning in Building Energy Analysis

RIGO Michel
Advanced Graph Theory and Combinatorics

2015

BARBIER Franck, RECOUSSINE Jean-Luc
COBOL Software Modernization: From Principles to Implementation with the BLU AGE® Method

CHEN Ken
Performance Evaluation by Simulation and Analysis with Applications to Computer Networks

CLERC Maurice
Guided Randomness in Optimization
(Metaheuristics Set – Volume 1)

DURAND Nicolas, GIANAZZA David, GOTTELAND Jean-Baptiste, ALLIOT Jean-Marc
Metaheuristics for Air Traffic Management
(Metaheuristics Set – Volume 2)

MAGOULÈS Frédéric, ROUX François-Xavier, HOUZEAUX Guillaume
Parallel Scientific Computing

MUNEESAWANG Paisarn, YAMMEN Suchart
Visual Inspection Technology in the Hard Disk Drive Industry

2014

BOULANGER Jean-Louis
Formal Methods Applied to Industrial Complex Systems

BOULANGER Jean-Louis
Formal Methods Applied to Complex Systems:
Implementation of the B Method

GARDI Frédéric, BENOIST Thierry, DARLAY Julien, ESTELLON Bertrand, MEGEL Romain
Mathematical Programming Solver based on Local Search

KRICHEN Saoussen, CHAOUACHI Jouhaina
Graph-related Optimization and Decision Support Systems

LARRIEU Nicolas, VARET Antoine
Rapid Prototyping of Software for Avionics Systems: Model-oriented Approaches for Complex Systems Certification

2007

BENHAMOU Frédéric, JUSSIEN Narendra, O'SULLIVAN Barry
Trends in Constraint Programming

JUSSIEN Narendra
A TO Z OF SUDOKU

2006

BABAU Jean-Philippe *et al.*
From MDD Concepts to Experiments and Illustrations – DRES 2006

HABRIAS Henri, FRAPPIER Marc
Software Specification Methods

MURAT Cecile, PASCHOS Vangelis Th
Probabilistic Combinatorial Optimization on Graphs

PANETTO Hervé, BOUDJLIDA Nacer
Interoperability for Enterprise Software and Applications 2006 / IFAC-IFIP I-ESA '2006

2005

GÉRARD Sébastien *et al.*
Model Driven Engineering for Distributed Real Time Embedded Systems

PANETTO Hervé
Interoperability of Enterprise Software and Applications 2005

Printed and bound by CPI Group (UK) Ltd, Croydon, CR0 4YY